Feeling in Theory

MW00849605

Feeling in Theory

Emotion after the "Death of the Subject"

REI TERADA

HARVARD UNIVERSITY PRESS

Cambridge, Massachusetts, and London, England

For Michiko

Copyright © 2001 by the President and Fellows of Harvard College
All rights reserved
Printed in the United States of America

Library of Congress Cataloging-in-Publication Data

Terada, Rei, 1962–
   Feeling in theory : emotion after the "death of the subject" / Rei Terada.
      p. cm.
   Includes bibliographical references and index.
   ISBN 0-674-00493-0 (cloth)
   ISBN 0-674-01127-9 (pbk)
      1. Emotions (Philosophy)   2. Subject (Philosophy)   I. Title.

B815.T47 2001
128'.37—dc21   00-054244

Imagine a case in which people ascribed pain *only* to inanimate things; pitied *only* dolls!

—WITTGENSTEIN, *PHILOSOPHICAL INVESTIGATIONS* §282

Contents

Acknowledgments

In writing this book, I've been influenced by Julie Ellison and Adela Pinch, friends whose work on emotion encouraged response. Writing has been in part a way of writing to them. Many other people have also helped me; those whose help was both intellectual and emotional include MindaRae Amiran, Timothy Bahti, Julia Carlson-Federhofer, Hank De Leo, Alice Fulton, Patricia Geldenbott, Sandra Gunning, Nick Halpern, Kerry Larson, Ian Leong, Yopie Prins, Eliza Richards, Sarah Riggs, Susan Rosenbaum, and Kelly Thomas. I'm grateful for all their support through long Michigan winters. I thank the graduate students in English and Comparative Literature, especially the members of the 1999 seminar on theory of lyric, for their contributions. Thanks too to Patrick O'Donnell and the faculty in English at Michigan State University. I learned from friends at North Carolina State University; from the conversation of Marjorie Levinson, John McGowan, Jim Morrison, Tom Reinert, Charles Stein, Michael Szalay, and David Wayne Thomas; and from participants in the 1999 UCLA Humanities Consortium on the politics of the passions. Neil Hertz encouraged the long-term development of this project; Lindsay Waters, Thomas Pepper, and Steven Shaviro have been perceptive and sympathetic readers. Eyal Amiran, whose ideas and passions show feeling in theory indeed, is the co-creator of this book. Jake supervised.

This project was supported by leaves from the Department of English, the Program in Comparative Literature, the College of Letters, Sciences and Arts, and the Office of the Vice-President for Multicultural

Affairs at the University of Michigan, Ann Arbor. Portions of Chapter 1 appeared as "Imaginary Seductions: Derrida and Emotion Theory," in *Comparative Literature* 51 (1999): 193–216; of Chapter 2, as "Pathos *(Allegories of Reading)*" in *Studies in Romanticism* 39 (2000): 27–50, reprinted by permission of the Trustees of Boston University; of Chapter 4, as "Psyche, Inc.: Derridean Emotion after de Man," in *Journal of the British Society for Phenomenology* 29 (1998): 47–62, reprinted by permission of the editors. I am grateful to the journals for permission to publish this material in revised form.

Abbreviations and Textual Note

AI   Paul de Man, *Aesthetic Ideology*

AR   Paul de Man, *Allegories of Reading: Figural Language in Rousseau, Nietzsche, Rilke, and Proust*

B   Jacques Derrida, "Biodegradables: Seven Diary Fragments"

BI   Paul de Man, *Blindness and Insight: Essays in the Rhetoric of Contemporary Criticism,* 2nd edition

EPS   Gilles Deleuze, *Expressionism in Philosophy: Spinoza*

D   Jacques Derrida, *Dissemination*

G   Jacques Derrida, *Of Grammatology*

M   Jacques Derrida, *Memoires for Paul de Man*

OCR   Jean-Jacques Rousseau, *Oeuvres complètes*

R   Werner Hamacher, Neil Hertz, and Thomas Keenan, eds., *Responses: On Paul de Man's Wartime Journalism*

RDR   Lindsay Waters and Wlad Godzich, eds., *Reading de Man Reading*

RE   Ronald de Sousa, *The Rationality of Emotion*

RR   Paul de Man, *The Rhetoric of Romanticism*

S   Gilles Deleuze, *Spinoza: Practical Philosophy*

SP   Jacques Derrida, *Speech and Phenomena*

TP   Gilles Deleuze and Félix Guattari, *A Thousand Plateaus*

WD   Jacques Derrida, *Writing and Difference*

YFS   Peter Brooks, Shoshana Felman, and J. Hillis Miller, eds., *Yale French Studies* 69 [*The Lesson of Paul de Man*]

Dates that appear in parentheses in the text refer to publication of the editions cited; first publication dates, where these differ, appear in brackets.

Within citations, spelling and italicization of words in languages other than the home language of the texts have been regularized.

Introduction: Emotion after the "Death of the Subject"

It may be difficult to imagine what the kinds of experience proposed by poststructuralist theory are supposed to feel like. Many readers have assumed that the very idea of strong emotion is inconsistent with poststructuralism. In the opening pages of *Postmodernism,* for instance, Fredric Jameson argues for a "waning of affect" in our time.[1] Comparing Andy Warhol's "Diamond Dust Shoes" with Van Gogh's shoe paintings and Munch's "The Scream," Jameson concludes that "concepts such as anxiety and alienation (and the experiences to which they correspond, as in *The Scream*) are no longer appropriate in the world of the postmodern" (14). Jameson's terms qualify one another in the course of his discussion; at times emotion itself seems to be in question, at times merely certain kinds of emotions. Jameson stipulates that "of course, it would be inaccurate to suggest that all affect, all feeling or emotion, all subjectivity, has vanished from the newer image" (10). Nevertheless, he circles back to what seems to be an essential friction between "the 'death' of the subject itself—the end of the autonomous bourgeois monad" (15)—and emotion as such:

> The end of the bourgeois ego, or monad, no doubt brings with it the end of the psychopathologies of that ego—what I have been calling the waning of affect. But it means the end of much more—the end, for example, of style, in the sense of the unique and the personal. . . . As for expression and feelings or emotions, the liberation, in contemporary society, from the older *anomie* of the centered subject may also mean not merely

a liberation from anxiety but a liberation from every other kind of feeling as well, since there is no longer a self present to do the feeling. (15)

Jameson memorably phrases what many people have suspected—that there is some kind of contradiction in attributing emotion, or at least strong and clear emotion, to anything other than a subject. Emotion and subjectivity seem to be deeply connected. Thus Manfred Frank remarks that "a dead subject emits no more cries of pain."[2] Although in poststructuralist theory the "death of the subject" figures the demise of a concept, Frank exaggerates the faux-reifying effect of the figure. Emotion in the "dead" subject evokes for him the oxymoron of a suffering corpse. As if developing this aphorism, another critic comments on Frank's philosophical position:

> In . . . *What is Neostructuralism?*, he pays particular attention to the problems created by the so-called Death of the Subject, the elimination of a thinking, feeling, and willing self as an existing part of what used to be called a person. Time and again Frank points out that the various systems or discourses offered as more up-to-date replacements of a subject/self always surreptitiously smuggle in effects supposedly created by such impersonal entities but that only such a self could really bring about.[3]

This testimony is offered as part of a symposium in the pragmatist journal *Common Knowledge* on reactions to the "linguistic turn" in theory. The context for the remark is a discussion of the things "linguistic" theories cannot do, and its assumption is that these theories cannot explain "effects" of thinking, willing, and—my concern here—feeling. Luc Ferry and Alain Renaut, provocateurs of an anti-poststructuralist philosophical movement in France, also assert that "the philosophists of the sixties could not thematize in their own discourses the resistance of subjectivity to its own 'vanishing,' due to the nature of their fundamental theoretical opinions." Believing this, they find something contradictory in Louis Althusser's calls for "class *consciousness*," "devotion," and "courage": "in this final foundation of history on consciousness and courage, or, in other words, on the classical attributes of the metaphysical subject . . . 'the elimination of the category of subject' seems again most decidedly at an abrupt standstill."[4]

Certainly, emotion after the "death of the subject" seems strange and worth inquiring into. Many scholars have found it so strange, however, that they simply presume its inconsistency. Some believe that poststructuralist theory describes a blank, mechanistic world; others point out with irritation that, nevertheless, certain theorists seem all too willing to claim and to represent strong emotion. Jacques Derrida, especially, has been criticized for appearing through his work to enjoy and to solicit suffering, sympathy, and animosity, supposedly against his reasoning.[5] Thus much of the secondary literature on poststructuralist theory assumes, first, that this theory does not have an account of emotion, and, second, that evidence of its own emotion belies its own nonbelief in the human subject. If one presumes in the first place that only subjects feel, then poststructuralist emotion looks like a symptomatic irruption, an unconscious contradiction. Yet if emotional effects are so terribly pervasive in poststructuralist theory—"*always . . .* smuggle[d] in"—it is time to consider the possibility that poststructuralism is *directly* concerned with emotion. In order for this to be so, emotion would have to be nonsubjective.

I will argue that these statements do describe the case. Poststructuralist thought about emotion is hidden in plain sight; poststructuralist theory deploys implicit and explicit logics of emotion and, as its very critics point out, willingly dramatizes particular emotions. It has reason to stress emotive experience, for far from controverting the "death of the subject," emotion entails this death. Not only poststructuralist thought, but the history of thought about emotion says as much. The purpose and the very existence of emotion have traditionally been associated with persistent difficulties in the philosophy of mind. Feared as a hazard or prized as a mysterious gift, emotion indexes strains in philosophy—the same strains that poststructuralist theory argues fracture the classical model of subjectivity. Thus "poststructuralist" dissatisfaction with the subject appears in *classical* thought about emotion: theories of emotion are always poststructuralist theories.

Poststructuralist readings of philosophy render visible both a *discourse of emotion* and an *ideology of emotion,* or narrative about the discourse that underrepresents its complexity. The discourse of emotion from Descartes to the present day describes emotion as nonsubjective experience in the form of self-difference within cognition. The ideology of emotion tells a supplementary story in which emotion fills in the difference it registers. These stories may be told within the same text, as in the works of Descartes (a paradigmatic author here). The discourse and the ideology are not equally untrue, however, since only the ideology makes a circular positive claim. Jerome McGann and Terry Eagleton, and others after them, have analyzed the ideological convenience of casting emotion as a basis for naturalized social or moral consensus.[6] I agree that this is ideological, and add that such a gesture depends on an even more fundamental one that casts emotion as proof of the human subject. Thematizing the discourse-ideology dynamic itself and emphasizing the phenomenology of philosophical narratives, texts like Derrida's *Of Grammatology* and Paul de Man's *Allegories of Reading* free a credible concept of emotion from a less credible scheme of subjectivity. I am arguing that a discourse and ideology of emotion exist; that poststructuralist theory shows their relation; and that the effect of this exploration is to suggest that we would have no emotions if we *were* subjects.

As we'll see, deconstruction intervenes in theories of emotion in a particularly mindful way. This may sound surprising, since deconstruction is often thought to be the truly glacial part of poststructuralist theory, the realm in which the death of the subject is most deathly. To explain this apparent irony, and hence my own emphasis, it's helpful to address some basic questions of vocabulary.

When I say that emotion requires the death of the subject, do I really mean *emotion* and not some sort of impulse, affect, sensation, intensity, or mood? Do I mean emotion and not the representation of emotion? How do the differences between modes of emotion such as passion and pathos, and between particular emotions such as grief and triumph, come into play? Emotion terms overlap in ordinary language; battling the vagueness, philosophers have developed the distinctions between them. Inevitably, emotion words are inflected variously by different writers. I try to steer a middle course between imposing a single vocabulary on all discussions of texts and giving up on terminological distinctions altogether. The terms seem to me to differ most valuably in connotation, and I've tried to preserve their shades of meaning. Some of those shades are as follows: by *emotion* we usually mean a psychological, at least minimally interpretive experience whose physiological aspect is *affect*. *Feeling* is a capacious term that connotes both physiological sensations (affects) and psychological states (emotions). Although philosophers reserve "feeling" for bodily conditions, I use it when it seems fruitful to emphasize the common ground of the physiological and the psychological. *Passion* highlights an interesting phenomenon, the difficulty of classifying emotion as passive or active. Emotions are often portrayed as expressions of a subject imposed upon the subject, as when someone is seized by remorse or surprised by joy.[7] Philosophers have taken sides on how this question should be dealt with; some address the ambiguity by dividing emotions into passive and active groups.[8] The whole quandary concentrates in the word "passion" (the same word in English and French). Although passion's Latin etymology connotes passive suffering, it has come to stand for intense goal-directedness as well—to mean "an aim or object pursued with zeal" *(OED)*. Following this latter track, Paul Ricoeur regards passions as so willful that "no passion can be placed *among* even the synthetic functions of the voluntary or the involuntary."[9] Of course passion's very force makes it seem compulsive. Thus passion drives intentional subjectivity to its self-undoing in senseless vigor—an undoing that does not have to be figured as decadent excess, but can be conceived as an interior limit of volition. Passion, therefore, characterizes the nonsubjectivity within the very concept of the subject. Finally, *pathos* conveys the explicitly representational, vicarious, and supplementary dimensions of emotion. Scenes are played not for passion, but for pathos; debates about pathos come to be about the relation between representation and intensity. If passion raises questions about the "upper" threshold of emotion—to use a spatial metaphor this time—pathos raises questions about its "lower" threshold and techniques of perpetuation. Since discussions of pathos acknowledge mediation, they play a large role in poststructuralist theories built on the significance of representation.

In this book I focus especially on emotion—emotion construed in a psychological and unremarkable way. Although emotion encompasses affect, passion, and pathos—and I grant a specialized privilege to pathos as perpetual emotion—I am most interested in the middle ranges of emotion. I assume, for example, that the meaningfulness implied by emotion is actually at stake in discussions of affect. The alleged authority of objectivity and subjectivity, the quality of affect and emotion alike, ultimately come to bear on the import of experience. Consequently, I believe that what we concede about emotion we will concede about rival terms. We tend to grant that physiological sensations are in some sense impersonal; this prompts Descartes to "prove that the mind [is] more easily known than the body"[10] and Michel Foucault and Jean-François Lyotard to use the body as a pedagogical introduction to self-difference. Emotion, however, is entangled in the mysteries of consciousness, its history locked inside the classical histories of mind and will. There does not seem to be anything unconventional, anything potentially radical in emotion. Hence emotion is seen as the territory that remains to subjects after one has admitted that even nonsubjects have affects. Emotions are usually described through the metaphor of expression, "the most classical of metaphors," as de Man writes.[11] For the very reason that emotion appears inseparable from expression and subjectivity in the first place, however, its capacity to criticize subjectivity is highly revealing. Proponents of subjectless experience find an unexpected ally in emotion. Emotion turns out to be "something perverse, under respectable appearances," Roland Barthes muses; "I was wrong when I used to see it wholly on the side of sentimentality, of moral illusion."[12]

Although focusing on alternatives to the term "emotion" doesn't contradict arguments against subjectivity, it does undersell the case to imply that the alternatives name what nonsubjects have *instead of* emotion. Here it's helpful to remain for a moment with my earlier example, Jameson's *Postmodernism.* Jameson does not want "to say that the cultural products of the postmodern era are utterly devoid of feeling, but rather that such feelings—which it may be better and more accurate, following J.-F. Lyotard, to call 'intensities'—are now free-floating and impersonal and tend to be dominated by a peculiar kind of euphoria" (15–16). For Jameson, to have "free-floating and impersonal" feelings instead of personal feelings is to be "[not] utterly devoid of feeling"—that is, to live in an age of waning affect. Similarly, Lawrence Grossberg disputes Jameson's ascription of weak affect to postmodernity, but only by drawing a distinction between emotion and affect that removes most of the point of disputing. Drawing on Gilles Deleuze and Lyotard, Grossberg specifies that "unlike emotions, affective states are neither structured narratively nor organized in response to our interpretations of situations."[13] Thus "the affective individual is not a single unified entity . . . nor is it a structured organization of its multiple possibilities," and the condition of postmodernity consists not in "a waning of affect but rather, an inability to anchor our will in something else" (125, 222). Grossberg's distinction between emotion and affect reinforces Jameson's association between emotion and centered subjectivity: there is not much disagreement here. My argument, unlike Grossberg's, is not that criticism of the subject requires a reconception of emotion-like states; it is that the classical picture of emotion already contraindicates the idea of the subject.

Championing affect is not the best way to debunk the supposed connection between emotion and subjectivity, in other words, because proponents of the subject are willing to compromise on affect. In comparison with the affect-centered Deleuze (whose texts I examine in Chapter 3), Derrida and de Man unfold fully the nonsubjectivism of emotion, as I want to demonstrate in the first and second chapters. In Chapter 3, I pursue the organization of emotion theories from the opposite angle, reading disparate philosophical texts to show their common investment in fixing the association between emotion and subjectivity—and complementarily, in the work of Deleuze, non-subjects and affects—and the common logical components on which these arguments rely. Philosophers of music, contemporary philosopher of mind Ronald de Sousa, and Deleuze and Félix Guattari demonstrate in various ways the circularity of the notion that subjects express emotions and emotions require subjects. Interlocking demands for subjects and emotions form a horizon of assumptions which makes it difficult to perceive anything outside it; I try to delineate that horizon and thus to situate subjective emotion as one scheme among alternatives—opposed, for example, to the modular account of experience offered by Daniel Dennett. In showing across Chapters 1–3 how Derrida, de Man, and Deleuze investigate the discourse of emotion, I also interpret Descartes, Husserl, Rousseau, and Spinoza at one remove. Classical philosophers, like contemporary ones, can be marshaled to show the terrain common to theories of emotion that belong to antagonistic philosophical systems. In Chapter 4, I return to deconstruction to connect Derrida's view of affection to his affiliation with de Man, and to trace the figuration of their alliance in the emotional rhetoric of Derrida's prose. Finally, in a conclusion I reflect briefly on how the metaphor of the dead subject and contemporary ideas of emotion influence one another.

De Man would seem to be a hardest case, someone whose acknowledgment of emotion is supposed to fit on a molecule. I contend, to the contrary, that de Man develops an unusually complete theory of emotion. This inversion of critical orthodoxy comes about not because I have chosen to find emotion in the most perverse possible corner, but because we have looked for poststructuralist emotion for years in exactly the wrong places—where subjectivity seems relatively robust, or else where notions of the body take priority, rather than where a genuine alternative to subjectivity has been conceived. "Deconstructive passion"—a phrase from a discussion that is exemplary for me, de Man's interpretation of Rousseau's *Julie*—is no oxymoron. Passion in Rousseau, de Man writes, is deconstructive because it supplements subjectivity, yet is called upon to efface its supplementary role (AR 198–199). My interpretations of emotion elaborate the logic of this passage, taking into account the prose as well as the reasoning of deconstructive texts. Although deconstruction is precisely relevant to the concerns I delimit here, there is reason to speak generally of poststructuralist emotion. Texts by Luce Irigaray, Julia Kristeva, Lyotard, and others, as well as the entire career of Barthes, are germane. Foucault is important not only thematically but methodologically: through *Madness and Civilization* and *The History of Sexuality* the theory of emotion becomes perceptible as a discourse. Although I reference this network of theories and theorists, I gravitate to harder cases.

In parallel to poststructuralist theory, scholarship in gender studies and psychoanalysis has also pursued the possibility of emotion after the death of the subject. Feminist writers have legitimated the whole idea of research on emotion, and have explored myriad emotive contexts—the way gendered social attitudes produce forms of emotion, for example, and fashion literary genres that cultivate certain kinds of emotions.[14] I differ with some feminist views of the discourse of emotion, especially in the literature before about 1990. Feminist criticism used to argue that philosophy slights thought about emotion and even emotion as such, much as it looks down on sentimental art. Erica Harth, writing about Descartes's influence on intellectual women of the *ancien régime,* contends that dualism "would make of emotion an object of investigation for the dispassionate mind."[15] Emotion tends, however, to occupy a high place in classical models of subjectivity. The example of Descartes is instructive: in *The Passions of the Soul,* Descartes knows that he has more to gain from tying emotion to reason than from dividing the two. In a complicated series of maneuvers, Descartes links passion, which indicates difference within reason, to a unitary *mind,* then ascribes subjectivity to that mind on the strength of its ability to encompass passion. For Descartes, thinking is the single employment of the soul as opposed to the body. Thoughts come in two sets, active and passive, the passive thoughts being passions.[16] Although Descartes classifies the passions as thoughts, and they therefore belong to the soul, they are that which, *within* thought and the soul, are not *of* them, "for it is often not our soul which makes them such as they are." "Soul" and "thought" ought by rights to be coterminous, since "there is nothing in us which we must attribute to our soul except our thoughts" (*Passions of the Soul,* 1:335)—the soul is what thinks, and that's all. The passions too are thoughts; Descartes does not assert, as he might have, that passions are nonthoughts that lie outside thought, yet inside the soul. Installing passion within thought allows Descartes to maintain that the soul is unitary, with the single duty of thinking. Still, he admits that "the passions of the soul differ from all its other thoughts" (1:338). The passions are a distinctive enough kind of thought that the category "thought" almost fails to contain them. The overlapping of thought and passion helps to explain Descartes's stake in the notorious pineal gland. For the very reason that Descartes's thought includes passions, he needs to find an apartment for the soul that avoids the dichotomy of "brain" and "body." He finds in the pineal gland an anatomical "analogue" of the passions.[17] The pineal gland, at the "innermost part of the brain" (1:340) and yet not just another part of the brain, symbolizes the possibility of an autonomous province, a Vatican City, within the brain. Defensively, it overlocalizes an entity—the soul—that is nowhere to be found. The gland literalizes the internal difference the passions make and the double edge of their location. Kicked upstairs within the thinking soul, passions are both circumscribed and dangerous. This kind of move is far more common than hostility to emotion as such: philosophy vies with emotion by elevating it, not by slighting it. Recent feminist work makes this point powerfully, showing that masculinist models of mind include and indulge emotion, and that nonsubjective engines drive the protocols of emotion and sentimentality.[18]

Any theory of emotion today, including nonsubjective theories, owes a debt to psychoanalysis. Freud's investigations of emotion are among a number of earlier approaches—Nietzsche's and Benjamin's work on pathos and allegory, Heidegger's theory of moods—that support the later texts I study here. Emotion in Freud operates very much as a differential force within experience.[19] My goal in these pages cannot be to construct a model of poststructuralist Freudianism, but I write informed by its possibility. The poststructuralist response to Freud matters to emotion in part because of the way it negotiates the tension between negation and repression. Freud recognizes that as a mode of representation, negation includes a positive dimension.[20] Damping feelings produces compensatory displacements that may seem inferior in kind; but negation raises questions for compensation, for it hints that negated feelings may not be less represented than other feelings, and that there may be no undisplaced feelings. Freud deals with such complications in his work on secondary repression; poststructuralist theory picks up the thread. In Foucault's *History of Sexuality,* repressive power creates displacements, "but also incitement and intensification." Foucault upgrades the intensity of displacements and their continuity with the "polymorphous techniques of power" that form them.[21] Emotion is not as easy to restrain and to release as it would be if it emanated from a subject. Far from implying that emotion is no longer emotive, however, this difficulty characterizes mainline emotion in the first place.

Poststructuralist theory's imagination of emotion differs from the decentered psychology offered by Lacanian psychoanalysis, since Lacan identifies certain discontinuities of experience with subjectivity itself. Thus Slavoj Žižek presents his reading of Lacan as an extension of classical thought. This orientation appears clearly in Žižek's recent conversation with Judith Butler: to Butler's assertion that subjectivity begins in the coerced attachment of a child to adults—"passionate attachment"—Žižek replies that the subject consists in a "primordial abyss of dis-attachment" that precedes attachment: "the need for 'passionate attachment' to provide for a minimum of being implies that the subject *qua* 'abstract negativity'—the primordial gesture of dis-attachment from its environment—*is already there.*"[22] Žižek discovers the subject as a neo-Kantian structure; subjectivity is read out of the experience of disattachment that makes it seem as though a subject were there to be disattached. Poststructuralist and Lacanian theorists thus interpret self-difference in mutually exclusive ways: the regress that, for poststructuralist theorists, impedes the closure of subjectivity just is what Žižek calls subjectivity. In a 1991 interview, Derrida slips away from the disagreement: "Some might say: but what we call 'subject' is not the absolute origin, pure will, identity to self, or presence to self of consciousness but precisely this noncoincidence with self," he notes. "This is a riposte to which we'll have to return. By what right do we call this 'subject'? . . . By what right, conversely, can we be forbidden from calling this 'subject'? Perhaps we'll pick this up again later on."[23] I agree with Thomas Keenan that questions such as "who speaks, reads, acts, takes responsibility or claims rights, if not me?" have "again and again" been answered: *"no one,"* and that "'no one' is not a new name or placeholder for what used to be called the 'subject.'"[24] It is true, however, that self-difference is a crossroads where the merits of subjectivity can be debated without anachronism.

Of the subtheses in this study, two are worth mentioning now. First, the relatively uncontroversial observation that expression is the dominant trope of thought about emotion. The ideology of emotion diagrams emotion as something lifted from a depth to a surface. "The term 'emotion,'" James R. Averill points out, "stems from the Latin, *e + movere,* which originally meant 'to move out,' 'to migrate,' or 'to transport an object.'"[25] It is so conventional to think at once of "expression and feelings or emotions," as Jameson puts it, that attacks on expression look like attacks on emotion. One might wonder whether it's really necessary to criticize expression; as an aesthetic doctrine, it seems rather outdated. Although people rarely advocate expression as such, however, current discussions of emotion are ubiquitously expressive. The purpose of expression tropes is to extrapolate a human subject circularly from the phenomenon of emotion. The claim that emotion requires a subject—thus we can see we're subjects, since we have emotions—creates the illusion of subjectivity rather than showing evidence of it. This sleight of mind, in which "expression" serves as the distracting handkerchief, strikes me as self-serving. It is this relatively large complex of circularity, naturalization, and inversion to which I refer as the *expressive hypothesis.* To object to the expressive hypothesis or any other mechanism of the ideology of emotion is not to discredit emotion, but to extricate it from expedient mythologies.

Mikel Dufrenne's *Phenomenology of Aesthetic Experience* [1953], cited sympathetically by Deleuze in *Cinema 1,* is a veritable encyclopedia of the ideologies of emotion to which poststructuralism reacts. In Dufrenne subjectivity's reliance on emotional expression is perfectly bare:

It is through what we have said of expression that we can gain an idea of the primordial reality of affective quality, wherein that part belonging to the subject and that belonging to the object are still indistinguishable. In fact, expression is that which reveals affective quality as total and undifferentiated. Expression exists prior to the distinction between body and soul, exterior and interior. The container and the contained are not yet differentiated within expression. Thus a certain melody *is* tenderness, without our having to effect a *rapprochement* between notes taken as a musical reality and tenderness as an emotional reality. As a word has a sense before being grasped as a phonetic reality and prior to the distinction between phoneme and semanteme, so the aesthetic object has a sense before it appears as a material object or as a signifying object. Affective quality is precisely this sense as immediately given through the sign. But to be prior to the distinction between interior and exterior is also to be prior to the distinction between subject and object, for the interior refers to a subject and the exterior to an object. Tenderness is at once a quality of Mozart and of a Mozartian melody, as tenderness is also a quality of the soul and countenance of the mother who smiles at her baby. Therefore, the creator appears immanent in the work only because there is a primary state of expression. . . . Feeling is as deeply embedded in the object as it is in the subject, and the spectator experiences feeling because affective quality belongs to the object.[26]

Like much of the ideology of emotion, Dufrenne's approach is transcendental. He contends that when we think we feel the "affective quality" of an object, we're not fantasizing; our feeling corroborates the existence of a "primordial reality" of expressiveness. Expression shapes interiority and exteriority "prior to the distinction between subject and object"—which explains circularly why everything fits together in this world. It is the special mission of feelings to identify correspondences, phenomenalizing the unity between subjects and objects. The semantic token of unity is the abstract noun ("tenderness," "quality"). Dufrenne closes with the most rapturous image of emotional connection, the smile exchanged between mother and child. As de Man remarks of similar ideas in Rilke, this kind of "perfect adjustment can take place only because the totality [is] established beforehand" (AR 38).[27]

To make the transmission of emotion maximally efficient, or in Dufrenne's words, to present "affective quality . . . as immediately given through the sign," voice and face become superconductors; the mother's countenance expresses her tender soul. In the case of elite media like the voice or music, de Man suggests, "the analogy between outer event and inner feeling" can be "so close that the figural distance between [outer event] and speech or even music almost vanishes."[28] Vocal and facial diaphaneity expedite the expressive hypothesis and the subject to which they bear illusionistic witness. For complementary reasons, poststructuralist theory's attention to voice and face should be seen as part of its study of emotion. Derrida's deconstruction of phenomenological voice, de Man's theory of prosopopoeia—the figure by which we perceive something as a face—and Deleuze's reflections on "faciality" and the cinematic close-up are episodes in poststructuralism's engagement with emotional experience.

Second, I will refer often to the *economy of pathos,* the recirculating infinity of feeling living on. In the discourse of emotion, specific emotions appear and disappear, carrying peculiar rationales with them, but there is no such thing as the absence of emotion. Emotions arise from others' subsidence, from reflection on emotions, and from the very absence of any particular thing to feel. While there are differences between individual emotions, second-order emotion is not less emotional as such than first-order emotion. When we're aware of the second-order nature of emotion we call it "pathos" and act as though it were something other than emotion. What is disturbing in the idea of second-order states is not finally position in sequence but supplementarity. Jameson brushes near this point in his meditation on Warhol's "Diamond Dust Shoes." Warhol's print, based on a photographic negative, uses an emotional rhetoric; Jameson notes that it exudes "a strange, compensatory, decorative exhilaration" (10). Ghostly negativity imparts to the shoes a "deathly quality . . . that would seem to have nothing to do with death" (9). Objects that seem to have no substance nonetheless seem to have characteristics; objects that seem never to have lived do seem to have died. Jameson contrasts Warholian exhilaration with the depth-effect and "immediacy" of Van Gogh's shoe paintings (8). Thus he associates pathos with mediation in images—with the realization that images are being produced in series. The image seems off-present, either too early or too late, a pre- or after-image. Parallel to this experience in the image-world is pathos in the emotion-world. Many questions surface here: Why should images that appear to possess a deathly quality invite less emotion than images that appear to possess a lively quality? Can we frame an emotionless moment for which compensatory exhilaration compensates? Is there, in real time, a sequence of reimbursement here, or is that only a way to narrate a complex simultaneity? How do we locate temporally an event that counts as an emotion? Is there anything to do other than feel? Even if the observer does not pity Warhol's shoes as though they were animate, she can still, with equal anthropomorphism, feel sorry for their inability to inspire sorrow. Any apparent ebbing of pathos makes more as well as less pathos: the less pathetic the end of pathos is, the more pathetic it is that it isn't pathetic any more. This regress typifies the structure of emotion (and I do mean *emotion*)—it describes diamond dust selves.

Keats affords a glimpse into a similar infinity in his poem "Drear-Nighted December." Keats's poetic narrator seems to wish he could stop feeling. "Ah! would 'twere," he sighs,

> But were there ever any
>   Writh'd not of passed joy?
> The feel of not to feel it,
>   When there is none to heal it,
> Nor numbed sense to steel it,
>   Was never said in rhyme.

By treating a "passed" emotion as an occasion for emotion, Keats implies that we do not have to understand an emotive state positively in order to writhe with it. "It" is an ambiguous pronoun, and its ambiguity is magnified here by a suite of negatives. Like Warhol's print, the poem reverses values to lead us into the opalescent end and beginning of feeling, where anesthesia hurts. While Keats's first "it" may refer either to "joy" or "passed joy," the later "its" can also refer to "the feel of not to feel it" itself. The point is not simply that poets lack the means to describe such states; arguably, the poem does say in rhyme what it says was never said. It is that feeling never quite disappears. Physicists speak of the "Planck length," the smallest something can get; shrinking circles that approach the Planck scale start to appear as though they are getting larger. Pathos is the Planck length of emotion, bounding the theory of emotion as the least that can be said.

This book coincides with a surge in the academic study of feeling. I am glad of this interesting development and glad to be part of it. I would seem not to have read my own words, however, if I didn't also wonder where the attraction to emotion comes from and why it comes just now. The texts discussed below suggest that historically, the idea of emotion has been activated to reinforce notions of subjectivity that could use the help. They also suggest that people deploy emotion in epistemologically defensive ways. Criticism's newfound thematization of emotion may be no exception; rising feeling may acknowledge and ward off antinomies in institutional life and thought, much as Rilke's *Duino Elegies,* de Man finds, "constantly appeal to the reader's emotion" just where they give up on classical reference (AR 49). Conversation about emotion often attempts to supply a sense of substantiality and purpose where there is and sometimes should be none. The discussion of critical emotions can always be ideological in this way. Respect for the power of emotion should encourage scholars to inquire closely into their assumptions about their own.[29] Of course, this does not mean there is anything unreal about the emotionality of experience, or that we ever could or should trade our emotions for the empty lucidity of a neutral world.

CHAPTER ONE

Cogito and the History of the Passions

While French feminists, Barthes, Deleuze and Guattari, Foucault, and Lyotard are all at least recognized for reinventing eroticism, deconstruction is regarded as a pathologically austere area of thought.[1] Pathologically austere or pathologically conflicted: Derrida's stance on emotion, especially, has been characterized as contradictory. No one argues that Derrida ignores emotion: themes of desire and loss suffuse his middle and later work; he has produced in the "Envois" section of *The Post Card* an epistolary novel about amatory writing and attachment, and in "Circumfession" a moving autobiographical reflection on his mother's death. Still, he is often considered a passionate writer whose ideas cannot fully comprehend his feelings. On this view, Derrida's emotive qualities burst the bounds of his thought. Separating Derrida's emotiveness from his philosophy ends in the idea that where Derrida exhibits emotion, he is out of control—in his sarcastic riposte to John Searle in *Limited Inc*, for example, or in his defense of his friend Paul de Man. The critical dispute about Derrida's willingness to show emotion, especially in the debate about de Man's wartime journalism, is itself impassioned; I will discuss some of the terms of the controversy in Chapter 4. First, however, I want to propose an interpretation of Derrida's work that lets us see how emotion engages the textual structures that belong to the paradigm of the death of the subject—the paradigm emotion is presumed to exceed.

To do this, I draw upon the same matrix of ideas that generates

Derrida's philosophy of différance. This matrix is less an argument than a configuration visible within and across texts—a picture composed by the discourse of emotion. Derridean emotion theory consists in relations between Derrida's "Cogito and the History of Madness," *Speech and Phenomena,* and *Of Grammatology,* Descartes's *Discourse on Method,* Husserl's *Logical Investigations,* and Rousseau's *Essay on the Origin of Languages* and *Letter to M. D'Alembert.* Reading (and writing) Descartes, Husserl, and Rousseau, sifting and reframing their premises, Derrida's texts approach a theory of emotion again and again; they prepare elements of such a theory without stating the theory itself. Even though no narrative but this one connects them, these elements—experiential notions of citation, différance, and textuality—are codependent and constitute a way of thinking about emotion without the expressive hypothesis of the subject and its contents. No necessary relation obtains between a writer's emotional or unemotional language and the ideas he or she holds; nonetheless, I'll show in Chapter 4 that Derrida's thematically emotional writings do unfold in a way predicted here. In this chapter, though, I leave aside the question of impassioned prose—and of consistency between ideas and textual behaviors—to gather together elements of an emotive set.

Derrida's response to Descartes, Husserl, and Rousseau reflects their awareness that emotion is an interpretive act and that positions on representation influence positions on emotion. The ideology of emotion is a "white mythology,"[2] a fiction of transparency and presence. Classically subjective schemes of emotion depend on the disappearance or insignificance of representation: Husserl and Rousseau affirm subjectivity on the basis of the representational translucence they figure as auto-affection. Auto-affection, the mode of transparent self-reflexivity, ensures passage from affect—mere corporeal sensations—to meaningfully interpretive emotions that can be ascribed to subjects. Conversely, the persistent differentiality of representation ushers in a textual scheme of emotional experience. Because mental representations are never equal to themselves, subjectivity remains an fictive threshold, a "finish line," as Dennett calls it, that is never actually crossed.[3] Auto-affection, Derrida argues, is necessarily second-order, and its secondariness both obstructs epistemology and enables emotion. Experience is experience at all only because of the self-difference of self-representation. Thus experience and subjectivity are incompatible. This, at any rate, is the tale that, by its own reasoning, the philosophy of subjectivity must tell.

Derrida also suggests dynamic relations between affect and emotion. Derrida's reflections on Husserl pertain mostly to development from affect to emotion, articulating a general theory of feeling; his readings of Rousseau reach into particularized social spheres. In both cases, affects appear to be unconscious and prereflexive; auto-affection demands a minimal registration of representation; and full-blown emotions respond to the representationality of mental representations as such. Since auto-affection involves representation, experience of any sort is already second-order; but emotions are explicitly mediated, registering registration. The existence of emotion reflects not just the content of mental representations but the fact that they are representations. Rousseau considers this phenomenon under the name of theatricality—the arena in which representation appears as such. Emotion in Rousseau responds to theatrical cues, attempting to "interiorize" them. Far from being diluted by representations of representations, then, emotions actually require them. A situation that Wittgenstein considers too absurd seriously to contemplate—in which people can feel emotions only through intermediate representations, which he likens to "inanimate things" or "dolls"—is the case even when the intermediary is oneself.[4]

Philosophy of Emotion

Before reading Derrida's texts on Continental philosophy, it's helpful to set them against the background of recent Anglo-American understandings of emotion, for this body of work is both opposed to poststructuralist positions and affiliated with earlier philosophies of intention to which poststructuralism replies. Michael Stocker notes that while philosophers have commonly believed that "emotions have, indeed are in part constituted by, cognitive, desiderative, and evaluative content," philosophy since the 1950s has given extra credit to emotions' ideational content.[5] The content approach to emotion comes in several variations, stressing background beliefs, attitudes, intentions, thoughts, propositions, or objects. The umbrella term for these approaches is often "cognitive theory," but I agree with Paul Griffiths that "the label 'cognitive' suggests a concern with the findings of cognitive psychology and with the study of emotions as part of human information processing[,] and nothing could be more misleading."[6] Like Stocker, I'll refer to this school of thought, understood slightly more broadly than Stocker understands it, as the "content approach" to emotion.

The content approach holds that emotions are both physiological and ideational, but that an individual emotion's character stems from the specific beliefs and desires involved. This line of thought flourished in the wake of Stanley Schacter and J. E. Singer's 1962 finding in experimental psychology that the physiological attributes of emotions are not very distinct (in the experiment, people interpreted injections of adrenaline differently according to context).[7] Although emotions are presented as blends of feelings and ideas, ideas are supposed to do the primary work of coloring emotions. "When we speak of a psychological state as an emotion," Amélie Rorty suggests, "we focus on the ways we are affected by our appraisals, evaluative perceptions, or descriptions."[8] Robert Solomon takes the subordination of feelings to an extreme, arguing that " 'feelings' and physiology and, with qualifications, dispositions to behave, do *not* play an essential role in the constitution of emotions and cannot be used in even the most rudimentary account of the definitive properties of either emotions in general or particular emotions."[9] Solomon's formulation is particularly inflexible, but many would at least agree that in addition to being affects, emotions have to be about something. Like intentions, emotions entail beliefs and apply to objects. To this extent, they are less sensations that happen to one than thoughts that one pursues.

Content approaches to emotion rely on theories of intentional content. As Helen Nissenbaum notes, most philosophers who see emotions as intentional acts "draw on the tradition of phenomenology for the key notion of intentionality."[10] Thus one precursor of the content approach is Edmund Husserl, the focus of Derrida's earliest research. Husserl claims that emotions come into being through their connections to intentional objects: "We do not merely have a presentation, with an added feeling *associatively* tacked on to it, and not intrinsically related to it, but pleasure or distaste *direct* themselves to the presented object, and could not exist without such a direction."[11] Thus Husserl distinguishes "feeling-acts" (emotions) from "feeling-sensations" such as bodily pain: emotions are about something, while pains aren't. And he solves the problem of our not always knowing what our emotions are about by positing formal objects for them. If an object is vague or indeterminate, that is no obstacle to its being an algebraic object: "Here we are dealing with intentional experiences, but with such as are characterized by indeterminateness of objective direction. . . . The idea we have when 'something' stirs, when there is a rustling, a ring at the door, etc., an idea had before we give it verbal expression, has indeterminateness of direction, and this indeterminateness is of the intention's essence, it is determined as presenting an indeterminate 'something' " (*Logical Investigations*, Fifth Investigation, §15). The advantage of having emotions exemplify subjective intentionality is that we can hold people responsible for their emotive reactions. (Thus Solomon's strictures on feeling, quoted above, come in an essay called "Emotions and Choice.") These conclusions become problematic if emotions are basically feelings or are modeled on feelings.

When Husserl writes about the content of intentions, he means merely representational content. He is not, in the style of Dufrenne, deploying metaphors of interiority and substance, but schematizing mental life using formal categories. Nonetheless, the notion of representational content gains its cachet from its proximity to substance. John McDowell, on his way to a very different conclusion, makes this point:

> When Kant says that thoughts without content are empty, he is not merely affirming a tautology. . . . "Without content" points to what would *explain* the sort of emptiness Kant is envisaging. And we can spell out the explanation from the other half of Kant's remark: "intuitions without concepts are blind." Thoughts without content—which would not really be thoughts at all—would be a play of concepts without any connection with intuitions, that is, bits of experiential intake. It is their connection with experiential intake that supplies the content, the substance, that thoughts would otherwise lack.
>
> So the picture is this: the fact that thoughts are not empty, the fact that thoughts have representational content, emerges out of an interplay of concepts and intuitions. . . .
>
> The very idea of representational content . . . requires an interplay between concepts and intuitions.[12]

McDowell returns substance to representational content because he believes that coherence accounts of mind and world that did *not* bridge content and substance would fail to address the anxieties that motivate people to think about mind and world in the first place. The philosophy of emotion bears McDowell out. The content approach takes emotions as evidence that subjective intentions connect to intuitions: affects—impacts on or in the living body—are intuitions, and emotion is thought to *be* the link between affect and subjective intention, for it combines affects and mental objects. "It has been thought that the contact between affect and cognition takes place primarily or even exclusively at the level of internal mental representations," write psychologists R. B. Zajonc and Hazel Markus.[13] According to the content approach, emotion shows that as McDowell contends, "the very idea of representational content" is more than merely representational. The fact that emotions possess content is supposed to fulfill a preexisting connectibility between the conceptual and the empirical. If emotion joins ideas and intuitions, however, it is also uniquely positioned to unhinge the philosophy of mind. Emotions "drag us from our dreams of pure reason," Ronald de Sousa writes, "yet just as surely they are mental phenomena" (RE 3).

Husserl and Rousseau both contribute to the content approach to emotion by maintaining that emotions rise to the level of concepts. In interrelated texts of the 1960s, Derrida considers this claim. Accepting for argument the distinction between affect and emotion, Derrida describes a surprising consequence: if one does accept that duality, then our own emotions emerge only through the acts of interpretation and identification by means of which we feel *for others*. Second-order emotion sounds like "emotion" in quotation marks, a mere miming of emotion, but Derrida's investigation suggests the opposite.[14] We are not ourselves without representations that mediate us, and it is through those representations that emotions get felt. Emotions are neither intentional nor expressive—not because they don't have objects, and not because we don't feel them on purpose, but because whether they are directed at objects or not, and whether we feel them on purpose or not, they take place on what must seem to be a mental stage peopled by virtual entities. Dennett calls this stage "the Cartesian Theater," and one of his main conclusions is that, contrary to Descartes's statements, the implied beholder of this stage is necessarily a virtual entity as well. Debate about that point lies ahead. The point at hand is that *in philosophy* the implied beholder—the Cartesian would-be subject—feels when it represents itself to itself, when it reads its self-representation.

Traditional aesthetics contemplates the sheer fact of mental representation less often than the meaning of fictionality, debating what kind of emotion, if any, we feel for mental objects with no empirical source. If it is granted that fictions inflame true emotions, that is usually explained by the thesis that fictional predicaments recall actual ones.[15] Under Rousseau's and Derrida's laws of theatricality, though, objects are not necessarily fictive, yet emotion always comes in a frame. *Speech and Phenomena* and *Of Grammatology* dwell on this curious state of affairs. They suggest that we feel not to the extent that experience seems immediate, but to the extent that it doesn't; not to the extent that other people's experiences remind us of our own, but to the extent that our own seem like someone else's.[16]

Cogito and the History of the Passions

Do our inmost experiences seem like someone else's? Do we have to imagine our way into ourselves? These are Cartesian questions, and poststructuralist theory depicts the Cartesian theater as a zone of auditory hallucination and oblique self-approach.[17] Derrida's early "Cogito and the History of Madness" [1964] takes the further step— a step I want to retrace—of defining this zone as that of emotive experience. "Cogito and the History of Madness" demonstrates a fundamental affinity between phenomenality and textuality, showing that emphasizing experience encourages a textualist stance toward life. Indeed, readings of Descartes's *Discourse on Method* generally predict the degree to which philosophers value experience: the more one honors Descartes's phenomenological description of the cogito over his rationalizations of it, the more one sees his subject as a mere defense against that description.[18]

Derrida takes Descartes's description very seriously, tuning in to Descartes's subtle references to what the cogito feels like. His disagreement in this essay with Foucault's *Madness and Civilization* is legend: Derrida attributes to Foucault the thesis that Descartes "executed . . . a summary expulsion of the possibility of madness from thought itself," and claims that, on the contrary, Descartes's cogito "is valid *even if I am mad.*"[19] Rather than excluding madness, the cogito for Derrida is a "zero point" ("Cogito," 56) at which both mad and sane thought are born as possibilities.[20] What interests me here is Derrida's fascination with the phenomenology of the cogito. Perhaps we mistake Descartes's "mad audacity," he writes, "because . . . we are too well assured of ourselves and too accustomed to the framework of the Cogito, rather than to the critical experience of it" ("Cogito," 56). As an "experience," Cartesian thought runs through emotional stages—"thought is announced to itself, *frightens* itself, and *reassures* itself against being annihilated or wrecked in madness or in death" ("Cogito," 61). The cogito consists at the broadest level of the maintenance of coherent discourse in inner speech—ideally, philosophical discourse. As one keeps talking to buy time, the Cartesian ego keeps thinking: "If I had merely ceased thinking," Descartes reflects, "I should have had no reason to believe I existed."[21] Sentence by sentence, "philosophy is perhaps the reassurance given against the anguish of being mad at the point of greatest proximity to madness. This silent and specific moment could be called *pathetic*" ("Cogito," 59). My point is not to italicize the emotion-words in Derrida's description of Descartes (Derrida already italicizes them), but to notice that the space between thinking and being—the self-difference that keeps experience short of subjectivity—fills up with fear and reassurance. Derrida underscores the pathos of the scene because "pathos" is the precise term for emotion *for another.* Pathos is indeed the Cartesian emotion, because in sustaining thought, I feel for myself as I announce myself to me.

Classical philosophies close self-difference either by claiming to have completed the process of subjectification or—in realism—by dismissing self-difference as a chimera. Vincent Descombes, for example, argues that poststructuralist "critics of the subject" and Cartesian "defenders of the subject" alike divide the transcendental subject from the person, the major distinction between the two being that "the critics of the Cartesian subject want the difference [between subject and person] to be more vigorously marked."[22] For Descombes "the quarrel of the subject is . . . when all is said and done, a scholastic quarrel," for "whether we speak of 'true subject' or of 'nonsubject' is a difference in terminology but not in thinking" ("Apropos of the 'Critique of the Subject,' " 133, 126): "The critique of the subject was not the critique of the philosophical subject, but rather a protest against the tendency to confuse subjectivity (defined by methods of doubt, of presupposition, or experience or postulation) with a person's mental life" ("Apropos of the 'Critique of the Subject,' " 125).

Where in this analysis is the phenomenology of the Derridean cogito? Despite his concern with mental life, Descombes does not mention what it is like. Arthur Danto similarly claims that "what is curious is that in our own case, the distance between ourselves and the world which the concept of truth requires is automatically closed."[23] "Automatically"? Can one recognize one's own experience of consciousness in this statement? In comparison, "Cogito and the History of Madness" pays attention primarily to the unremitting difference of mental life as it seems to us. In this it is unironically phenomenological, or to put it the other way around, here post-Cartesian phenomenology anticipates poststructuralist theory. Musing on modern revivals of the cogito, Foucault notes that "phenomenology is . . . much less the resumption of an old rational goal of the West than the sensitive and precisely formulated acknowledgment of the great hiatus that occurred in the modern *episteme* at the turn of the eighteenth and nineteenth centuries"; its fondness for detail overcomes its ideology, as "the phenomenological project continually resolves itself . . . into a description—empirical despite itself—of actual experience" (*Order of Things*, 325, 326).[24] Derrida's work extends the descriptive fineness of phenomenology but reformulates the meaning of such description. It implies that self-difference—falsely resolved in the Cartesian tradition, rejected as nonsense in the realist tradition—is experience itself, nonsubjective experience. In Derrida's memorable phrasing, "to be Cartesian . . . is to attempt to be Cartesian" in a way that can no longer be encompassed within Cartesianism ("Cogito," 61). By the same token, not being Cartesian can no longer be encompassed within *anti*-Cartesianism, either, since Cartesian experience itself consists of not being Cartesian in the first place. Derrida's sketch of experience as not-being-Cartesian in "Cogito and the History of Madness" conforms poorly to Descombes's expectation of how criticisms of the subject behave. Because Derrida conceives subjective incompleteness as a "critical experience," he proposes precisely an identity between the nonexistence of subjectivity and "a person's mental life."[25] Subjectivity should not be "confuse[d]" with mental life, not because Derrida cuts mental life out of the picture, but because mental life *should* be confused (so to speak) with something else: with the nonexistence of subjectivity. The "death" of the subject institutes mental life; dismissing self-difference therefore forecloses emotion even as it posits subjectivity.

Feeling and Phenomena

Do we have to imagine our way into ourselves? Derrida argues in *Speech and Phenomena* that Husserl's first concern is to make sure we don't. Derrida locates the crisis of this endeavor in Husserl's concept of auto-affection, a peculiarly refined form of self-reflexivity.

Auto-affection has had a long, strange career in philosophy. It appeals to philosophers of subjectivity because it promises self-sufficiency. "Cogito ergo sum" can be interpreted as an auto-affective motto.[26] In the guise of the self-causing first cause, auto-affection underpins metaphysics; Nietzsche complains that philosophers believe "everything of the first rank must be *causa sui*. Origin in something else counts as an objection, as casting a doubt on value."[27] Thus auto-affection is sometimes thought to typify living systems; Husserl, Derrida finds, figures "life as self-relationship."[28] Husserl's idea of a "primal impression" of time claims mythic self-causation: "it does not come into existence as that which is generated," Husserl declares, "but through *spontaneous generation* [Derrida's italics]."[29] Simultaneously spontaneous and second-order, auto-affection is the putative distortion-free form of representation, the mode of representation of one's own sensations and ideas to oneself. In such a language we could form mental representations free of the side effects of all media. Emotions would be felt toward these mental objects—emotions modeled on cognition as opposed to affect, individuated by particular contents, and authenticated by intending subjects.[30]

Derrida contends, however, that just because auto-affection *is* self-enclosed, it raises the question of representation where its consequences are most damaging, inside for-itselfness. Husserl's "dream of a mode of being that would not have to borrow from outside itself anything foreign to its own spontaneity"[31] is also a vision of experience mediated all the way in. In *Of Grammatology*, reading Rousseau's *Essay on the Origin of Languages*, Derrida writes:

> Auto-affection is a universal structure of experience. All living things are capable of auto-affection. And only a being capable of symbolizing, that is to say of auto-affecting, may let itself be affected by the other in general. Auto-affection is the condition of an experience in general. This possibility—another name for "life"—is a general structure articulated by the history of life, and leading to complex and hierarchical operations. Auto-affection, the as-for-itself or for-itself—subjectivity—gains in power and in its mastery of the other to the extent that its power of repetition *idealizes itself*. Here idealization is the movement by which sensory exteriority, that which affects me or serves me as signifier, submits itself to my power of repetition, to what thenceforward appears to me as my spontaneity and escapes me less and less.[32]

Derrida turns the paradox of immediate representation inside out, into the antithetical paradox of produced immediacy. Auto-affection constitutes the representationality of object and subject-production; in experiential terms, it is the feeling of self-relation: "Ideality and substantiality relate to themselves, in the element of the *res cogitans,* by a movement of pure auto-affection. Consciousness is the experience of pure auto-affection" (G 98).

According to Derrida, Husserl thus winds up making clearer than ever the problems that beset classical considerations of mental life: (1) While consciousness is presumed to occur in the present, there is nonetheless something retrospective about it, since it kicks in with representation; the temporality attributed to it is not the temporality it describes. (2) The self-enclosure of auto-affection upsets the distinction between conceptual emotion and mere empirical affect. Because auto-affection is self-enclosed, it is difficult to say whether it is intentional or empirical, an "act" or a "sensation" in Husserl's terms. When what I sense is my sensing something, my feelings' relation to their content is even tighter than (one of Husserl's examples) "the relation of pleasure to the pleasant" (*Logical Investigations,* Fifth Investigation, §15). Husserl writes of feeling-sensations that "our sensations are here functioning as presentative contents in perceptual acts," and this is true of auto-affections as well. Yet in contrast to feeling-sensations, it cannot be said of auto-affections that "they themselves are not acts" (*Logical Investigations,* Fifth Investigation, §15). Neither passive nor active, substance nor idea, yet not *non*substance, *non*idea, auto-affection cannot be assimilated to affect or to cognition as these states are classically defined. (3) Classical and realist descriptions of consciousness notice effects of self-difference, but discount them as stray antinomies. Manfred Frank argues, "Husserl would not dispute this internal differentiality of self-consciousness (contrary to his teacher Franz Brentano, Husserl describes self-consciousness as self-*relation*). He would, however, emphasize that in the case of this differentiality of self-consciousness, it is actually only a matter of a *virtual* difference" (*What Is Neostructuralism?* 233). From a poststructuralist perspective, in contrast, even if self-differentiality is virtual there is nothing insignificant about our needing to experience this virtual difference in order to be conscious. Ignoring it is like saying, like one of Bob Dylan's ballad narrators, that you don't have to worry about dreams because they're "only in your head." The real differentiality is not between ideality and substance but between the virtuality of this division and its experiential persistence; not between the subject and the person, but within the experience of the person. If one grants Derrida's point in this regard, experience appears enmeshed in a fiction—the seemingly fabulous notion that we deal with ourselves through reports. In Rousseau, as we'll see, internal differentiality, while sometimes unwelcome, has effects in emotional life. But in the realist tradition, it casts no shadow; it is simply a mirage that we must expunge from our picture of the world.

Derrida claims that Husserl attempts to isolate expression in the privileged medium of "phenomenological voice," "the expressive discourse" that "has no need of being effectively uttered in the world" (SP 32). Voice is

> a medium which both preserves the *presence of the object* before intuition and *self-presence*, the absolute proximity of the [subjective] acts to themselves. . . .
>
> The subject can hear or speak to himself and be affected by the signifier he produces, without passing through an external detour. (SP 76, 78)

Voice, the vehicle of expression, extends the translucence of auto-affection to emotive content. There are nonvocal auto-affections, Derrida observes, but Husserl sees these as insufficiently transparent. On the one hand, auto-affection performed through writing or gesture has to "pass through what is outside" (SP 78) and so cannot secure self-immediacy; on the other, there are "forms of pure auto-affection in the inwardness of one's own body" that "remain purely empirical," since they can't be idealized or willfully repeated. Only "hearing oneself speak is experienced as an absolutely pure auto-affection," both subjective and ideal:

> As pure auto-affection, the operation of hearing oneself speak seems to reduce even the inward surface of one's own body; in its phenomenal being it seems capable of dispensing with this exteriority within interiority, this interior space in which our experience or image of our own body is spread forth. This is why hearing oneself speak [*s'entendre parler*] is experienced as an absolutely pure auto-affection, occurring in a self-proximity that would in fact be the absolute reduction of space in general. (SP 79)

Husserl's preference for ideal over empirical auto-affection inflects his semiotic theory, and vice versa, through an opposition between "expression" and "indication." Voice delivers "expression" *(Aus-*

druck)—by which Husserl means not just any externalization, but "a purely linguistic sign" that can reveal the relation of intending consciousness to "an objective ideality" (SP 18, 22). Expression is contrasted by Husserl to "indication" *(Anzeigen)*, an indexical gesturing-toward things by vocal or other signs. In an illustration of Derrida's, "the canals of Mars *indicate* the possible presence of intelligent beings" (SP 27). Now—this is important—the contrast between indication and expression transposes the contrast between feeling and emotion and vice versa. Indication and expression, affect and emotion, share common roots. One term in each pair is opaque and empirical, the other transparent and conceptual. Like expression, emotion links intending subjectivity with ideality; like expression, it is a "white mythology" that escapes the unconsciousness of bodily processes and gains ideal lucidity without suffering any loss of immediacy. Not accidentally, emotion is proverbially what is expressed. Husserl's technical sense of "expression" and casual usage, in which expression means any articulation, but especially the articulation of an emotional state, intertwine. Jameson notes, "the very concept of expression" culminates in a moment in which " 'emotion' is then projected out" (*Postmodernism*, 11).[33] Emotions appear to be exemplary inner contents, however, *because* the history of thought about emotion has invested in theories of expression, with the result that emotions have had to become "cognitive" in order to fit those theories. Thus Derrida's attack on Husserl's security-obsessed theory of ideal expression enables an attack on the expressive hypothesis of subjective emotion.

In Chapter 6 of *Speech and Phenomena*, "The Voice That Keeps Silence," Derrida shows how expressive voice introduces its own distortions—with consequences for ideas of emotion built to match it. According to Derrida, Husserl isolates voice not only from everything empirical but from a threat within itself; in performing this maneuver, Husserl exposes an internal digression, an envelope of theatricality. Husserl's "strange prerogative" (SP 70) of the vocal figure, Derrida notes, makes an exception of interior address—imaginary dialogue in which I address myself as "you." In Husserl's example, "someone says to himself: 'You have gone wrong, you can't go on like that' " (*Logical Investigations*, First Investigation, §8, quoted in SP 48).[34] The whole point of Husserl's project is to assure subjective immediacy; inside this project, I can't represent myself to myself because I have neither the need nor the ability to get information about myself *indirectly* (§8, SP 49). Like Wittgenstein, for whom self-knowledge obviates interpretation—"one does not infer one's own conviction from one's own words"[35]—Husserl concludes that interior address must be, as Derrida phrases it, "only a false communication" (SP 70), "only *representation* and *imagination*" (SP 48). Only expression—that is, "expressing oneself about something"[36]—animates ideality, while "in the interior monologue, a word is thus only represented. It can occur in the imagination [*Phantasie*]" (SP 43). Husserl's exemption of interior address from voice parallels J. L. Austin's exemption from performative utterances of words "said by an actor on the stage . . . or spoken in soliloquy."[37] Words the mind addresses to itself as "you" do not convey idealities: they therefore aren't, in Husserl's sense, really expressive. Because it is *theatrical,* Husserl's mind addressing itself is no better off than those auto-affections inside the body that remain merely *empirical.* Much as Kant's thoughts without content are empty, while his intuitions without concepts are blind, Husserl's empirical auto-affections are blind and his theatrical ones are empty.

Derrida observes that the exclusion of interior address produces a weird result: silently addressing yourself is less immediate than speaking aloud to someone else. "If one is heard by another, to speak is to make him *repeat immediately* in himself the hearing-oneself-speak in the very form in which I effectuated it" (SP 80). When I talk to someone else I reduce the distance between us, since there *is* a distance; when I talk to myself I take the long way around, since I shouldn't need to address me. Thus the ruling figure of this part of *Speech and Phenomena* is involution, which curves space and creates a theatrical echo.[38] As soon as one takes this figure as a model, the rest is grammatology: Derrida contends that all voice is "*representation* and *imagination*," cloaked as it may be in rhetorics of immediacy. The sentence that Husserl specifically excludes from voice—"You have gone wrong, you can't go on like that"—actually exemplifies it. Indeed, it exemplifies experience itself, for experience appears with "you." If, for Husserl, auto-affection was the non-space that made self-reflection immediate, for Derrida it is the self-differential encounter of experience itself.[39] Henry Staten notes, "the detour by which the self comes to itself, becomes longer and longer—becomes, indeed, interminable. But this interminability only intensifies the auto-affection involved." Staten goes on to state that attention to auto-affection gives Derrida's "erasure of the subject . . . a very different sense than one might have thought. But it is not yet clear to me just what this sense is."[40] I am suggesting that the effect of this "erasure" is indeed different than one might have thought: it makes possible phenomenological life.

Derrida's Husserl, then, unwillingly describes an auto-affection that is experiential because it includes representation. This conclusion recalls the structure of the sublime, with its positive relation between emotion and cognitive struggle. In *The Critique of Judgment,* anxiety and what Kant calls "a liking emotion [*rührendes Wohlgefallen*]" result from the mind's collision with obstacles and its self-congratulatory inference that it can conceive greater things than it can imagine.[41] Similarly, fright and reassurance spring from the Cartesian ego's inability to complete its project of subjectivity. The similarity of these narratives lies not only in their movement from anxiety to reassurance but in their implication that the very existence of emotive experience assumes the incompleteness of subjectivity.

Poststructuralist theory has often pondered emotion's contribution to such a scheme. Neil Hertz contends, using Descartes's *Second Meditation* as his illustration of a general phenomenon, that welling emotion can smooth cognitive resolution: "An affect—a sense of loss—bound up in a specific temporal structure . . . is experienced at a moment when an ongoing process of cognitive inquiry is about to post a conceptual gain, to affirm a proposition about the nature of mind."[42] According to Hertz, such emotion accompanies images of lost life—in the case of the *Second Meditation,* the piece of wax transiently anthropomorphized by Descartes as an exemplary body—that distract the reader from mental difficulty. When Descartes kindles pathos on behalf of the wax,

> an operation that can be thought of epistemologically (as the registering of impressions of things in the mind) or semiotically (as demonstrating the power of signs to represent things) has been rewritten as the touchingly irreversible passage from life to death. If we take in that difference *as feeling* we are not likely to reflect on or to question the appropriateness here of the distinction between being alive and being dead. A wobble yields to a stance: a sense of difference [between body and soul] is consolidated, and it is that consolidated awareness that is purchased at the expense of the wax-as-figure. ("Dr. Johnson's Forgetfulness," 176–177)

The difference of the soul from the body which Descartes pushes across with emotion is paradigmatic of subjectivity. By encouraging the reader to feel emotion for a body, Hertz implies, Descartes allows the reader to acknowledge a sense of injustice toward the idea of the body while deflecting that sense from its proper object, Descartes's own argument. The ideology of emotion here channels emotion rather than downplaying it. In the Derridean narratives of the cogito, emotion too is sublime in responding to difficulty: the phenomenology of the sublime and the phenomenology of the cogito are similar. The object of emotion in the latter, however, is not the loss of something cognition sacrifices or subordinates; it is the struggle of cognition itself. The plot of sacrifice and compensation can be conceived, in de Man's vocabulary, as a rhetoric of temporality, a defensive schematization of an alarming condition—namely, being conscious—larger and less orderly than the plot implies. It is an understatement to assert that emotion compensates for cognitive difficulty, for, logically, the first emotion *is* cognitive difficulty.

Emotion demands virtual self-difference—an extra "you." The theatricality of self-representation might seem to cast doubt on the reality of experience. Yet while theatricality causes trouble for subjective expression, as Husserl worries, it does not suspend or weaken emotion. It seems to do so only if emotions are envisioned—as in fact they are by Husserl and others—as affective cognitions with none of the disadvantages of affects. Of course, it is unusual to think of emotions in any other way, but this is just what Derrida shows we must do in *Of Grammatology.*

Imaginary Seductions

Speech and Phenomena and *Of Grammatology* were both published in 1967 and are intricately related—almost parts of the same work. Although tonal and stylistic differences make it hard to see, Husserl and Rousseau are counterparts in Derrida's work.[43] Like Husserl, Rousseau protects self-presence with the voice and against writing (G 237). He bases self-presence on "emotional self-affection," as Rodolphe Gasché remarks (*Tain of the Mirror,* 18). *Amour de soi* is to Rousseau what phenomenological voice is to Husserl—an allegedly immediate form of self-consciousness which Derrida reveals as self-deconstructive in practice. The comparison can be embarrassing to

Husserl, as when his nervousness about interior address pairs up neatly with Rousseau's nervousness about masturbation. In both masturbation and interior address the "danger is that of the image," as Derrida writes of the *Confessions* (G 151)—or more generally of the imaginary. "This vice, which shame and timidity find so convenient," Rousseau writes in his *Confessions*, "possesses, besides a great attraction for lively imaginations."[44] Masturbation generates plural virtual entities, affecting the body from without by caressing its surface, as though the body belonged to someone else: "affecting oneself by another presence, one *corrupts* oneself [makes oneself other] by oneself [*on s'altère soi-même*]" (G 153). To Derrida in the early 1960s, writing his dissertation on Husserl, Rousseau must have seemed to *literalize* Husserl's precepts. Keeping Husserl in mind, then, I turn now to Rousseau's ideas about literal theater. Theatricality may sound like an overblown figure for mental representation; its magnification, however, clarifies the implications of Husserl's fragile internal partitions.

Michael Fried contends, "Rousseau not only argues that the theater is beyond redemption . . . but strongly implies that there is no aspect of social life that is not comprised within the dangerous."[45] Fried cites a footnote in Rousseau's *Letter to M. D'Alembert* that criticizes contemporary drama, yet "attempt[s] to imagine a valid theatrical experience" based on the biblical episode of the hand writing on the wall at Balthazar's feast:

> The idea alone [*cette seule idée*] makes me shudder. It seems to me that our lyric poets fall short of these sublime inventions; seeking to terrify, they deploy a riot of decorations without effect. Even on the stage it is necessary not to address everything to the sense of sight, but to shake the imagination. (OCR 5:110n, quoted in Fried 171)

In the first of a series of civilizing acts, imagination appears as a moral force that redeems the stage. Rousseau shudders when he merely thinks about the hand writing on the wall. He has not seen the moment enacted; thus he can say quite literally that "the idea alone" frightens him, and Fried can say quite literally that Rousseau "attempts to imagine" valid theater. The incidental fact that contemporary poets have not come up with anything as delicious as the awful hand matters less than the moralized difference between devices aimed at "sight" and those aimed at imagination. Thus Derrida asserts that imagination is to Rousseau what auto-affection is to

Husserl: "Imagination alone has the power of *giving birth to itself. . . .* it receives nothing that is alien or anterior to it. It is not affected by the 'real.' It is pure auto-affection. It is the other name of différance as auto-affection" (G 186–187).[46] The parallel goes even further: the opposition between theatricality and imagination recalls Husserl's opposition between indication and expression. Theatricality and imagination use empirical, exoteric signs and ideal ones, respectively. Shifting from theatricality to imagination, Rousseau shifts from the eye to the mind's eye and from affect to emotion. Imagination overleaps obstacles—potentially, the confines of dramatic media as well as of our own finite powers of observation. We can't see supernatural happenings, so we imagine them; we can't see a disembodied hand writing, even in a play, so we imagine we see it. But although Rousseau prefers imagination's inward eye to external artifice, a minimal theatricality—something that makes one *recognize* an impediment—remains necessary to spur imagination to action. According to Rousseau, theater can grow more moving by inviting imagination, by staging its sublime boundary, by reminding us that it is theater. Burke, similarly, opines that words and sounds arouse sublime emotions because they do not arouse images;[47] complementarily, contemporary plays fail to terrify not because they lack visual representations—"they deploy a riot of decorations"—but because the visual images themselves lack nothing. Failing to trigger imagination, the plays necessarily fail to trigger terror. The object of emotion must not only be represented: it must be apprehended as representation.

The point pertains to more than stagecraft. In one sense, imagination names the capacity to create whole fictive scenes or beings (the fantasies that accompany masturbation, a ghostly hand writing on a wall, or the phantasm of an inner self to encourage or abuse). In another, imagination merely animates perceptions, some more than others. Winfried Menninghaus points out the double valorization of imagination in Kant: "Imagination in its pure form . . . produces 'tumultuous derangements' that shatter the 'coherence which is necessary for the very possibility of experience.' On the other hand, as the 'faculty of intuitions' and of 'presentation,' imagination is precisely the guarantor, indeed, the producer of all reality."[48] The second sense of imagination can be thought of as stronger than the first, since imaginative perceptions are more vivid than fabrications. Rousseau affirms the presentational capacity of imagination: not only is drama effective only when it encourages imagination, but imagination performs best in a theatrical context. Despite his objections to artifice, Rousseau recognizes the necessity of imagination to the work of enlivening perception—work that theatricality supplies. The second, lesser sense of imagination suffices to stir the emotions and deserves to be distinguished from the cognition with which it may coexist. Although I may form a cognition about something that has also struck my imagination (I see the ruined castle clearly), I do not cognize it *where* I imagine it (it is such a romantic place). The imagined side of the object *carries* the emotion. If one sees theatricality as a menace, uncomfortable questions emerge here. If imagination corrects theatricality and brings emotion, then we need to suffer theatricality in order to get the emotive benefits of its cure. Worse, imagination is a remedy that replicates the problems it solves; it is another, inner, better, supplementary theater.[49]

Derrida points out that pity is a good emotion through which to study such questions. Since Aristotle pity has been the prime emotion inspired by theater. Indeed, "Rousseau's entire theory of the theater . . . establishes a connection, within representation, between the power of identification—pity—and the faculty of the imagination" (G 184). We pity only others, and exercise imagination to feel on their behalf; thus, "pity does not awaken with reason but with imagination which wrenches it from its slumbering inactuality" (G 182). Rousseau backs Aristotle's claim that "whatever men fear for themselves they pity when they happen to others."[50] Yet more works in it than difference of person; what matters is not whether something concerns me or someone else, but rather whether I treat my concern *as* mine or—in self-pity—*as* another's, and another's concern *as though it were* hers or mine. "It is in the difference between absolute proximity and absolute identity," Derrida argues, "that all the problematics of pity are lodged" (G 174)—between total awareness of one's own suffering and "*simply experienc[ing]* the suffering of others *by itself*" (G 189). Aristotle writes that suffering without distance is not pitiable, but "terrible"; thus "Amasius did not weep when his son was being taken off to be executed, as they say, but did when his friend was begging him" (*Rhetoric*, §6, 2.8). Similarly, Derrida concludes that without "a certain nonidentification" (G 190), pity loses its grip. The full meaning of pathos, with its positive association between emotion and difference, crystallizes here, where "we neither can nor should feel the pain of others immediately and absolutely" (G 190).

Charting the development from affect to emotion, Rousseau locates a qualitative shift in the emergence of pity. Pity separates the empirical from the conceptual, the unrepeatable from the expressible, and animality from humanity. While Rousseau grants pity to "all living beings," animal pity is too visceral to be a meaningful emotion; for Rousseau as for Hegel, "animality has no history because feeling and understanding are, at root, functions of passivity" (G 183). The instinctive gentleness that horses, according to Rousseau's *Second Discourse,* can feel—"it is well known that horses show a reluctance to trample [*fouler aux pieds*] on living bodies" (OCR 3:154)—recalls those inner bodily affections that are empirical, unrepeatable, and in that respect unavailable even to those who feel them.[51] Equine pity is a mere affect, waiting for idealization to raise it to emotion. Derrida picks up another echo of Husserl here: "Identification pure and simple would be immoral *because it would remain empirical* and would not be produced in the element of the concept, of universality, and formality" (G 191; my italics). Rather like Kant in the *Critique of Practical Reason,* Rousseau concludes in *Emile* that "to prevent pity degenerating into weakness we must generalize it and extend it to mankind" (OCR 4:303–304, quoted in G 191).

Rousseau's attraction to plots that progress and regress at the same time takes over the story when emotion spills over into passion. Exorbitantly idealized, passion reverses emotion's ideal fortunes. Rousseau points out in the *Second Discourse* that "moral love," for example, artificially "limits our attachment to a single person" (G 175, on OCR 3:157–158). While one might expect Rousseau to praise this artifice—it certainly elevates love above instinctive attachment—he does not, because it works to excess and concentrates love into "a terrible passion":

> The imagination, which causes such ravages among us, never speaks to the heart of savages [*l'imagination . . . ne parle point à des coeurs Sauvages*], who quietly await the impulses of nature, yield to them involuntarily, with more pleasure than ardor, and, their wants once satisfied, lose the desire. It is therefore incontestable that love, as well as all other passions, must have acquired in society that glowing impetuosity, which makes it so often fatal to mankind. (OCR 3:157–158)[52]

Although we are used to thinking of emotion as spontaneous, it is often a card played on the side of the ideal cognitivization "acquired in society." Without idealization, we would have only instinctive "impulses." With too much of it, we have "fatal" passions. In the best-case scenario of Rousseau's fables, emotion absorbs the authority-effect of feeling and transfers it to ideality, the form of mental representation supposed to befit the enlightenment subject. For Rousseau, emotion moves people from needs to desires. The need/desire axis organizes the *Essay on the Origin of Languages* especially, in ways that both Derrida and de Man discuss. Here Rousseau rejects the idea that language is utilitarian, arguing that needs—exemplarily food and water—disperse populations, while the passions bring them together in language. At the same time, passion infuses and re-creates need; in a delicate mini-myth of Rousseau's, water is evanescently poeticized by sexual desire: "Girls would come to seek water for the household, young men would come to water their herds. . . . Imperceptibly, water becomes more necessary" (quoted in G 262). Rousseau's economy of needs and desires expedites philosophy's project to model emotion on cognition—to define emotion by the ideality of its contents and to legitimate subjectivity by its association, through emotion, to affects. He implies that the right balance between idealization and affect—if we can find it—affords love that is not terrible and pity that is not automatic. The tremulousness of the formulation, however, generates its own anxiety, especially in debates about theatricality.

Since Rousseau makes imagination a condition for emotion, he winds up implying that potentially emotive situations *must* elicit imagination if emotion is to occur. This circumstance leads to high comedy. Real-life objects of potential pity follow Rousseau's recipe for effective theater, appearing as appearance to draw out imagination. De Man writes in *Blindness and Insight* that "pity, the arch passion in Rousseau[,] is itself, as Derrida has very well perceived, inherently a fictional process that transposes an actual situation into a world of appearance, of drama and literary language: all pity is in essence theatrical."[53] Continuing this train of thought in *Allegories of Reading,* de Man muses on the episode in *Remembrance of Things Past* in which the servant Françoise, who feels no sympathy for her real-life pregnant kitchen maid, sobs over the medical book that describes her pains (AR 76). The challenge of the scene is its implication that in order to be able to feel for the maid, Françoise needs to see her as something in a book. Intrigued by similar episodes, Rousseau protests that such people only fancy themselves sympathetic. "There is a type that weeps at a tragedy, yet has never had any pity for the suffering," Rousseau complains (OCR 5:378n, quoted in G 239n and discussed in BI 132). Yet he goes on to grant this "type" a pervasive normalcy: ultimately, we're all this type.

In the *Second Discourse* Rousseau himself proves the fundamental naturalness of pity by means of theatrical examples:

> Such is the force of natural pity, which the greatest depravity of morals has as yet hardly been able to destroy! For we daily find at our theaters men affected, nay, shedding tears at the sufferings of a wretch who, were he in the tyrant's place, would probably even add to the torments of his enemies.

In a note Rousseau continues that such a man is

> like bloodthirsty Sulla, who was so sensitive to ills he had not caused, or that Alexander of Pheros who did not dare to go and see any tragedy acted [*qui n'osoit assister à la représentation d'aucun tragédie*], for fear of being seen weeping with Andromache and Priam, though he could listen without emotion to the cries of all the citizens who were daily strangled at his command. (OCR 3:155n)

In contrast to Rousseau's meditation on Balthazar's feast, which at least superficially praises the emotional utility of imagination over the ineffectuality of theatrical presentation, this passage reclaims the emotional utility of theatricality. While Rousseau wonders how pity persists in people who spend most of their time "destroying" it in themselves, his anecdotes demonstrate the even more curious fact that theatrical pity outlives natural pity. Sulla and Alexander have too much at stake in murders to be able to *afford* pity for their victims: "When our interest is involved, our sentiments are soon corrupted" (OCR 5:22). Their actions not only demonstrate that objects of pity *may* be theatrical, but demand it. Thus Rousseau extends theatrical into natural pity. Alexander discovers theatrical emotion both inside and outside the play: when he goes to tragedies, he is not just a member of the audience—or so he assumes—but a display for others. Through his fear of the audience, Alexander implies that both he and they take his moaning seriously. Rousseau himself apparently pays as much attention to his neighbors' reactions as to spectacles, since he claims he spies such things *"tous les jours"* (making one pity the celebrity who has to sit near Jean-Jacques). Outside the emotions of theater begins the theater of emotions.[54]

While it presents no threat to conceive pity as vicarious, theatricality is an attribute of all emotion, not pity alone. In a passage Derrida adduces from the *Letter to the Prince of Würtemberg*, Rousseau declares that "as reason has little force, interest alone does not have as much force as one believes. Only imagination is active and one excites *the passions* only by imagination" (quoted in G 183; my italics). Rousseau concludes in the *Letter to M. D'Alembert* that theatrical emotions serve no social purpose—they are "fleeting and vain" because they don't make people more feeling in life (OCR 5:23)—yet if theatrical emotions are worthless, he must question the global worth of emotion. For interior address, a structure like knowing myself through a report, has turned out to be indispensable: I need imagination to "excite" sorrow even at a loss of my own.

David Marshall has argued that in the philosophy of Shaftesbury and Smith, as in Descartes's, "the model of theater . . . would seem to be contained in the structure of the philosophical method."[55] Marshall believes that for Rousseau, as well, the debate about theater forms a pretext for an inquiry into mental space. Derrida clarifies the historical relation of such inquiries. As a couple, Rousseau and Husserl embody a structural homology between eighteenth-century "imagination" and modern "expression," suggesting that expression is a refinement of imagination. Eighteenth-century worries about theatrical falseness and weakness persist in contemporary worries about the emptiness, emotional dilution, and attenuated humanity of second-order domains. The resemblance between imagination and expression also suggests, however, that phenomenological voice can only miniaturize theatricality, not eliminate it.

Where might Derridean emotion stand in contemporary philosophy? The content approach to emotion is currently under siege from many directions. Materialist cognitive science offers more epistemological sophistication. Dennett, for example, holds that "there is no reality of conscious experience independent of the effects of various vehicles of content on subsequent action (and hence, on memory)."[56] The content approach has not thoroughly incorporated such revisions of presence and retrospect. As Griffiths protests, it has too often excluded feeling-based research on "affect programs"—automated systems of chemical, reflexive, and other physiological responses that endanger concepts of emotional depth and the division between animal feeling and human emotion. Speaking up for the capaciousness of feeling, Griffiths complains that "the mainstream philosophy of emotion has little interest in empirical research and has systematically ignored the ways in which our understanding of the mind/brain has been enriched during the last thirty years" (*What Emotions Really Are,* 2—3). Finally, tight versions of the content approach risk parsing emotion into nonexistence. Stocker charges that the content approach "fails as an account of affectivity" because it "hold[s] that there is nothing more to emotions or emotionality than . . . affectless content" (*Valuing Emotions,* 26). Against Stocker, I would agree with Dennett that clarifications should use terms other than the ones they seek to clarify (Dennett, *Consciousness Explained,* 64), so that affects need to be explained by something nonaffective. My complaint is rather that the content approach explains things only circularly. The content approach often looks like a shell game of concepts that claims to establish a subject actually given from the beginning.

The content approach struggles most of all with aesthetics, the land of imaginary objects. Here, as Griffiths remarks, "the beliefs and desires of the propositional attitude analysis are ones the subject explicitly does not possess" (*What Emotions Really Are,* 29). Preserving the expressive hypothesis under these conditions forces some very odd gambits, such as Jerrold Levinson's idea that because music seems expressive "it disposes us to construe it as if it is or harbors an individual externalizing its inner life."[57] Dissatisfaction with this sort of strategy has riddled the content approach with exceptions and eroded its coherence. Yet even commentators critical of the content approach tend to sympathize with the motivations that get it into trouble in the first place. Thus E. M. Dadlez notes that in some strong versions of the content approach, "existential commitment is necessary" to emotion, which tends to imply that emotions for nonexistent objects are either "irrational" or unreal. She argues that "the adoption of a cognitive characterization of emotion cannot provide grounds for an ascription of irrationality or inconsistency without thereby classifying a number of seemingly unproblematic responses as equally irrational"—in other words, many nonaesthetic emotions are likewise "affective response[s] to which no existentially committed belief could be said to correspond."[58] If aesthetic emotions are "quasi," we will have to concede that a great deal of life is "quasi." Dadlez herself defends the reality of imaginary emotions, however, only in order not to have it the other way around, not to assent to the imaginariness of real emotions. The emotions of life apparently *cannot* be "quasi."[59]

Richard Moran, however, distinguishes the fictive character of aesthetic content offered to imagination from "the *way* in which it is imagined": "to imagine something with feeling is not the same as to imagine having that feeling."[60] This makes room for productive effects of "the ornamental features of artworks," Moran notes, "for it would appear to be the very features of the work that do indeed detract from the realistic presentation of the fictional world that actually *enhance,* and don't inhibit, the intensity and richness of one's emotional involvement with it" ("Expression of Feeling," 82–83).

Moran's insight may be pushed farther. In Derrida's texts emotions are "quasi" in that they respond not just to mental representations but to their perceived representationality as such. Unlike the expressive hypothesis of emotional response, this account is normatively aesthetic: it has no difficulty fitting aesthetics because aesthetics fits it. There is no reason to guard mental life against theatricality, to guard emotion against representation, or to worry that layers of mediation diminish emotional intensity as copies degrade. Its only cost is that we do not like to think of our personal feelings as of the second order. But we might have a different opinion if we thought that citational structures brought the unexpected bonus of emotion. Derrida discovers such a windfall in Rousseau's description of the relationship between emotion and spoken words which, according to Rousseau, "penetrate to the very depth of the heart, carrying there the emotions they wring from us":

> The thing disappearing, the voice substitutes an acoustic sign for it which can, in the place of the object taken away, penetrate profoundly into me, to lodge there "in the depth of the heart." It is the only way of interiorizing the phenomenon; by transforming it into *akoumène;* which . . . supposes that the disappearance of presence in the form of the object, the being-before-the-eyes or being-at-hand, installs a sort of fiction, if not a lie, at the very origin of speech. Speech never gives the thing itself, but a simulacrum that touches us more profoundly than the truth, "strikes" us more effectively. Another ambiguity in the appreciation of speech. It is not the presence of the object which moves us but its phonic sign: "The successive impressions of discourse, which strike a redoubled blow, produce a different feeling from that of the continuous presence of the same object. . . . I have said elsewhere why feigned misfortunes touch us more than real ones" (*Letter to M. d'Alembert* [OCR 5:377, 378n]). If the theater is condemned, it is thus not because it is, as its name implies, a place of spectacle; it is because it makes us hear and understand. (G 240)

Although "voice" ought to be diaphanous to its ideal object, this meditation on voice ends in "the theater." Ending there, it arrives at emotion as well: Derrida passes from "the thing" to "the voice" to a "sign" that "moves us." When the sign substitutes for the thing, the substitution sounds like loss—at least that's how it sounds if we fear either the destructive or the attenuating effects of any representation worthy of the name. The term "sign" emphasizes this difficulty of representation. Yet Rousseau's signs carry *to* the heart "the emotions they wring *from* us," importing the very emotions that we call our own to express. Therefore, it is neither the "feigned" nor the spectacular character of theatricality that Rousseau condemns. Like Alexander of Pherae, Derrida's Rousseau flinches precisely at theater's capacity to "penetrate profoundly," indeed its exclusive capacity to move. Exchanging an object for its mental representation "is the only way of interiorizing the phenomenon." Not only is there a *conceptual* gain when phenomena are converted into signs; there is an *emotive* gain when we see those signs *as* signs. As signs, they "penetrate" better, they really move us now.

Idea-Signs of Passion

Foucault's reproach that Derrida effects a "reduction of discursive practices to textual traces" ("My Body," 27) is frequently repeated. Usually readers draw from the idea of such a reduction the inference that it disallows access to experiences such as emotion. Critics have complained that deconstruction, obsessed with the reduction to language, discusses representations of things rather than things themselves. It is not possible to talk about what emotion is, however, apart from arguments about how it can be conceived. It is only possible to construct a theory of emotion—or of anything—by asking how to represent it. The difficulty of representing emotion, in other words, *is* the difficulty of knowing what it is, not just for poststructuralist theory but for any theory. To claim that for Derrida, emotion cannot be represented by expression, is exactly to make a claim about what he thinks emotion might be. What lies beyond expression? What does the fact that emotion demands this "beyond" say about emotion?

Derrida ponders the representation of emotion in his reading of Rousseau's *Second Discourse* and *Essay on the Origin of Languages*, especially the famous passage in the *Essay*—also explicated by de

Man, and after that ubiquitously discussed—in which Rousseau illustrates the figural and passional roots of language:

> Upon meeting others, a savage man will initially be frightened. Because of his fear he sees the others as bigger and stronger than himself. He calls them *giants*. After many experiences, he recognizes that these so-called giants are neither bigger nor stronger than he. Their stature does not approach the idea he had initially attached to the word giant. So he invents another name common to them and to him, such as the name *man,* for example, and leaves *giant* to the fictitious object that had impressed him during his illusion. That is how the figurative word is born before the literal word, when our gaze is held in passionate fascination; and how it is that the first idea it conveys to us is not that of the truth.

As representations of internal states, such metaphors as "giant" for "man" "signify an affect or a passion," Derrida claims:

> It is the *inadequation of the designation* (metaphor) [to an object] which *properly expresses* the passion. If fear makes me see giants where there are only men, the signifier—as the idea of the object—will be metaphoric, but the signifier of my passion will be literal. (G 275–276)

> It is not fear itself that the word *giant* expresses literally—and a new distinction is necessary which would infiltrate as far as the literalness [*propre*] of expression—but "the idea that the passion presents to us." The idea "giant" is at once the literal sign of the representer of the passion, the metaphoric sign of the object (man) and the metaphoric sign of the affect (fear). That sign is metaphoric because it is *false* with regard to the object; it is metaphoric because it is *indirect* with regard to the affect: it is the sign of a sign, it expresses emotion only through another sign, through the representer of fear, namely through the *false* sign. It represents the affect literally only through representing a false representer. (G 276–277)

This intricate passage outlines the following scenario. I spy a strange man approaching and feel afraid; fear inspires in me—"presents"—the idea that he is gigantic. The word "giant" represents my idea literally (inaccurate as it may be regarding the man). The "sign of the representer [the idea] of the passion" rather than of the object, "giant" catches the object's effect on me only, at the expense of the facts. The word "giant" is at best metaphoric with respect to the man, and not even metaphoric, but rather more loosely figurative, of the fear—not even metaphoric because it's not a question of similitude: fear is not like a giant. The asymmetry is significant. If I can't say what the approaching man is, I can at least say what he is like for me—the word "giant" allows for likeness—but *my fear is not like anything.*

At what point, then, does the fear itself enter representation? It seems not to be there—so let's back up and go over this ground once again. The sign that's "false" of the man, Derrida writes, is "literal" regarding the idea that he appears gigantic to me, excited by my feeling about the man. So far in this formulation, my emotion influences representation rather than being represented itself. It is not the sign's literalness with respect to the idea, then, that represents my fear itself (hence, two of Derrida's formulations—"the signifier of my passion will be literal" and " 'giant' is literal as sign of fear" [G 276]—are revised more precisely in a third: "it is not fear itself that the word *giant* expresses literally").[61] Nor is it the sign's imprecision regarding the man (its being able to say at most what he is like, not what he is). It is the *difference between* the sign's falseness with respect to its object and its accuracy with respect to its idea that represents the passion: "the *inadequation of the designation* (metaphor) . . . *properly expresses* the passion." This "inadequation," this remainder between "man" and "giant," *measures* my fear of the man:

> The fact that "giant" is literal as sign of fear [again, this is revised one page later; I would read here "literal as sign of the idea"—RT] not only does not prevent, but on the contrary implies, that it should be non-literal or metaphoric as sign of the object. It cannot be the idea-sign of the passion without presenting itself as the idea-sign of the presumed cause of that passion, opening an exchange with the outside. (G 276)

Derrida comments that Rousseau believes he "restores to the *expression of emotions* a literalness whose loss he accepts, from the very origin, in the *designation of objects*" (G 275). In other words, Rousseau suggests that the restorative, supplementary faculty of emotion retreats to a confined but securer sphere of subjective truth. Accepting "loss . . . in the *designation of objects*," he appears to anticipate that expression will pay indication's debts. But Derrida's close reading of the scene shows that this is not what happens in it. Derrida registers the echo of Husserl in his explication, in free indirect discourse, of this turn: "we must . . . come back to the subjective affect, substitute the phenomenological order of passions for the objective order of designations, *expression for indication,* in order to understand the emergence of metaphor" (G 276; my italics). It is true that by such a substitution, we understand that "giant" does express my idea even though it doesn't indicate the man coming toward me. The correspondence between my idea of his giantism and the sign "giant" makes this sign what Husserl calls an expression. Yet in this same example, emotion is not expressed as that idea is. The idea of a giant and the emotion of fear are not the same thing; expression does not express the emotion as it expresses the idea. Rather, the emotion is at most implied by comparison between the idea-giant and the actual man, "opening an exchange with the outside." Emotion is not expressive, not subjective: it is the difference between subjective ideality and the external world, appearing within experience.

Nor is emotion indicative. Geoffrey Bennington hints that it is when, explicating Derrida's reading of Husserl, he uses a sign of emotion as his own example of indication: "the canals on Mars are *perhaps* an indication of intelligent life, my blushing *perhaps* betrays an embarrassment, but meaning is here subject to mistake and is at best no more than probable; meaning is not *expressed* in such signs."[62] Derrida also opines that "the whole of the visible and spatial as such" belongs to indication (SP 35). Emotion, however, confounds and exchanges the features of expression and indication. Let's recall what those features are:

> In indication the animation has two limits: the body of the sign, which is not merely a breath, and that which is indicated, an existence in the world. In expression the intention is absolutely explicit because it animates a voice which may remain entirely internal and because the expressed is a meaning [*Bedeutung*], that is, an ideality "existing" nowhere in the world. (SP 33)

In the episode of the giant, "the *inadequation of the designation* (metaphor)" that represents fear takes over all the traits of expression. An "inadequation" is not a body. It is certainly not limited by "the body of the sign," since as we've seen, emotion is not directly represented by either signs or ideas: its representation is negative, in the cracks. Fear itself "exist[s] in the world" no more than an idea does, except in its representation that also exists nowhere in the world, since it is not a body itself. As Derrida notes, Rousseau acknowledges indication's expressive power even though he also asserts its inferiority. He claims in the *Essay*, for example, that "what the ancients said in the liveliest way, they did not express in words but by means of signs. They did not say it, they showed it" (quoted in G 236).[63] According to Husserl, only expressions are supposed to be able to *show* only permanent relations: "While in real communication existing signs *indicate* other existences which are only probable and mediately evoked . . . when expression is *full,* nonexistent signs *show* significations [*Bedeutungen*] that are ideal (and thus non-existent) and certain" (SP 43). Wittgenstein declares in a similar spirit that "what *can* be shown, *cannot* be said."[64] Derrida's description of fear violates these principles: is representation through difference among signs an indication that works like an expression, or an expression that works through indication?

Unrepresentable by any individual sign, emotion is represented by traces in a differential network. Textuality offers an alternative to expression and indication. Textuality plays in poststructuralist theory the double role that expression plays in philosophy, being both a means of representing emotion and an explanatory scheme of the operation of emotion. Textuality, in other words—and différance, its dynamic force—models Derridean emotion. Throughout his work Derrida locates emotion in relations rather than in subjects. *The Post Card* (1980) portrays affection as a postal system: Derrida's narrator pens a series of love letters, "open but illegible."[65] Reenacting Cartesian interior address, the narrator addresses letters to someone dubbed "you," who may be himself, a lover, or the reader. Through the *pas de deux* of the indefinite "I" and "you," affection thrives on successions of person and place rather than emanating from a source. In "Passions: 'An Oblique Offering' " (1992), Derrida tucks passion into the category of secrecy. Defined with maximum strength, he proposes, a secret could never be other than a secret. Such a secret "remains secret under all names and it is its irreducibility to the very name which makes it secret."[66] Passion, open but illegible, fits the definition of a secret: the uncertainty of recognizing emotion is one of the proverbial loci of anxiety about emotions. The impossibility of identifying particular emotions by signs leads to the deeper worry that it is not possible to know what emotion is.[67] But although it isn't possible to state or point to an emotion, one can have a concept of emotion as the phenomenology of the textual difference between ideality and substance.

It might seem that when a text becomes a text—can represent emotion and index itself as emotive mechanism—there must be a subject there to write or read it. If you think so, then using textuality to model emotion will seem either to imagine emotion inhering in textual relation in a personifying way or to project emotion into an interpreting subject who perceives the relations. Let's keep the alternatives distinct: (1) the classical perspective: only subjects have emotions, so emotions must be "cognitive" idealities expressed by subjects. (2) The poststructuralist perspective: the presence of emotion signals that in practice, experience is différance. As expression is criterial of subjectivity, textuality is criterial of experience. This may sound bizarre, but why should it sound more bizarre than the idea that when something is expressive, the ideality expressed must be perceived as belonging to a subject? To demand that if textuality is experienced, it must be experienced by a subject—however strongly or weakly subjectivity is construed—is to impose the requirements of (1) on (2).

So it is not the case that emotions are a subject's interpretations of texts. That would be Husserl's position:

> That one may eventually "interpret" gesture, facial expression, the nonconscious, the involuntary, and indication in general, that one may sometime take them up again and make them explicit in a direct and discursive commentary—for Husserl this only confirms the preceding distinctions. This interpretation [*Deutung*] makes a latent expression *heard*, brings a meaning [*Bedeutung*] out from what was still held back. Nonexpressive signs mean [*bedeuten*] only in the degree to which they can be made to say what was murmuring in them, in a stammering attempt. Gestures mean something only insofar as we can hear them, interpret [*deuten*] them. (SP 36)

"Gestures mean something only insofar as we can hear them, interpret [*deuten*] them": this is true—so true that it applies to our *own* gestures. When I must interpret my own mental representations, whose is the subjectivity to whom the emotion finally belongs? No one but a string of Humean "whos" who are all the I's I have. There should be no confusion that the "death of the subject" necessitates a poststructuralist rehabilitation of subjectivity itself.[68] Passion in *The Post Card* or "Passions" does not demand a subject, unless an infinite abysm of transpersonal perspectives is your idea of a subject. It does, however, preserve experience. By showing how différance possesses a phenomenology, emotion demonstrates how experience survives subjectivity.

Arguing that in a textual theory "whether and how 'passion' refers to personal and interpersonal affects—envy, anger, love, hate . . . never becomes clear"[69] underestimates the difficulty of gathering individual emotions into a general theory. Requiring emotion to appear by itself and not as part of some other kind of thought forgets the one fact everyone agrees on, that emotion is a construct of thought. To protest that "when we habitually speak" about emotion "we do not mean something like" experience that cannot belong to subjects, and that for this reason, poststructuralist emotion theory isn't really a theory of emotion, would be to be satisfied with nothing less than the echo of one's own presuppositions.[70]

Finally, the reduction to textuality, in this instance, not only makes logical room for emotion, but summons emotion out of the economy of pathos:

> When there is no longer even any sense in making decisions about some secret beneath the surface of a textual manifestation (and it is this situation which I would call text or trace), when it is the call [*appel*] of this secret, however, which points back to the other or to something else, when it is this itself which keeps our passion aroused, and holds us to the other, then the secret impassions us. (Derrida, "Passions," 24)

The experience of being impassioned is itself an outcome of feeling compelled to look for passion although we cannot finally identify it. Because one does not find the source of it, one also does not run out of it. Such a theory does not debunk emotion, but debunks the ideology of emotion and in particular, the expressive hypothesis. Exploring emotion in Derrida's theory reveals that the expressive hypothesis underwrites subjectivity, not emotion; discarding the expressive hypothesis discards subjectivity, not emotion. To claim that emotion is homologous with experience is to estimate emotion highly. Such a theory can begin to help us consider particular emotions; it shows that if emotion replies to representation, it is literally "a manner of speaking" (Brothers, *Friday's Footprint*, 111). To go further requires not a theory of subjectivity but a theory of kinds of emotion as kinds of rhetoric.

CHAPTER TWO

Pathos (Allegories of Emotion)

In Rilke's poems, de Man observes, "whatever pathos is mentioned refers to the suffering of others" (AR 36). The same would seem to be true of *Allegories of Reading,* in which de Man urbanely dissects some of the most passionate writers in European literature. In comparison, *Blindness and Insight* is tense, labored, and disquiet. *Allegories* unfolds almost reposefully, proceeding, as Barthes would say, "without hysteria."

The inverse ratio between the ardor of de Man's chosen authors and his own apparent ease is interesting. De Man comments on his texts' emotionality in the preface to *Allegories:* "The choice of Proust and of Rilke as examples is partly due to chance, but since the ostensible pathos of their tone and depth of their statement make them particularly resistant to a reading that is no longer entirely thematic, one could argue that if *their* work yields to such a rhetorical scheme, the same would necessarily be true for writers whose rhetorical strategies are less hidden behind the seductive powers of identification" (AR ix).[1] De Man associates pathos with thematics: pathos urges the reader toward an "entirely thematic" interpretation. By "thematic," de Man also means "referential"—not in the direct sense in which everything represented would be understood as having occurred, but in an indirect one in which the general meanings of the texts would be located in their authors' intentionality and psychology. Thus de Man connects pathos to the popular idea that keenly affecting texts must be based in the real—in real, not fictive, emotions.

According to de Man, then, his book undertakes an exposé of "ostensible pathos" in literary texts; it calls our attention to the deployment of pathos as a persuasive tactic. This self-description helps to create the impression that de Man is hostile to emotion, or at least believes it to be a mere illusion behind which lurks a "rhetorical scheme." De Man is indeed skeptical about emotions in that he questions our motives for representing them and even having them: we use emotions, he argues, to mitigate epistemological uncertainties. When we don't know what to think, emotions give us something to feel; they make our unstable perceptions and sensations seem more stable and nameable. The analysis of emotions therefore reveals self-consoling elements in the way we think about ourselves. To inquire into the motivation of emotions, however, is to doubt neither their existence nor their ability to affect us. Indeed, de Man's preface assumes the power of emotions not only to move individuals but to become "seductive," or contagious. Still less does his inquiry underestimate, neglect, or somehow fail to face up to emotion.

Quite the contrary: *Allegories of Reading* constructs a theory of emotion, propelled by de Man's response to Rousseau, and tests it on a wide variety of texts and contexts. It ranges over aesthetic, erotic, social, moral, and theological emotions, and over increasing levels of self-consciousness. De Man has a reputation for intense but detached prose, infused with only the most Alpine *apatheia*. Eric Santner comments that while "de Man's writings do in fact deploy elegiac procedures," de Man "vehemently denies that any of this has anything at all to do with human grief, pain, or survival." Rather, "depleted of affect, unfolding in the polar stillness of an exquisite isolation, mourning can never be anything but a repetitive looping through the abstract procedures of so many purely structural operations."[2] The metaphor of "polar stillness," or of empty spaces where no human race is, pervades the reception of de Man's work.[3] Lindsay Waters mentions the "emotional undertow" of de Man's writing, yet compares de Manian deconstruction to "the snow falling on top of Mont Blanc, falling interminably, not in accord with any concerns of humanity."[4] The economy of pathos tells us what to expect from someone with such a reputation: heightened emotional effects. De Man's emotive significance overflows the level of effects, however, for his theory of emotion is as direct as Derrida's is oblique. While one can count the few occurrences of the *word* emotion in Derrida's writing, de Man at least mentions "emotion" in nearly everything he wrote after 1971. Unlike Derrida and Deleuze, he tends to use "emotion" and "passion" synonymously, retaining just a dash of intensified compulsion in "passion." In *Allegories of Reading* he is comfortable as few of us would be with defining passion outright, as when he writes that "passion is not something which, like the senses, belongs in proper to an entity or to a subject but, like music, it is a system of relationships that exists only in the terms of this system" (AR 210), or that "passions all have, by definition, the self-deceiving structure . . . that forces the narrative of their deconstruction to unfold" (AR 197). Almost all of de Man's texts after his reading of Rousseau's *Essay on the Origin of Languages* purvey a coherent model of emotion as tropic structure. This theory sees emotions as practical interpretive acts which are yet not classically subjective; as such, it constitutes a very effective attack on the expressive hypothesis.

The originality and controversy of de Man's view lies in its isomorphism of emotions and figures. When de Man writes that "the referential representation of what Rousseau calls a passion . . . is in fact the representation of a rhetorical structure" (AR 172), it sounds as though passions, in contrast to rhetorical structures, were something comparatively fanciful—as though after stripping away apparent passions, one struck the reality of rhetoric. We can read de Man's formulation in a different but equally possible way, however, as saying that passions *themselves* are rhetorical structures, a fact which becomes especially clear when we examine representations of passions. In de Man's account of the discourse of emotion, emotions regulate analogies and transactions between perceptible things and possible inner states. Love in Rousseau, for example, is a complex network of analogies in which lovers exchange features and even entire identities. Love "crosses from '*visage*' ('outside') to '*âme*' (inside) by way of '*traits*' ('*les traits de l'âme*') which are said to be both inside and outside," while "simultaneously, we pass from '*sens*' and '*yeux*' (outside) to '*sentiments*' by means of the synecdoche '*organe*'" (AR 211). "Love" in this passage names an entire set of interpretations—a picture of the world—while the affect of love links and justifies the various connections in the set: lovers believe that their emotion leads them from outer traits to inner states and back. Love, then, is not merely an inner content but a would-be means of access to others' feelings: one's own emotion, an "inner" quality, throws a line through the external world to someone else's emotion. Thus far, de Man's account reflects the eighteenth- and nineteenth-century ideology of expressive emotion.

He goes on, however, to develop his texts' implication, at the same time, that one's own emotion comes to be known in the first place only through connection with and confirmation from others. Emotions in interaction with observations of other people and their professed or apparent emotions lead us to believe that perceptible things express unknown inner states, and therefore project the unity of outsides and insides. Of all the means of encouraging such belief, de Man writes, emotions work "most effectively of all" (AR 219).[5] As rhetorical structures, emotions are "blind metaphorization[s]" (AR 156), over-forceful interpretive acts that trigger the effects of rhetorical structures: narratives of their own undoing and repetition. Yet to say this does not discount emotion—suggest that "'love' does not mean or intend or desire anything"[6]—but rather unhinges it from the expressive hypothesis of emotional interiority.

De Man's theory of emotion begins with a reading of Rousseau's *Essay on the Origin of Human Languages*. In the first part of this chapter, I'll consider de Man's analyses of Rousseau, which move from the paradigm case of solitary fear to ambitious investigations of social and aesthetic emotion. De Man's debate with Derrida regarding Rousseau pivots on what de Man takes to be Derrida's acceptance that the word "giant" in Rousseau's *Essay* represents an inner idea homologous with fear. He claims that Derrida uses emotion in the classical way, to posit a relationship between an outside and an inside. De Man evolves counterideas about emotion that also use Rousseau's example of fear; I'll contrast de Man's thoughts on fear to his thoughts on love, self-love, and vanity in readings of Rousseau's *Narcisse* in order to trace the internal ambiguity of de Man's view of emotion. De Man contends that emotion arises in uncertainty and that emotional interpretations form suspensive hypotheses; yet he also contends that emotions tend to put a stop to uncertainty. Duplicity is characteristic of de Manian figures, fictional structures that mask their own fictionality through reality-effects. Exploring the dual purposes of emotion, de Man walks the line between its value and its potential destructiveness. This line of thought reaches a dramatic conclusion in his lecture on Kant and Schiller, in which emotion can trump even self-preservation. De Man pursues the effects of emotion's ambivalence in his reading of Rousseau's *Julie*, in which resistance to sensual emotion only suggests the power and strange prevalence of pathos, the emotion that lives on in others' wake.

De Man's theories of moral and social emotion, developed through dialogues with Rousseau's "Profession of Faith" and *Social Contract*, recount relations between judgments and sentiments and between individual and collective well-being. Judgments and sentiments, de Man suggests, collude to disguise their common basis in comparison, a figurative procedure. Comparing individual well- or ill-being to Rousseau's notion of collective will—an unconscious force exerted by an executive power—de Man shows that emotion is predicated on a self-differentiality missing from executive power. The sovereignty of Rousseau's State exemplifies action independent from consciousness, significance, and emotion. Because sovereign power is not internally divided, it acts but cannot feel; the example of the State thus helps us to see that in contrast to mere action, emotion assumes a strongly differential, subjectless model of selfhood. De Man's Rousseau-based analyses, moving from *Narcisse* to the *Social Contract*, from individual to collective examples, form a narrative in which emotions hypothesize uncertainty, deny their own hypotheses, and then repeat the process. By conforming to this pattern, emotions display the allegorical behavior of figures.

Finally, I touch upon de Man's interest in Kantian *apatheia*, the paradoxical thrill of affectlessness. *Apatheia* is crucial because it suggests the fundamental incoherence of conceiving nonemotional experience. This incoherence appears in interpersonal and intrapersonal forms. First, *apatheia* exercises the general economy of emotional transactions: one person's *apatheia* inspires another's passion. But *apatheia* does not merely generate emotion outside itself. In de Man's Kant (and in de Man's readings of other philosophers at parallel moments), intellectual freedom from emotion constitutes its own emotion. Such elasticity suggests that emotion does not bear a solely compensatory relation to the supposed coldness of theory.

Even so brief a sketch, I think, shows the extent to which *Allegories of Reading* is a book about emotion. Arguing consistently for emotion's interpretive force, de Man details its advantages and disadvantages, its aesthetic, moral, and social implications, and its logical conclusion in perpetual emotion—the absence of any experiential state that is nonfigurative and nonemotional.

De Man's work on prosopopoeia, the figure that bestows face, reflects his preoccupation with the shaping of information and of the emotionality of information processing. Through prosopopoeia "voice assumes mouth, eye, and finally face" (RR 76). Nor does prosopopoeia stop once we have built a face: faces themselves are read more than other parts of the body, studied for signs of emotion. Darwin indexed facial expressions to emotional correlates, and behavioral psychologists and anthropologists today—indeed, scholars of all sorts—still recognize the preeminence of the face in emotional transactions.[7] Faces, like figures, facilitate the crossing of inward and outward properties (love, as I mentioned, crosses in and out by way of "traits"). The face is to visibility what the voice is to audibility: of all physical surfaces, it has the greatest reputation for expressivity, an alleged ability to externalize invisible emotions in a virtually unmediated way. Emmanuel Levinas follows the tradition of phenomenology in which he was trained, though in an idiosyncratic, outdoing fashion, when he calls "face" "the way in which the other presents himself, exceeding the idea of the other in me."[8] For Levinas, face is defacing, affective, and self-differential for the beholder, but what appears as a face displays a precisely expressive self-presence. Because of its classically auto-affective nature, it does not even have to be interpreted, as Jill Robbins explains: "The face *is* a face, and not a mask . . . it is without clothing or covering or attributes . . . it divests itself of its form and signifies as an expression, *kath 'auto,* as Levinas has said, having reference only to itself."[9] De Man's prosopopoeia, in contrast, confers only appearance on the face.

The relation of these concerns appears in a well-known piece of de Man's work: his reading, in "Wordsworth and the Victorians" (1983), of the "Blessed Babe" passage of Wordsworth's *Prelude,* with which it may be helpful to begin. In its most general form, the problem with which de Man concerns himself is the relation of mental representations to signs. In the context of facial expressiveness, de Man attends to the exchange of glances between Wordsworth's mother and child. Writing well after his analyses of Rousseau's *Essay on the Origin of Languages,* de Man notes that the "Blessed Babe" passage "can be considered Wordsworth's essay on the origins of language as poetic language" (RR 90):

> the Babe,
> Nurs'd in his Mother's arms, the Babe who sleeps
> Upon his Mother's breast; who, when his soul
> Claims manifest kindred with an earthly soul,
> Doth gather passion from his Mother's *eye!*

"The enigmatic phrase: to 'gather passion,'" de Man writes, refers to "a process of exchange" (RR 91). A Rousseauvian "poetic language" commences in this meeting of glances because a fictive transfer of properties occurs in it, as in metaphor. Cathy Caruth notes that "this scene is also governed by the figure of passage, present here in the word *passion* as a sort of originary movement."[10] The infant "gather[s] passion from his mother's eye" in that he infers it; but, as de Man points out, this is a nursing scene in which the word "'eye' . . . displace[s] 'breast' where one would most naturally expect it" (RR 90).[11] Because the Babe draws sustenance from his mother's body, his gathering of passion is modeled after nursing, the transmission of substance. This comparison suggests that the Babe also gathers *in* his mother's passion for him and mixes it into his passion for her. Wordsworth may even be attributing this elemental metaphor— the idea that passion is like milk, the eye like the breast—to the infant. If so, this first metaphor is indeed poetic, and also a first error. Of course, milk can be treated *with* passion; its substantiality does not preclude its also becoming, in Rousseau's terms, an object of passion rather than of need. Wordsworth portrays a part of the process by which milk becomes more than a required sugar.[12] But that does not mean that passion is like milk; someone else's passion cannot be drawn into the body and transmuted into one's own. It cannot be "gathered" with any reliability even in the weaker sense of gathering as inference. The child could mistake what he believes he sees: if the mother's eye is reflective, the face he lends his mother may be his own.

Nevertheless, through the trade of meaningful glances the eye comes to be regarded as part of the face and the face in turn "open[s] the way to a process of totalization which, in the span of a few lines, can grow to encompass everything" (RR 91). According to de Man, Wordsworth's scene underlies all perception, beginning the assembly of a world. The infant metaphor grows up to be a myth. Yet, de Man continues, "this same face-making, totalizing power is shown at work in a process of endless differentiation," a "sea of infinite distinctions in which we risk to drown" (RR 92). In this oceanic metaphor, the hint of "passage" that Caruth perceives in de Man's focus on passion sounds again in an ominous tone. We cannot make sense, de Man suggests, without overloading sense and re-creating chaos: "somewhere in between, at the interface of these contradictory directions, words such as 'face' can be said to embody this very incompatibility. They do not master or certainly do not resolve it, but they allow for some mode of discourse, however precarious, to take place" (RR 92).

This reading typifies de Man's approach to emotion in several ways: the source of emotion is ambiguous, since emotion involves circular relations, making it hard to tell emotions from one another; the experience of emotion is buoying but wobbly, maintaining a "precarious" claim on the world; and emotion coincides with the shaping of sense, suggesting that emotion itself is a figure—here it serves as prosopopoeia and as metaphor—that consolidates an outside, a face, an inside, and a precarious means for getting back and forth between them. The affect of the figural exchange prompts us to think the exchange is substantial. The security of feeling—palpable in the drowsiness of Wordsworth's nursery—appears to sustain the figurative claim of relation, in this case of literal kinship. Emotion not only colors the world, then, but designs it. De Man's commentary on this state of affairs is neutral and descriptive: one's own emotion does not really provide access to the feelings of others or reflect the structure of reality, he seems to be saying, but the affective force of emotion understandably persuades us to think so.

Emotion and Figure

Like Derrida's, de Man's theory of emotion replies to the expressive hypothesis of emotional response that appears in Rousseau's *Essay*. Here is Rousseau's giant again, this time in de Man's translation:

> A primitive man [*un homme sauvage*], on meeting other men, will first have experienced fright. His fear will make him see these men as larger and stronger than himself; he will give them the name *giants*. After many experiences, he will discover that the supposed giants are neither larger nor stronger than himself, and that their stature did not correspond to the idea he had originally linked to the word giant. He will then invent another name that he has in common with them, such as, for example, the word *man,* and will retain the word giant for the false object that impressed him while he was being deluded.[13]

In Chapter 1, I argued that Derrida can be read as proposing that emotions constitute and measure the difference between the figural and the literal. De Man comments on Derrida's analysis of the *Essay* twice, in "The Rhetoric of Blindness" (1970–71) and in *Allegories of Reading;* in neither work does he consider the possibility I develop above. In both texts he assumes that for Derrida as well as for Rous-

seau, the primitive man's fear justifies his resort to the word "giant."
According to de Man, Derrida introduces emotion to reestablish the
"correspondence between . . . properties" that suffers when "giant"
fails to match the approaching man (AR 150). While I believe that
Derrida views emotion as the remainder that keeps the figural and the
literal from matching, de Man believes he views it as what must be
added to make them balance out. Emotion thus recuperates in subjectivity an authority lost with objectivity.[14] I am concerned now not
with de Man's reading of Derrida, however, but with his own ideas
about emotion, which begin in this encounter with Derrida. In exploring this material, I will not be revising the available critical understanding of de Man's theory of figuration, but will place that understanding in an emotive context. De Man's adjustments to what he
takes to be Derrida's stance toward emotion involve the origin of
emotion in uncertainty, its figurative structure, and its deceptive behavior.

In "The Rhetoric of Blindness," de Man contends that Rousseau re-
buffs the expressive aesthetic of the eighteenth century. In order to
make his argument, he opts to view the giant episode not as evidence
of Rousseau's expressivism, but as a "badly chosen" example of passionate figure. "Fear," he claims, is "distinctively utilitarian" in the
first place, "much too practical to be called a passion," and Rousseau
slipped when he used it to illustrate passion's bond to language: "the
third chapter of the *Essay*, the section on metaphor, should have been
centered on pity, or its extension: love (or hate)" (BI 134, 135). Wherever Rousseau adhered to real passions such as pity and love, he "said
what he meant to say" (BI 135), namely that "the metaphorical language which, in the fictional diachrony of the *Essay*, is called *'premier'*
has no literal referent" (BI 135).

In *Allegories*, however, de Man shifts his position. He notes that in
the giant fable "the reaction [of fear] is not obvious: it is certainly not
based on objective data" (AR 149). If this is true, then fear is excessive, like a passion, and does not "[belong] to the world of *'besoins'*"
as de Man had previously written (BI 134).[15] De Man goes on to remark of Derrida's analysis,

> Derrida is certainly right in stating that the act of denomination . . .—
> calling the other man a giant, a process that Rousseau describes as a
> figural use of language—displaces the referential meaning from an out-

ward, visible property to an "inward" feeling. The coinage of the word "giant" simply means "I am afraid." But what is the reason for the fear, if it is not due to observable data? It can only result from a fundamental feeling of distrust, the suspicion that, although the creature does not look like a lion or a bear, it nevertheless might act like one, outward appearances to the contrary. The reassuringly familiar and similar outside might be a trap. Fear is the result of a possible discrepancy between the outer and the inner properties of entities. It can be shown that, for Rousseau, all passions—whether they be love, pity, anger, or even a borderline case between passion and need such as fear—are characterized by such a discrepancy; they are based not on the knowledge that such a difference exists, but on the hypothesis that it might exist, a possibility that can never be proven or disproven by empirical or by analytical means. A statement of distrust is neither true nor false: it is rather in the nature of a permanent hypothesis. (AR 150)

Again, de Man presumes that "giant" refers "to an 'inward' feeling." But he is also saying that while "'giant' simply means 'I am afraid,'" so that its figurative status need not disturb referentiality in any way (we can simply translate it from a figurative to a literal register), fear itself—the emotion, not the word—has a function more complicated than that of "giant." Fear not only expresses the inner state of the frightened person, but forms a hypothesis about something in the outside world as well. Pointing in two directions, it means not only "I am afraid," but "This may be frightening"; even in the latter instance, however, it makes no objective claim. As an interpretation of a predicament, "fear" is "in the nature of a permanent hypothesis." Thus de Man differentiates the impulse to call the approaching man a giant from fear of him as such—"because it presents as certain what is, in fact[,] a mere possibility":

> The fear of another man is hypothetical; no one can trust a precipice, but it remains an open question, for whoever is neither a paranoiac nor a fool, whether one can trust one's fellow man. By calling him a "giant," one freezes hypothesis, or fiction, into fact and makes fear, *itself a figural state of suspended meaning,* into a definite, proper meaning devoid of alternatives. The metaphor "giant," used to connote man, has indeed a proper meaning (fear), but this meaning is not really proper: it refers to a condition of permanent suspense between a literal world in which appearance and nature coincide and a figural world in which this correspondence is no longer *a priori* posited. Metaphor is error because it believes or feigns to believe in its own referential meaning. (AR 151; my italics)

The "giant" metaphor diverges from fear because "fear" is definitionally hypothetical while "giant" is ontological. The primitive man "end[s] the uncertainty of his feeling," as de Man puts it, by attributing to the stranger "the size corresponding to his suspicions" (AR 169).

These passages have been read over and over again for what they say about language, but not for their attention to emotion. In them de Man attacks the assumption that emotions act simply as the stuff of subjective reality. One would expect that if "giant" figures fear, fear itself would not represent anything. De Man conceives their relation almost the other way around, since the emotion does interpretive work which its metaphor papers over: "the figure literalizes its referent and deprives it of its para-figural status" (AR 151). Even more than the metaphor, the emotion behind the metaphor is another interpretation that works in the spirit of figuration. Thus "giant" has a proper meaning but "this meaning is not really proper"[16]—because fear itself is a figure. In shifting from fear to the figure that follows it, we move not from the literal to the figurative, but from the openly figurative to the faux-literal. Carol Kay draws out the pragmatic implications of such a shift; she points out that the suspension of emotions recognized as hypothetical may seem to afford a safety zone, as though nothing further could happen for as long as the suspension lasted. But the hypothesis of fear, she argues, may create violence, as "delay in Hobbes's state of fearful competition makes room for 'anticipation,' one of the most important causes of the war of all against all."[17] Nor does fear's figurative status—what Kay calls its "literary" quality—dispel the affect of fear. Rather, commentary on fear generates a pathetic economy of fear: "the attempt to assert powerfully that there is no occasion for fear multiplies the occasions for fear" (Kay, "Hobbesian Fear," 100).

In his discussion of the *Essay*, then, de Man divides emotion (fear) from metaphor ("giant") for the unexpected reason that emotion is figurative, while metaphor works toward literalization. In other places, however, emotion itself operates more ambiguously. De Man's reading of Rousseau's early play *Narcisse*, especially, "allows for a parallel with the fable of the *Essay*" (AR 164). *Narcisse* "tells the story of a character named Valère so inebriated by vanity that he falls in love with his own portrait, barely disguised as a woman" (AR 164; the retouching of the portrait turns out to have been commissioned by his sister to make a point). De Man ponders an interpretation of *Narcisse* that corresponds to Derrida's "expressive" exegesis of the *Essay,* in which Valère's conceit accounts for his mistake:

> On the level of identifiable bad faith the fantastic image that originates in the mind of the subject and that blots out the world can simply be identified with the mode of consciousness that created it; the reductive reading of the situation is also the correct one. Once the assumption is made that the character is vain, the kind of aberrations to which it is to fall prey are entirely predictable and the author's skill will consist only in the invention of more or less surprising situations in which the predictable reaction will choose to fit. The semantic pattern is straightforward: the misreading of the portrait as being the image of a pretty girl simply means: Valère is vain. (AR 166)

According to this reading of the play, Valère's "aberrant substitution" of a nonexistent woman's image for his own is "neither a metaphor nor any other trope" (AR 166). It is subjectively literal, in the way that Derrida claims the primitive man's substitution of a giant's for a stranger's image is literal: it is "simply the representation of a consciousness" (AR 167), in this case a vain one.

De Man takes issue with the suggestion that "subjectively candid" (AR 151) emotive representations are literal, offering an alternative reading of *Narcisse* in which Valère's substitution is itself a trope. In Rousseau's thought, de Man writes, *amour propre* is the realm of the literal and *amour de soi* the realm of figure, even though *amour propre* is more "aberrant" in the sense that it is more narcissistic. Although *amour propre* is aberrant because it is pathological, by being pathological, it is, as Husserl would say, "merely empirical": where all is vanity, there's nothing to figure out beyond the subjective candor of the moment. But "the actual narcissistic moment when Valère falls in love with his own image," de Man suggests, "is not a moment of pure *amour propre*" (AR 168). Far from being pathological, this event reflects the structure of *amour de soi*—auto-affection, the bedrock of experience. As such, de Man heralds it as a cogito, an instance of the self-differential emergence of experience as such:

> The actual narcissistic moment when Valère falls in love with his own image is not a moment of pure *amour propre*. It comes closer to the situation summarized by [Valère's valet] Frontin: "*il est devenu amoureux de sa ressemblance*" ["he fell in love with his resemblance"; OCR 1:1006], a moment suspended between self-love and the transi-

tive love of others, not quite *"je m'aime"* or *"j'aime X"* but rather *"je m'aime comme si j'étais X."* The self/other tension, latent when the feeling, as in the *Second Discourse,* is that of pity, has become objectified in an autonomous entity, the portrait, that is not entirely fictional but exists in the mode of a simulacrum. The portrait has been substituted for the reflexive pronoun in *"je m'aime"* and it can do so because it is and is not the self at the same time. It both resembles the self sufficiently to allow for the possibility of self-love, but it also differs enough from it to allow for the otherness, for the *"pieuse distance"* (Valéry)[18] that is a constitutive part of all passion. (AR 168)

De Man's version of the cogito mediates between alternatives regarding the pronouns of consciousness that I mentioned in Chapter 1. Manfred Frank, speaking for Husserl, opined that the differentiality between the two I's of the cogito can be set aside because it is merely virtual. I suggested that if we consider the pronominal difference virtual, self-differentiality persists, because the virtual difference appears as actual, so that experience consists of this second differentiality between the virtual and actual. *Narcisse* can be interpreted in this Cartesian way, as a fable of consciousness: Valère experiences his fictive self as though it were someone else, and without doing this, cannot be self-aware. De Man comments that the portrait "is and is not the self at the same time," interpreting Valère's predicament as a rendezvous with *resemblance.* The portrait (like all self-images) is effective because it only resembles Valère, so that he couldn't be sure who it was; the notion of resemblance supersedes the polarity identical/different. *Narcisse* stages aesthetic experience, and resemblance defines the aesthetic object. For de Man, not only art is semblance, but any image or idea one can have of one's own self: "aesthetic generality is the precondition for resemblance" (AR 183). In the course of the plot Valère understands his mistake and trades the painting for a live woman, Angélique. Still, he tells her, referring to himself in the third person and as the portrait, that henceforward he will be able to love the person in the painting "only because he adores you" (OCR 1:1017, quoted in AR 170). According to de Man, this ending produces the new cogito *"Je m'aime aimant,"* in which "the 'self' to which [the statement] claims to point is in fact itself an infinitely deferred condition of indeterminacy between self and other" (AR 170). Whether Angélique is in the picture or not, Valère more or less gets it right the first time: not only does the portrait resemble Valère, but *Valère* resembles Valère, approaching himself through a chain of mediations in which both the portrait and Angélique take part. Self-reflection takes an infinite detour. If love, like "all passions," hypothesizes the possibility of a discrepancy between inner states and outer properties, then we can infer that Valère cannot know who the portrait depicts from the very fact that he falls in love with it. His loving the painting *presumes* his not knowing whose portrait it is.

De Man divides the functions of emotion when love in his discussion of *Narcisse* begins to differentiate itself from fear. Emotion seems to do more than hypothesize discrepancies between insides and outsides:

> The portrait is a substitution, but it is impossible to say whether it substitutes for the self or for the other; it constantly vacillates between both, exactly as *in the condition of fear, one constantly vacillates* between the suspicion that the reassuring outside might or might not conceal a dangerous inside or, in the opposite situation, that the frightening surface may or may not be appearance rather than evidence. . . . in the case of love the polarities involve a subjective as well as a spatial model and the fluctuation occurs between self and other, between ipseity and alterity here reduced to the empirical polarity of man and woman. . . . From the moment Valère/Narcisse gives in to this fascination, he considers the portrait "beloved" and *transforms the suspended vacillation* into the definite identity of an other. The pattern runs parallel to that of the fictional primitive man in the *Essay* who, upon encountering another man, ended the uncertainty of his feeling by attributing to him the size corresponding to his suspicions. (AR 169; my italics)

In this passage, de Man compares Valère's love for the portrait not to the primitive man's fear, but to the moment when he sees a giant. Valère's love does not vacillate between suspicions. Rather, from the moment he falls in love ("considers the portrait 'beloved'"), Valère attributes a "definite identity" to it: even though he doesn't know who is in the portrait, he knows the portrait depicts his "beloved." He bestows his love upon a formal object. The passage from fear to love corresponds to the passage from uncertainty to certainty, as shown by the italicized phrases in the quotation above. Earlier de Man contrasts fear to metaphor; he now likens love to metaphor. At the same time, the purpose of emotion shifts before our eyes from registering the vacillation between possible interpretations to ending it.

This shiftiness turns out to be characteristic of emotion. On the one hand, emotions hypothesize uncertainty, acknowledging the difficulty of negotiating interpretive alternatives. Thus de Man lists several of Rousseau's outbursts and comments, "the pathos of these statements, regardless of whether they are expressions of terror or assertions of prophetic exaltation, *stems from* the referential indeterminacy of the metaphor 'man'" (AR 197, my italics). On the other, emotions hastily resolve confusing feelings and hermeneutically perplexing situations as though they were not only "based" on the hypothesis of uncertainty but wanted to deny it. In "Semiology and Rhetoric," for example, de Man notes that Archie Bunker gets furious at a verbal confusion between himself and his wife Edith: he erupts when she takes a rhetorical question literally. Archie's anger reveals his "despair," de Man writes, "when confronted with a structure of linguistic meaning that he cannot control" (AR 10); his emotion sallies forth as though to resolve the issue by force. What's more, Archie does not think he is in confusion; his anger displaces his not knowing what to make of it all and disguises it from him. (In fact, if emotion begins in uncertainty, in Archie's case there are two displacements, from uncertainty to "despair" and from despair to "ire" [AR 9].) But to Archie, the subjective candor of the situation might be phrased, "Edith is stupid." Emotion behaves in the same defensive way in de Man's discussion of Rousseauvian religious faith. Rousseau's faith invents "innate and natural moral feelings" (AR 221–222) to deflect "genuine and intolerable confusion" (AR 227). Similarly, Valère's love causes him to overlook the fact that he knows nothing at all about the person depicted in the portrait, including whether or not the original is lovable.

The gradual resolution of an uncertain feeling into a named emotion is sealed in Rousseau's *Pygmalion*—in lines singled out by de Man—when the sculptor encounters his finished statue: "I don't know what I feel in touching this veil; I am seized by terror [*frayeur*]" (OCR 1:1226, quoted in AR 176). This bit of dialogue gives an uncanny impression of internal fluctuation. As Pygmalion talks to himself, he seems to be unveiling his emotion as well as his sculpture. The movement from the first to the second clause seems to show confusion modulating into "terror." Alternatively, perhaps it shows that Pygmalion, having lived with his feeling a little longer, *decides* that what he feels is terror. Either way, Pygmalion's conclusion seems hurried. His uncertainty gives way suddenly, in a seizure that dispels the ambiguity with a kind of violence. Rousseau reinforces the hint of haste by making Pygmalion announce that he is terrified *before* removing the veil, breaking the parallelism between the unveiling of the sculpture and the unveiling of his emotion. It is emotion that jumps the gun: Pygmalion feels terrified before he knows what to be terrified at.

How are we to conceptualize the idea that emotion both hypothesizes discrepancies and "postulate[s] a continuity between . . . signs and their signification" (AR 219)? Marc Redfield, one of the few who perceives that "'literal' affect does have its place in the de Manian allegory of reading," argues eloquently that fear is suspensive only "prior to becoming properly affective." For Redfield, affect "derives . . . from the effacement of undecidability that produces the possibility of literal meaning" and "manifests itself as a dimension of a referential imperative in flight from its own impossibility."[19] Building on Redfield's metaphor of flight—which captures the impression of emotion as a speeding force—we might say that emotions run from the dilemmas they describe and describe what they run from. Kinds of emotion reflect kinds of self-interest: fear serves the primitive man's interest because it takes no chances where the stakes are high; love serves Valère's since it ratifies his good opinion of himself where the stakes are relatively low—as we can see in lines Valère speaks of the image in the painting: "On my word, she is charming. . . . her taste bears witness to her intelligence. The girl is an expert in the merits of men!" (OCR 1:984, quoted in AR 166). Emotions hypothesize uncertainty by fleeing it, their flight acknowledging an unwanted indefiniteness; in flight, they change their colors and restart the process. To form an emotional "hypothesis" at all is to be out ahead of perception in the syncopation of ideas and facts. When one is forced to narrativize the double role of emotion, emotions seem to reverse themselves, converting nameless experiences into nominative acts. Although this reversal seems contradictory, I would argue that for de Man it is built into the very notion of emotion, just as the *trompe-l'oeil* that turns a hypothetical proposition into an ontological name "is built into the very notion of trope" (RR 242).

Safety and the Sublime

The figurative strength of emotion seems more useful than truthful. Like forgetting in Nietzsche, it makes the unbearable bearable temporarily at the cost of ensuring its recurrence. In their very deceptiveness emotions may be beneficial. Figurative power has a destructive side, however, and at extremes of persuasiveness may overwhelm even an instinct as strong as self-preservation. So goes the burden of de Man's late lecture "Kant and Schiller" (1983), which quietly revisits a scene of danger like the one in Rousseau's *Essay*. De Man asserts that Schiller appropriates the Kantian sublime for practical psychology, thus misreading and ideologizing the sublime in a way that "result[s] in a total loss of contact with reality."[20] For de Man's Schiller, sublime experience is "practical" because it helps you "survive, psychologically, the assault to which you are subjected" (AI 140). Terrifying episodes "get your faculties going" (AI 142), and the sublimity that ensues wins a psychological triumph separate from but compatible with physical extinction. The sublime "succeeds," as de Man puts it, in genuinely terrifying but "not . . . immediately threatening" situations that allow the time necessary to work through the process of sublimation (AI 142). In de Man's words, which again liken passion to passage,[21] "it's better not to be on the boat that's being tossed up and down, it's better to stand on the shore and see the boat being tossed up and down, if you want to have a sublime experience" (AI 142). This sheer temporality of sublimity forms a space of imaginative theatricality, as in Aristotle and Rousseau. The perfect sublime domain is literal theater, vicarious, yet "vivid" enough to awaken "'actual'—the German word is *ernstlich*, serious, taken seriously"—sublime reactions or, at the very least, "analogous" ones (AI 143). Through the transfers of the sublime trope,

> the notions of seriousness and of playfulness are now no longer pure—it is serious but only by analogy, it is not an actual fear but it is the trope of fear—one plays at danger as in a fiction or as in a play, but one is sheltered by the figurative status of the danger. It is the fact that the danger is made into a figure that shelters you from the immediacy of the danger. The tropological figuration here, this passage to the imagination, is what allows you to cope with the danger. Again, the figuration appears as a defense by means of which we cope with danger, by replacing the danger by the figure, by the analogon, by the metaphor, if you want, of danger. (AI 144)

Sublime defenses try out what it means to "cope with danger." Sublime elevation may inspire the sometime serenity of the besieged mind and heroic acts performed on automatic pilot. But there is also peril in a figure that "shelters you" not from the danger but from "the immediacy of the danger."

Sublime autonomy, in other words, teeters between ability and disability, like Freudian anxiety, which warns one to act or paralyzes action. It is certainly convenient that Schiller's emotions of triumph over danger can occur independent of any actually dangerous situation. Because emotions proceed as hypotheses, we do not have to wait for a true threat in order sublimely to rise above it. Through what de Man again calls a "tropological exchange" of fictive for literal danger (AI 144), we can eat our sublime cake without having it. Yet Schiller's psychological state of transcendence—which would certainly be a passion in Rousseau's opposition of passions and needs—conflicts with the ultimate need of self-preservation, as becomes clear when de Man moves from fictive to physical danger. In "really physically overwhelming" danger (AI 145), the independence of the intellect, drawing on its fund of confidence in immortality, abandons the doomed body. When we really are "on the boat that's being tossed up and down" the mind finds it preferable to be somewhere else and simply jumps ship, as in this alarming passage de Man quotes from Schiller:

> We call practically sublime any entity which makes us aware of our weakness as a natural creature, but which at the same time awakens an entirely different sort of resistance in us, resistance to the terror. This counterforce in no way rescues us from the physical existence of the danger, but, what is infinitely more, it isolates our physical existence from our personality. It is therefore not a particular and individual material security, but an ideal security, which extends to all possible and imaginable situations, and of which we have to become conscious in the aesthetic contemplation of the sublime. It learns to consider the sensory part of our being, the only part of us that can be in danger, as an exterior natural object that is of no concern to our person, to our moral self.[22]

Schiller reverses all the expected connotations of physical danger and mental autonomy. At the beginning of the sublime transfer, "knowledge is representation, fantasy, an imaginary thing, whereas self-preservation is a concrete physical thing and therefore of the order of the real" (AI 144). But as Schiller turns the trope of the sublime, these various attributes are crossed so that "self-preservation becomes imagined instead of being really real, and therefore self-preservation now relates to representation" (AI 144). As de Man points out, it is ironic that Schiller would call this operation "practical." By substituting passion for need, here in a fashion compatible with conventional theologies, Schiller bargains away life itself. In life and death circumstances—where "giant" may be a wishful understatement—sublime emotion plays out its final double cross, costumed as a "counterforce" yet resisting not the danger, but "the terror." Schiller's version of the battle between successive emotions—here, terror and sublime self-satisfaction—verifies de Man's earlier intuition in *Blindness and Insight* that fear is "much too practical to be called a passion" (BI 134).[23]

The Allegory of Emotion

The duplicity of de Manian emotion recalls Derrida's observation that the idea-sign "giant" "cannot be the idea-sign of the passion without presenting itself as the idea-sign of the presumed cause of that passion" (G 276). The notion of falsely self-presenting signs for passion draws upon Nietzsche's idea that pathos initially appears as ethos. When living through an experience, Nietzsche writes, "we always assume that it is the only state that is possible and reasonable for us and—to speak with the Greeks and adopt their distinction—an *ethos* and not a *pathos*."[24] Nietzsche is fond of the topos of conflict between inner and outer properties, especially in classical contexts. In *The Birth of Tragedy,* for example, he declares that "Dionysus speaks the language of Apollo; and Apollo, finally, the language of Dionysus."[25] Ruben Berezdivin has argued that Nietzsche influences Derrida's view of the affections;[26] de Man also owes a great deal to Nietzsche's attraction to misleading experiences and concepts, and like Nietzsche and Derrida, aligns emotions and signs on the basis of their common illusiveness. Metaphors seem figural but establish a faux-literal order, in comparison to emotions; but emotions, which as it were know the uncertainty of interpretation, can also act to establish a faux-literal order which contradicts their own knowledge. Here we enter a particularly bizarre corner of de Man's world, in which personified concepts and figures of speech go around deceiving themselves and one another at a kind of masked ball for abstractions. The effect is strongest in de Man's early work on Yeats, in which "natural images" are actually "disguised, not yet understood emblems," while "emblems are in reality pseudo-emblems," and so on (RR 168, 172). Figures disfigure, while disfiguration is infinitely susceptible to refiguration; this dynamic forms the basis for de Man's nonprogressive hermeneutic theory. Within this theory, "allegory" names a sensitive phase of a text's constitution and tendency to come apart, when the unraveling of a figure begins to look like the point of a text. All of this conforms to a common understanding of de Man's notion of trope. What is interesting for my purposes is that de Man works out his entire argument using emotions as examples, so that *Allegories of Reading* offers not just a weirdly emotive view of reading, but a hermeneutic theory of emotion. De Man's account of emotion, too, contains an allegorical phase, which arrives (to continue in de Man's mode of personification) after emotion has betrayed its awareness of uncertainty by acting as an agent for the literal order. Beyond the deceptiveness of emotion, de Man tells a new story about second-order emotions, emotions that compose an allegory of emotion.

For de Man, "allegory" presumes that a self-deceiving structure has revealed itself as self-deceiving: "allegory" describes what happens at and after that point, when a text tells the story of how it has so far told (or failed to tell) its story. Rousseau's epistolary novel *Julie ou la Nouvelle Héloïse* (1761) exemplifies the allegorical turn for de Man, for several reasons. *Julie* portrays emotion from the beginning as self-deceiving, and according to de Man, Rousseau tries not to compensate the reader for this unwelcome message with thematic or linguistic sensuality. A stiff, didactic text, *Julie* makes a small claim to verisimilitude and none at all to direct reference (allusion to real people). The letters that make up the novel "appear to be reflective and retrospective musings," de Man notes; they issue "no invitation to a shared erotic or passionate experience" (AR 194). In fact, the lovers' letters resemble nothing so much as criticism: they offer "interpretations of events rather than being themselves the events" (AR 194). Throughout, the lovers, Julie and Saint-Preux, comment explicitly on the wishfulness and phenomenality of their own love, which operates on the principles that de Man discovers in *Narcisse* and *Pygmalion*. De Man argues that in the "ethical" second half of the novel especially, Julie and Saint-Preux describe their love as "a process of figural substitutions . . . based on the presumption of an analogy between body and soul, between inside and outside" (AR 210) and opposed to "the contractual agreement of marriage, set up as a defense against the passions and as the basis of social and political order" (AR 216). "Mov[ing] against the 'natural' logic of the narrative," *Julie* draws a

moral, renunciatory conclusion "from the discovery of its earlier aberrations" (AR 216). Thus de Man portrays *Julie* as an inquest for so-
called emotion, just as he portrays *Allegories of Reading* as an exposé
of "ostensible pathos."

Yet since love is born of uncertainty, *Julie's* criticism of love reproduces uncertainty and generates more love:

> Like "man," "love" is a figure that disfigures, a metaphor that confers
> the illusion of proper meaning to a suspended, open semantic structure.
> In the naïvely referential language of the affections, this makes love into
> the forever-repeated chimera, the monster of its own aberration, always
> oriented toward the future of its repetition, since the undoing of the illu-
> sion only sharpens the uncertainty that created the illusion in the first
> place. (AR 198)

Love's efflorescence out of its own dubiousness is reflected in *Julie's*
reception when readers just cannot take allegory for an answer: "The
more Rousseau tried to avoid particularization, for example by reduc-
ing distinctive physical traits to the minimum need for allegorical
signification or by making the epistolary style almost intolerably uni-
form, the more readers have felt compelled to fill the space allotted to
their fantasy with trivia" (AR 189). Although it may seem naively romantic to discuss a didactic text as though it were personal "trivia,"
or overly generous to read it "as a novel of inward self-reflection"
(AR 189), de Man sees these reactions as moments of subjective candor that actually fulfill the contract of *Julie*. Love now takes its turn as
the "arch passion," for it shares its capacity for self-perpetuation with
emotion in general. "In the case of *Julie*, the passion happens to be
love," de Man claims, but "it is not the prevalence of love rather than
fear that sets apart *Julie* from the *Discourse*, since the determining
structure is that of passion which both have in common" (AR 197–
198).

Mirroring de Man's own enterprise so far—or, at least, what it may
look like to some readers—*Julie* establishes "the figurality of the language of passion," and by doing so, "return[s] in fact to a referential
model" (AR 198):

> However evanescent the referent of the passion may have become [*"le
> néant de mes chimères," "le néant des choses humaines"*; OCR 2:693],
> it is clear that once the figurality of the language of passion has been es-
> tablished [*"son langage est toujours figuré"*] we return in fact to a refer-

ential model. The unproblematic figurality of the metaphor restores its proper meaning, albeit in the form of a negating power that prevents any specific meaning from coming into being. The very pathos of the desire (regardless of whether it is valorized positively or negatively) indicates that the presence of desire replaces the absence of identity and that, the more the text denies the actual existence of a referent, real or ideal, and the more fantastically fictional it becomes, the more it becomes the representation of its own pathos. Pathos is hypostatized as a blind power or mere *"puissance de valoir,"* but it stabilizes the semantics of the figure by making it "mean" the pathos of its undoing. (AR 198–199)

In de Man's usage here, "pathos" does not necessarily involve lack, since it can be "valorized positively"—as desire's boundless persistence, for example. Rather, pathos is a generic second-order emotion. This secondary status grows clear when de Man attaches pathos to "desire," which in the amorous sense that applies here is an emotion itself. The advent of allegory draws the line between a "desire," which "replaces the absence of identity," and the "pathos of the desire," which *"indicates that* the presence of desire replaces the absence of identity" (my italics). Strictly speaking, pathos belongs not to desire (or any emotion) as such, as de Man writes in this first formulation, but to "its undoing," as he adds at the end of the passage. Arising "of" the knowledge that desire "replaces the absence of identity," pathos is the revenant emotion of allegory, the deconstructive passion. As Werner Hamacher has pointed out, it marshals the "power of disillusionment" toward a negative epistemology, "the certainty of the unreliability of the world and of all assertions that can be made about it."[27] In Hamacher's analysis, pathos bids to be the negative double of auto-affection, since by disconnecting itself from nonlinguistic referents, it appears as a "language of pure understanding in the medium of negativity" ("'Lectio,'" 194). Hamacher goes on to say that since for de Man no sign is ever "disburdened of its semantic gravitation," "pathos is always also and always at first an effect of language and of *another* language than that of pathos of itself" ("'Lectio,'" 196–197). The phoenix emotion, pathos assumes the death of other passions and fixes the conditions for their revival. Despite its explicitly second-order status, it acts like any emotion. Like the emotions it follows, it presents itself as meaning and thereby reinstates referentiality in a negative form. Henceforth the "work can be read as the 'portrait' of its own negative gesture," complete with "a pathos in which all can share" (AR 199, 200). According to de Man, this infinity of pathos appears on the level of *Julie*'s plot in (for example) Julie's assertions of love for God after she repudiates love for Saint-Preux. Following the pattern set with her lover, de Man writes, Julie seeks to gain her own self from God "by recognizing the signs through which the divinity manifests itself: a face, a voice, or most effectively of all, certain emotions that postulate a continuity between these signs and their signification" (AR 219). The result of her theological transposition of romance is that "virtue will later be identified . . . as being a passion among others, with a structure similar to that of love" (AR 219). It is here that *Julie* becomes allegorical, showing the "undoing" of its moral conclusion and making us reread the book, at least in memory.

Through his discussion of *Julie,* de Man also considers how phases of his own readings may look and how they are connected to emotion. He highlights the parallel between *Julie* and *Allegories* in the very title for the chapter, "(Allegory) *Julie.*" Julie's career of "virtue" corresponds to his own audit of passions—their recurrent patterns, their structural networks, their status as self-interested interpretations, and their concealment of their own interpretive activities. All of this exposure stirs up more pathos, as de Man points out. Since pathos proper can occur only after previous incarnations of emotion have been anatomized, pathos—the dominant emotion of de Man's prose, according to his explicators[28]—would indeed be the emotion criticism is most likely to induce. Thus de Man calls Julie "the best conceivable critical reader." As Jane Marie Todd observes, de Man "actually signs with Rousseau, *as* Julie";[29] Julie becomes de Man's Rrose Sélavy, a twin whom he praises for "the rigor of [her] insight into the aberrations of 'romantic' love" as though she were, after all, a portrait of—someone (AR 219n36; all of this comes in a footnote appended to the word "emotion"). Through its resemblance to *Julie,* criticism too becomes a "portrait" of "deconstructive passion" (AR 199).

Reflecting on de Man's work on pedagogy and aesthetic education, Anita Sokolsky concludes that "a reflex of sentimentality is triggered even by the attempt to fend it off."[30] Sokolsky states both that de Man's "austere discussion of the dismantling of the philosophical project by the grammar/rhetoric oscillation is meant to escape the pathos of abyssal logic" and that he "endorses the inescapability of the structure of fetishism" that produces pathos ("Resistance to Sentimentality," 79, 80). The question of whether de Man consciously embraces pathos is not of primary importance to her, as her main point regards sentimentality:

> The sentimental may be described as the something more which subtly mocks the declaration of sincerity by being more than sincere. It is possible to be insincere; but too sincere? too much oneself? one's words too much meant? . . . Unabashed sentimentality would be understood not as a search for an encompassing substantial unity, but instead as an attempt to render unintelligible both this search and the counterargument that one must fail to be adequate to oneself. Sentimentality in this sense can only be accused of taking too seriously the claim that the heterogeneous configuration of investments which is the self is all that we have to work with. If that configuration *is* the self, then we have lost not only the self which would guarantee that these configurations belong to a single subject . . . but also the conceptual means to describe this loss as a loss. (83)

Although Sokolsky uses a compensatory logic to explain de Man's pathos, her reflection on sentimentality goes beyond that logic. By Sokolsky's reasoning, sentimentality challenges subjectivity, but for different reasons than emotion does. Although Sokolsky does not put it in these terms, sentiment is opposed to emotion to this extent. Pathos assumes distance, she notes (82); as we've seen, the Cartesian form of self-distance, fatal to subjectivity, is a prerequisite for emotion. A separate, sentimental alternative to subjectivity is being "too much oneself." Sokolsky is right to point out that the logic of sentimentality is distinct from that of emotion; de Man's texts are indeed emotional but not sentimental. It is worth thinking further about sentimentality's challenge to subjectivity and about whether we might want theory to be sentimental.[31] But I do not take this to be the purpose of the widespread criticism that de Man displaces emotion, since these criticisms tend to seek the genuine. The distinction of sentimentality—its witless brilliance—is that it exposes the overlap between the genuine and the disingenuous. If one did want to recommend the sentimental self—a self neither self-differential nor unified, but overpresent—it would be difficult to do it in the name of the subject, much less in the name of emotion.

The chain of interpretations and emotions in *Julie* posits not subjects but networks, since emotions do not lodge in containers to whose contours their own presence can testify. The suspension of subjectivity does not suspend emotion unless you believe, in the first place, that emotions are not emotions unless subjects precede and intend them. This point is passingly debated with regard to authorship in Rousseau's Second Preface to *Julie,* at a moment de Man considers. Rousseau's Preface features disputants named N. and R. who debate the authorship of the novel, whether it was "merely copied (or quoted?) from a previous document or whether [R.] invented it" (AR 202). As so often happens, the idea of authorship metaphorizes subjectivity.[32] And as de Man's own preface to *Allegories of Reading* might lead us to expect, N. and R. try to use emotion as a guide to authorship:

> Asked whether he can respond to the pathos of the text, [N.] replies: "I can conceive of this effect with regard to you. If you are the author, the impact is easy to understand. If you are not, I can still conceive of it . . ." [OCR 2:18]. What he could not tolerate, however, is the impossibility of distinguishing between the alternatives. (AR 202)

N.'s anxiety demonstrates the divergence between emotion and the conceptualization of emotion—between perceiving or believing one perceives others' emotions and feeling emotions oneself on the one hand, and on the other, deciding what that means. Apparently, N. has already responded to the pathos of the text even though he does not know who wrote it and thus where the pathos comes from. He has no problem acknowledging the pathetic "effect" or "impact" of the text; he has trouble understanding and conceiving that impact. Having already engaged emotion in all the ways the situation allows for, N. now wants to know to what to attribute his own engagements. The dialogue shows the experiential precedence of emotion over its conceptualization as a reflection of subjectivity—an "easy" understanding of how emotion works—or as a nonsubjective phenomenon (not so easy, but tolerable). For de Man, the "impossibility of distinguishing" evidence for one model from evidence for the other returns N. to the inception of emotion. As we know from de Man's reading of *Narcisse,* emotion restarts from its own failure to find an object and thus reflect a source. Why, then, does N. insist on knowing where it comes from?

Inner Voices, Hostile Strangers: Moral and Social Feelings

The allegory of emotion in *Julie* seems to push the narrative of emotion as far as it can go: the story begins in disorientation, asserts the natural affinity of love, then moves through critical self-reading to moral sentiments which are themselves romantic and libidinal. Further, de Man predicts the recurrence of this story in readers in a position to ironize *Julie*'s ironization of emotion. Now, in Chapter 10 of *Allegories of Reading*, de Man comments that Rousseau's "Profession of Faith of the Savoyard Vicar" in *Emile* is "structured exactly like the *Nouvelle Héloïse*" (AR 247): in it, too, "virtue becomes finally justified in terms of an erotic pleasure principle" (AR 243). The distinction between affects and emotions here is vague, for in the eighteenth-century style, Rousseau describes highly socialized mores in terms of supposedly intuitive qualities. This does not raise a real question about the emotionality of the sentiments at issue, but demonstrates how the distinction between emotion and affect can readily be sharpened or softened for polemical purposes. De Man's explication of the "Profession of Faith" does not so much advance a fresh thesis about the specificity of moral and theological feelings as undertake, by focusing on them, a philosophical basis for the analysis of erotic emotions he has already conducted—for the set of nonerotic emotions may be empty. The target of the new discussion is not only moral judgment, but judgment in general. In addition, de Man couples his treatment of the "Profession of Faith" with his treatment of the *Social Contract* in order to make a distinction between judgments of any kind (as shown by *Julie* and the "Profession of Faith" alike) and executive force. Romantic and moral emotions both form judgments, but de Man will argue that the executive power of the State neither judges nor feels.

As Derrida finds différance within auto-affection in interior address, de Man finds in Rousseau's experience of self-presence a "condition of uncertainty" (AR 227) that both provokes the fiction of an inner voice of conscience and removes its authority to prescribe. De Man notes that while the "Profession of Faith" sometimes propounds the existence of "innate and natural moral feelings"—a notion that relies on "inwardness, innateness [*inéité*], voice" and so on—it also demonstrates that "reduction to a condition of mere self-presence . . . does not result in a constitutive cogito." Rather, this condition produces "a moment of genuine and intolerable confusion" (AR 227), as noted above. The indecisiveness of moral feeling appears on the surface of the text, de Man points out, in comical incongruities: Rousseau exhorts us to "look into ourselves" for the fount of virtue, all the while mentioning the examples of people whose inner passions destroy them or whose self-absorption deadens them (AR 241).

De Man asserts that the contingency of Rousseau's supposedly autonomous *"assentiment intérieur"* is revealed by its predication on prior ideas and judgments which may themselves be groundless. Unable to create ideas, the inner voice whispers "yes" or "no" to them in degrees of intensity, as though responding to the terms of a referendum: "turning over in my mind the various opinions that had successively swayed me since my birth, I saw that . . . my inner assent was given to them or withheld from them in varying degrees" (OCR 3:569, quoted in AR 228). Rousseau draws his notion of "inner assent" in part from the Aristotelian and Stoic idea that "assent" screens belief or judgment from mere appearance.[33] Moral feeling therefore depends on judgment, and Rousseau's judgment depends on "compar[ing] all those different ideas" (OCR 3:569, quoted in AR 228).[34] Yet, de Man goes on, a judgment grounded in comparison only confirms "the critical theory of metaphor that underlies the argument of the *Second Discourse*" (AR 230). Neither reason nor feeling, then, accounts for moral choice. Moral judgments and moral feelings supplement one another, deferring moral certainty around their circle. De Man's discussion of comparison recalls his reading of the "Blessed Babe" passage of *The Prelude,* in which Wordsworth's child converts simultaneous experiences (nursing and reading his mother's eye) into analogous ones. Because drinking milk and reading an expression line up with one another on at least one of the axes of his existence—the temporal one—he begins to believe that they line up on others. Built like all living creatures to notice structural patterns, the infant crosses levels of pattern to form chiasmus and metaphor. He not only compares objects, but compares and likens grounds of comparison—and this is his mistake, produced by a hypertrophism of the pattern perception that enables him to survive. De Man now treats this comparative capacity in general terms, under the name of "the act of judgment," or "the possibility of elaborating systems based on the correlation of differential with integrative moments" (AR 232).[35] For de Man, "the process is a manipulation, a displacement that upsets the 'truth' of things as they are, for sensation, unlike judgment, is truthful to the extent that it leaves things in their proper places." Earlier in *Allegories of Reading,* "what appears to be the inwardness of things" in a lyric of Rilke "is not a substantial analogy between the self and world of things but a formal and structural analogy between these things and the figural resources of words" (AR 37); judgment now proves to be another name for the ability "to create systems of relationship that are not substantial but merely structural" (AR 232). Once again, structural relation (which may also be found in mechanicity, grammar, and so on) is opposed not to emotion in de Man but to substantial relation. Sense requires the moment of judgment or structure, since "the unity of perception is an act of judgment"; unjudged perceptions—to continue in a Kantian vocabulary—can never offer "access to true knowledge" (AR 234), but only construct the world of precipitous surface that de Man later explores through the Kantian term *Augenschein* (for example, AI 80–90). The sensical, comparative but always possibly erroneous mechanism of judgment "warrants the equation of judgment with figural language, extensively conceived" (AR 235).

While emotions conduct tropic transactions, they would seem now not to be the only phenomena that do. In de Man's view, judgment of the most basic sort imaginable is also figurative, "extensively conceived." Emotions and judgments are hard to distinguish, forming an oscillating blur that decoys the mind from their cooperation. De Man's evaluation of judgment as we have followed it so far, then, consists of two phases: one which reveals innate moral sentiments as built on comparative judgments and a second in which asymmetries of judgment produce a narrative of errors. The process circles back on itself as judgments in turn fall back on feelings:

> As the confusion between structure and value increases, the tone and the terminology of the text glide almost imperceptibly from the language of judgment to the language of the affections, and judgment finally openly declares itself to be another name for "sentiment" (still distinct, at this point, from "sensation," *against* which, it will be remembered, judgment was originally defined). The ambiguously "inner" world of consciousness, of which it can no longer be said whether it is the seat of good or evil, becomes the affective space engendered by this ethical indecisiveness. . . . Virtue becomes finally justified in terms of an erotic pleasure principle, a moral libido that seems not easily compatible with the piety of the inner voice of conscience but that consistently acts out the rhetorical system of the text. (AR 242–243)

In earlier chapters of *Allegories,* emotions try to rescue the mind from indeterminacy; here, similarly, Rousseau calls upon "the affections" "as the confusion between structure and value increases." Now the affections save the mind from themselves. Because the voice of moral feeling responsible for judgment no longer sounds clearly "good or evil," we must throw ourselves upon—our feelings: "ethical indecisiveness" has "engendered" an "affective space." Judgment returns to its starting place; we must feel our way around our own feelings, reintuiting the trustworthiness of each "inner voice of conscience" in a potentially infinite regress of *"assentiments intérieurs."*[36]

When de Man moves from Rousseau's moral theory to his social theory, the concomitant problem for emotion becomes the question of connection between "individual and collective well-being" (AR 254). According to de Man, moral feeling for Rousseau is either a matter of one's own inner qualities or of divine justification ("divine activity" itself being "described by the same terms that were used to define judgment" [AR 238]), not a matter of social contract, consensus, or statistical norms. To undergird a theory of moral judgment, then, de Man's Rousseau needs only a unity of perceptions, but for a theory of the State, he needs a unity of unities of perceptions. The idea of the State as a higher-order unity clarifies individual experience by contrast, especially emotional experience.

The emotional significance of the contrast is borne out by de Man's choice to focus on another emotive text, more emotive than the *Second Discourse* to which it bears some relation: namely, the fragment "Du bonheur public." The fragment and its appearance in *Allegories of Reading* present something of a puzzle: despite the anticipatable liabilities of the figure, Rousseau seems to go out of his way to cast social success as a form of *happiness*. Since anthropomorphizing the State predictably creates problems for Rousseau's project, we must ask what advantage he saw in this approach. Similarly, we might ask why de Man goes out of his way to read this humble scrap of Rousseau's oeuvre, this "reply to a questionnaire sent out by the Société économique de Berne" (AR 250).

De Man summarizes the initial problems of the text as follows:

> "Du bonheur public" . . . considers the possibility of a readable semiology of private happiness that would be based on analogies between inside feelings and their outside manifestations only in order to reject it out of hand: "Happiness is not pleasure; it is not a fleeting stirring of the soul, but a permanent and entirely inward feeling, that can only be evaluated by the person who experiences it. No one can therefore decide with certainty if someone else is happy, nor can he, as a result of this, come to know with certainty the *signs* that bear witness to the happiness

of individuals" [OCR 3:510, de Man's italics]. Consequently, there can be no easy metaphorical totalization from personal to social well-being, based on an analogical resemblance between both: "It is . . . not by the feeling that the citizens have of their happiness, not consequently by their happiness itself that one can judge the prosperity of the State" [OCR 3:513]. . . . Yet . . . [Rousseau] at once replaces the dismissed, natural affectivity of the individual subject by a natural affectivity of the group that can be interpreted precisely as the self has just been shown *not* to be. . . . This being granted, the totalization is bound to ensue without further delay: "[men] will be united, they will be virtuous, they will be happy, and their felicity will be the well-being of the Republic." (AR 250–251)

De Man stresses the advanced nature of Rousseau's assumptions about emotions at this point: his entire discussion "reject[s] . . . out of hand" the "natural affectivity of the individual subject." Moreover, public happiness cannot be understood as an accretion of private emotions. Rousseau "undo[es] the 'natural' metaphor" of happiness as inner property by claiming that "the moral condition of a people is less the result of the absolute condition of its members than of the relationships among them" (OCR 3:511, quoted in AR 253). Yet in the face of all this, Rousseau reinstates "a natural affectivity" and even a happiness "of the group." Why does Rousseau seem so suddenly to become naive about group emotion? Since it postdates Rousseau's critique of emotion, the naturalism of public emotion looks like either a great mistake or a great enigma. There is, indeed, something careless and all too happy about the return of happiness in Rousseau's argument: as the dubiousness of moral feelings circularly generate a second, philosophically weaker, blatantly empirical and eudaemonic reappearance of moral feeling in "Profession of Faith," here the irrelevance of individual happiness to that of the State just happens eventually to make people happy anyway. Disconnected in principle from the happiness of the State, happiness nevertheless wells up in the system, diluted to empirical happenstance but no less pleasant for that.

Yet for de Man, the naturalness of Rousseau's public happiness cannot be put down to mere wishfulness: it stems instead from a distinction in kind between the executive power of the State and individual experience. This conclusion is important for my purposes because it clarifies by opposition what individual experience is, with surprising results: individuals and states must be seen as feeling nonsubjects, but the executive power of the State must be seen as a nonfeeling subject. Thus we must go slowly at first through de Man's theses about State sovereignty.

Executive power's singularity, for de Man, can be seen when Rousseau sets "the entire set of relationships among members of the State" against "the relationship of one State to another" (AR 254) and, ultimately, the relationship of the State to anything that is not itself, including each of its individual members. De Man claims that because Rousseau's *Social Contract* must articulate these various relationships, its most important verbal act is generalization, which "ha[s] a very different figural structure than such metaphorical processes as, for example, conceptualization, love, or even judgment" (AR 261).[37] De Man explains Rousseau's use of generalization through the illustration of a piece of property. "The contractual instrument" that construes a plot of land both as the property of an individual citizen and as part of the geographical State itself "exists as a paradoxical juxtaposition or interference of relational networks":

> On the one hand, as private property, objects of possession used for the fulfillment of individual needs and desires [*jouissance*], the relationship between the owner and the land, or dwelling, is entirely literal. . . .

> The relation of one private property to another is a relationship between two units that are similarly constituted. . . . But the same is not true when the property is considered within a context of public interests, especially when they involve the interests of the State with regard to other States. The contractual constitution of a State may or may not be similar to that of another, but this question is irrelevant with regard to territorial conflict and integrity. From that point of view, the other State is, per definition, a hostile stranger. . . . When considered privately, property is a structure based on similarity and on the integration of shared needs and desires; when considered publicly, the same property functions as a structure of necessary estrangement and conflict. (AR 262, 263)

De Man sees the plot of land, and the individual who owns it, as imbricated in "two entirely divergent texts" (AR 264) using "two distinct rhetorical models, the first self-reflective or specular, the other estranged" (AR 265). Not only does the relation of two properties within the State differ entirely, for him, from the relation between two States which include the same properties; synecdoche does nothing to assuage the difference between the two sets of relations. Private interests "do precisely *not* derive" from public interests "as part derives from whole" (AR 265). As in my reading of the Derridean cogito, the differentiality of the individual is not pure, consisting only of estrangement, but rather consists of an incommeasurability between virtual experiences and conceptual beliefs. In the phenomenology of the cogito, I feel divided, although the cogito states that I am not: my nondivision is inaccessible to me. The aporia regarding subjectivity that de Man finds in the preface to *Narcisse* offers another version of this simultaneity of incommensurable classical and nonclassical schemes. De Man's present example occurs still higher, in the relation between interpersonal and international relations, and its polarities are reversed. Interpersonally, according to de Man, as owners of property, we act literally or specularly, our actions "perfectly defined" by "objective dimensions, and the inscribed signs by means of which these dimensions are designated" (AR 262). In contrast, States are definitionally and symbolically alienated in relation to others. The estrangement in principle of States to one another—States amassed necessarily of individuals and properties—bears no relation, not even a metaphoric relation, to the individual's experience of other individuals that make up the State as it can be known from the inside. The individual has what Rousseau calls a "double rapport" with the State—the State can be engaged from within or without—but the State's sovereign power does not have a double rapport with anything. It is self-identical, and anything outside it is potentially its enemy.

The fascination of this situation for de Man, and its importance for emotion, lies in the asymmetry he discovers between the differentiality of the individual and the unity—we could say the self-presence—of the State's sovereign power:

> What the individual is estranged from is precisely the executive activity of his own State as *souverain*. This power is unlike him and foreign to him because it does not have the same double and self-contradictory structure and *therefore does not share in his problems and tensions*. The *souverain* can consider himself "under one single and identical relationship" and, with regard to any outsider, including the individual citizen, it can become "a single Being or an individual" ["*à l'égard de l'étranger, il devient un Etre simple ou un individu*"; OCR 3:291]. Unlike the "individual," who is always divided within himself, the executive is truly individual, un-divided. (AR 265, my italics)

De Man goes on to argue that the legal generalization that binds the individual into a double rapport with the State is the paradigm of a text, "any entity that can be considered from such a double perspective" (AR 270), and as such, can be expected to unwind. But I must pause here in order to draw the emotive conclusions of de Man's reading. We know that there are such conclusions, not only because Rousseau's public "happiness" must somehow be related to his vision of sovereignty, but because de Man's sketch of defensive Leviathans, in which "the other State is, per definition, a hostile stranger" (AR 263), recalls Rousseau's fable of the giant, in which the fear of possible violence causes one individual to misperceive another as a monster. What sort of "happiness," if any, does the State attain—what can "happiness" possibly mean here? And how, if at all, can this happiness accommodate the alienation manifest in the standoffs between States?

In "Du bonheur public," the "happy" State is structured like a mind, so to speak. It "does not remain . . . satisfied to consider the other State as a pure stranger," but "is forced to enter steadily into comparison in order to know itself" (OCR 3:605, quoted in AR 256). The happy State *knows* that it is happy, and to the extent that it knows itself, it isn't independent of what lies outside it. It does not form a "(non)relationship of pure estrangement"; it is "dialectical" (AR 256), self-differential, allegorical, like a living thing, like something that can feel. All of this is entailed in the mere proposition that this State is "happy," even if Rousseau insists that the ground of its happiness does not resemble an individual's. Sovereign power in the *Social Contract*—although it seems an extension of the same independence—is *not* aligned with the happiness of the state. Sovereignty, or "executive power" in de Man's updated terminology, is that "active" aspect of the State exclusively defined as oriented toward outsiders "including the individual citizen" (AR 265). It is the side of the State, in other words, that turns outward and is *constitutionally incapable* of self-relationship. It follows that the sovereign power of the State is an *unconscious* power, and that as an unconscious power, it acts but does not feel emotions. As Rousseau moves from "Du bonheur public" to the *Social Contract*, his anthropomorphization of the socius comes to consist of a reflective, differential State that feels and an undivided, unconscious power that violently acts. (Thus, for de Man "the differentiation between the State as a defined entity [*Etat*] and the State as a principle of action [*Souverain*]" duplicates the tension "between the constative and the performative function of language" [AR 270].) In a passage de Man cites, Rousseau attaches some of these associations to his terminology: "This public person thus constituted by the union of all the others . . . is called by its members the

State [*Etat*] when it is passive, the *Sovereign* [*Souverain*] when it is active" (OCR 3:290, quoted in AR 265). As sovereign, de Man's State, I would argue, is not afraid. Unlike the individual man who fears another, it isn't conscious enough to be afraid. Sovereignty has no psychology; collective psychology would be inappropriate here, just as it would be in the individual realm if unconsciousness were all there were. The world of sovereign powers does not deal in metaphorical monsters, but real monsters—vigorous, unconscious, hostile entities that are not afraid of one another.

The brake on such power, supplied by de Man, is that these entities depend for their very existence on the legal text that binds the individual to the general will in "double rapport" (where "text" means not just a written code, but also the system of relationships itself). The asymmetry of the State's founding, the fact that "the general will is rarely that of all," as Rousseau puts it, creates, "in the wheels of the State"—these are still Rousseau's words—"an equivalent of the principle of inertia in machines [*dans les ressorts de l'état un equivalent aux frottements des machines*]" (OCR 3:287, quoted in AR 272). This and other founding paradoxes ultimately make of "the general will" "a helpless and 'mutilated' giant, a distant and weakened echo of the Polyphemos we first encountered in the *Second Discourse*" (AR 274).[38] To write about sovereignty in this way, however, in its connection to legislation and "the sum of individual strengths" (OCR 3:287, quoted in AR 272), is already to step outside its definitional lack of connection. It is to say tautologically that in conjunction with other things, sovereignty is not sovereign. It remains true that to the extent that sovereignty is sovereign, it acts as an unfeeling unconsciousness (much in the way that positional power acts without the power to know in "Shelley Disfigured" [RR 103]). And *this, for de Man, is what a real "subject" would be like.* Far from containing emotions (or, for that matter, judgments) or possessing a consciousness capable of directing feelings, a "truly in-dividual, un-divided" being would lack the self-differentiality that makes experience possible at all.

Emotion Degree Zero

The allegories of emotion in *Allegories of Reading* feed into an economy of pathos, a reproduction of emotion out of its diminution. As I indicated earlier, de Man might seem to be a hardest-case scenario for emotion; he can alternatively be understood to be confronting the strongest case for emotionlessness, and by way of answer, describing an exceptionally resilient form of emotion. While minimal cases of emotion are not, of course, the only ones available, much turns on how one takes minimal experiences. Emotions at the end of the mind such as Aristotelian shock or Cartesian astonishment are sometimes envisioned as sensory overloads. They seem to show experience staggered by its own intensity. When the mind has received an astonishing impression, Descartes writes, it is "so wholly occupied with the preservation of this impression" that it comes to a halt; "as a result the whole body remains as immobile as a statue" (1:354). Other limit cases figure emotion not as excess but as an ebbed tide, and the mind as a dry but alert shell, its life entirely encompassed by mechanical and formal processes. Some readings of the sublime see the mind reaching a traumatic state in which, because form and content no longer coincide, only form remains. The lower reaches of emotion are not typical of the experience described by poststructuralist theory, but are important to the question of subjectivity because they evoke the nightmare of "living death." They convey the fear that experience without a subject is, somehow, experience without experience.

De Man addresses this fear by tracking the consequences of Kantian *"apatheia"* in the late lecture "Kant's Materialism" (1981) and the overlapping essay "Phenomenality and Materiality in Kant" (1984). De Man pays special attention to the following note in *The Critique of Judgment*:

> *Affects* differ in kind from *passions*. Affects relate merely to feeling, whereas passions belong to our power of desire and are inclinations that make it difficult or impossible for us to determine our power of choice through principles. Affects are impetuous and unpremeditated, passions persistent and deliberate. Thus resentment in the form of anger is an affect, in the form of hatred (vindictiveness) it is a passion. Passion can never be called sublime, no matter what the circumstances; for while in an affect the mind's freedom is *impeded*, in passion it is abolished. (132n39)

In "Kant's Materialism" de Man uses Kant's "affect" specifically to negate the expressive hypothesis:

> What exactly is affectivity in Kant? It is easier to say what it is not: certainly not Shaftesbury's enthusiasm, nor the valorization of an inward-

ness which, in the Augustinian and pietistic tradition, unites the voice of consciousness . . . with the discourse of feeling, a tonality associated with Rousseau and with pre-Romanticism. Kant carefully distinguishes between affects and passions [*Leidenschaften*], which belong for him to the order of arbitrary and coercive desire: "in the affect, the freedom of the soul may be curtailed, but in a state of passion, it is eliminated altogether [*aufgehoben*]." Kant's discussion of the affects does not start out from the inner experience of a subject, from the sort of interpretive sensitivity, the affective cogito that one can capture in Montaigne, in Malebranche, or in the Romantics. (AI 123)

Kant's discussion is indeed related in a complex way to the mainstream of the philosophy of emotion since Aristotle. Kant does not share the common desire to degrade feelings (what goes in Husserl by the name of "merely empirical" affections and in Rousseau, "sentiments"). Atypically, he values "impetuous" feelings over "deliberate" passions; while deliberation is more easily keyed to idealization and repeatability, Kant, thinking a move ahead, sees in this very capacity a potential for *"mania" (Wahnwitz)*—an obsessive overrepetition all the more "ruleless" for being unaccountably persistent (*Critique of Judgment*, 136). As many people have noted, Kant is generally phobic about addiction.[39] Within what he calls affect, however, Kant resubscribes to the usual philosophical bias toward ideal and repeatable principles. Unsurprisingly, Kant admires "admiration [*Bewunderung*], which is lasting," over "surprise [*Verwunderung*], which is fleeting and transitory" (*Critique of Judgment,* 133, quoted in AI 123), a revulsive impulse like shock—and so on. Elsewhere Kant uses similar criteria to insulate sublime affects from "emotions [that] belong only to *motion,* which we welcome for the sake of our health" (*Critique of Judgment,* 134); "VIGOROUS" affects based on moral ideas from "LANGUID" affects based on dumb, feminine sympathy; and even *"interesting* sadness" from *"insipid sadness"* (*Critique of Judgment*, 133, 137). Awarding merit to emotions the less arbitrary and coercive they are leads to a conclusion which, Kant writes, "may appear odd": "the absence of emotion *(apatheia, phlegma in significatu bono),* when found in a mood that adheres emphatically and insistently to its principles, cannot only be sublime but most admirably so" (*Critique of Judgment,* 132–133, trans. de Man, quoted in AI 125). De Man believes that the sublimity of *apatheia* inhabits Kant's idea of nature as well, nature "just as one sees it [*'wie man ihn sieht*']" (AI 128), not correspondent or even related to "any mind or judgment": "the dynamics of the sublime mark the moment when the infinite is frozen into the materiality of stone, when no pathos, anxiety, or sympathy is conceivable; it is, indeed, the moment of a-pathos, or apathy, as the complete loss of the symbolic" (AI 127).

Kant postulates that zero degree of emotion—corresponding to a way of thinking "entirely devoid of any substitutive exchange," figure, or trope (AI 127)—of which de Man's work, and Kant's as well,[40] shows the impossibility. Pygmalion's "I don't know what I feel in touching this veil" is hotly emotional in comparison, since Pygmalion already knows that he is supposed to feel something and has gone looking for it. A statement of *apatheia* would read "I see what I see, and feel nothing." *Apatheia* would see nature as an eye sees it, as *Augenschein*, without emotions and figures, a display of sheer optics belonging to the formal and material world of physics.[41] "It is this entirely a-referential, a-phenomenal, a-pathetic formalism that will win out in [Kant's] battle among affects," de Man concludes, "and find access to the moral world of practical reason" (AI 128).

While *apatheia* has a side that faces out, we cannot, in Kant's own terms, experience that side. It also has a side that faces in, the feeling of the failure of feeling—Keats's "feel of not to feel it." The first evidence that Kant acknowledges such a feeling is interpersonal: Kant implies that when emotion drains away from a noble mind, this very circumstance excites emotion in others. After asserting that "*being without affects* . . . in a mind that vigorously pursues its immutable principles is sublime," he goes on to note that "a cast of mind of that sort is called noble . . . if it arouses not so much *amazement* [*Verwunderung*]. . . as *admiration* [*Bewunderung*]" (*Critique of Judgment*, 132–133). The distinction between amazement and admiration, adduced by de Man to show Kant's enthrallment by rhyme, itself prefers the paler feeling, but is drawn by Kant in the act of announcing that admiration is *aroused*. Under the generally economic law of emotive thermodynamics, the total amount of feeling is not diminished by the affectlessness of a noble mind. More revealingly, Kant classifies "loss or absence of affect [*Affektlosigkeit*]" (AI 125) "among affects" in the first place. A kind of phantom-limb reasoning emerges here; there is not only no negative in the unconscious, but no negative in experience. By Kant's own expressive logic, *apatheia* could only be experienced as a sense of the grammar of forms. "Feeling" is a sensitive slot independent of any specific object: when empty, it sends back the (positive) message "empty." Formality is therefore perfectly thematizable as a content, and does not fail to be thematized in Kant's text. While de Man underlines the divisibility of grammar from content or substance, grammar can also find its own content in *apatheia*.

The possibility of *apatheia* as a minimal emotion is an outcome of freeing emotion from definition by expression. Gasché also reads "Kant's Materialism" to claim that de Man resists the "unifying and universalizing" conception of classical pathos.[42] For Gasché, however, making this claim seems to require claiming that de Man abandons pathos altogether. "Kant's Materialism" can be seen instead as employing a concept of pathos that Gasché does not recognize because it does not use emotion to validate a fit between inner and outer domains. As Gasché points out, de Man finds Kant's reasoning motivated by "merely formal . . . verbal distinctions" (*Wild Card*, 99); de Man catches or pretends to catch Kant contrasting *Verwunderung* to *Bewunderung* because of the words' rhyme. Gasché asserts that these "verbal distinctions" are "entirely without affect, which means that they do not possess any connecting and unifying potential" (*Wild Card*, 99). By describing Kant's resort to them de Man is proposing that "a moment of absolute singularity that is thematized here in terms of a complete lack of pathos" is "constitutive of the formal, the thematic, and also the technical level of aesthetic experience" (*Wild Card*, 102). According to Gasché, the "apathetic linguistic elements" are "cut loose from meaning and universality, remaining on this side of affection," hence capable of being "usurped for (cognitive) purposes" but incapable of "*lend[ing] themselves* to any meaning intention" (*Wild Card*, 105, 109). Rather, "whatever they may possibly come to mean, will always have been the result of an imposition" (*Wild Card*, 109). The intrinsic value determining Gasché's recognition of feeling, however, is compatible only with a classical view of feeling. For the kind of feeling, and thus the kind of apathy, Gasché seeks, it does not matter whether someone happens to feel affected or not, but rather whether that affection is motivated and "unifying" if and when it occurs. Here, feeling unsupported by a larger coherence does not count as real feeling. Gasché looks specifically for feeling that corresponds to potentials in elements of semiology that "lend themselves" to being felt about: he looks for *expressive* feeling that validates a mind-world coherence. Therefore, Gasché only casually notices the actual or likely occurrence of emotion. He quarantines empirical instances of emotion from his definition of emotion as the vehicle of relation and self-relation:

> One could, of course, argue that apathy is still a pathos and that apathy cannot entirely avoid being "pathetic." This is certainly the case as far as the tone and the language itself of de Man's writings are concerned. The question, however, is whether this pathos of apathy that derives from the historical and psychological conditions under which de Man's texts have been written can be brought to bear on the philosophical attempt of *conceiving* of apathy not only as an absence of all emotions and feelings but also as having no emotional relation to itself anymore. If the apathetic in de Man's sense is to preclude all (emotional) relations, it can no longer have the identity of an emotion. (*Wild Card*, 282n48)

Gasché moves axiomatically: pathos that "derives from . . . historical and psychological conditions" is not pathos in principle. Apathy is not an emotion "if the apathetic in de Man's sense is to preclude all (emotional) relations," yet this latter statement is Gasché's burden to prove. He approaches this proof through the idea that in real feeling, "constituting elements, rules, or acts" must conspire in the production of their meaning (*Wild Card*, 109).[43] While this consent of world to mind—sometimes figured as the passivity of one or the other—is entailed by the expectation that emotion be expressive, it is exactly, not accidentally, excluded from the alternative of nonexpressive emotion which, I have been arguing, de Man's narrative describes. In this account, emotion arises *because* of the lack of fit between mind and world and between the mind and itself. Such emotion can no longer verify unities, but then it no longer has to; indeed, it has *not* to.

De Man invokes Nietzsche in *Allegories of Reading* in a way that parallels his exploration of *apatheia* in the Kant articles—to show that feeling *nothing* is *feeling* nothing, a feeling like any other, not an anesthetic suppression. In his reading of Nietzsche's *On Truth and Lie in the Extra-Moral Sense*, de Man emphasizes Nietzsche's belief that the unveiling power of art is a "truth of appearance." Seemingly outside emotion, such a truth "is not a threat or a passion that could be described in terms similar to those used in *The Birth of Tragedy* to evoke the Dionysian pathos of truth" (AR 113–114). Yet Nietzsche's claims for this passion-free mode of being remain affective, as we can see in de Man's paraphrase:

It can therefore be said that it [the truth of appearance] stands above pleasure and pain, in the ordinary sense of those terms. The artist, who is truthful in his recognition of illusion and of lie for what they are, thus gains a special kind of affective freedom, a euphoria which is that of a *joyful* wisdom or of the Homeric *Heiterkeit* and that differs entirely from the pleasure principle tied to libido and desire. . . . *On Truth and Lie* describes the euphoria of this type of "truth." (AR 114)

Again proper emotions are differentiated from needs, here in the form of "the pleasure principle tied to libido and desire." Beyond the orbit of pleasure and pain, yet within the constellation of experience, "euphoria" is "affective freedom," a phrase that implies both freedom from affect and freedom that is affective. A "euphoria" of freedom from pleasure is no freedom from pleasure at all, but a *trompe-l'oeil* substitution of one pleasure for another that accomplishes an increase in illusionistic efficiency. In other words, it is strange to take theory's sometime promotion of *apatheia* at face value when it is simultaneously depicted as the greatest thrill. This performative contradiction is a staple well understood by drug culture and rock music ("I don't feel and it feels great," sings the band Modest Mouse).[44] Similarly, it is odd to conclude that the sublime is emotionless because in its intensity, the besieged imagination does not keep pace with the representation demanded: its not coming up with the right representation does not mean it comes up with nothing.

De Man's theory of mind comes closer to Heidegger's theory of moods, in which states of mind are givens around which perception works. Heidegger bothers to differentiate between modest emotional states and normalizes all: "the pallid, evenly balanced lack of mood . . . which is often persistent and which is not to be mistaken for a bad mood, is far from nothing at all" (*Being and Time*, 173). He holds moods' interest independent from cognition; rational suppositions about the sources or lack thereof of moods "[count] for nothing as against the phenomenal facts of the case. . . . From the existential-ontological point of view, there is not the slightest justification for minimizing what is 'evident' in states-of-mind" (*Being and Time*, 175). Heidegger not only respects moods, but grants them existential priority over judgments and even affects (*Being and Time*, 177); de Man, however, gives emotion and pathos no edge. He rather, as the secondary criticism amply demonstrates, spends as much time on their deceitfulness as on their power. But he does share Heidegger's belief in their continuousness as "phenomenal fact." Nietzsche's affective free-dom, Julie's desire for self-criticism, and Kant's sublime *apatheia* de-scribe what it is like to feel the endlessness of pathos, the "deconstruc-tive passion" that tells the difference between the concept and the actuality of emotion's negation. While Hamacher observes that "the language of pathos does not speak but, almost in a stammer, only re-peats its own incapacity to speak" ("'Lectio,'" 193), in a later phase of de Man's argument and Hamacher's reading of it as well, pathos is always talking about how mute it is. Expanding with the expansion of signifying and interpretive discourse, "the language of pathos is infinitely eloquent" (AR 186), de Man remarks.

In light of de Man's rhetorical theory of emotion, the chestnuts of his critical canon appear startlingly new. De Man writes, for example, that questions like Archie Bunker's, or like Yeats's "How can we know the dancer from the dance?" contest "the possibility of conver-gence between experiences of consciousness such as memory or emo-tions—what [Yeats] calls passion, piety, and affection—and entities accessible to the senses such as bodies, persons, or icons" (AR 12). Throughout his investigation of rhetorical questions de Man specifies that he is thinking not just about poems, but about all "entities acces-sible to the senses." Yeats's "Among School Children" fosters this generalization by comparing religious icons to people: "Both nuns and mothers worship images." While Yeats differentiates animate and inanimate objects of affection, he notes that even the inanimate ones are effective: "they too break hearts." Pivoting on Yeats's word "icon," de Man shifts easily from images to words, that is, from idols to poems; at the same time, Yeats's association between images and children warrants viewing bodies, too, as objects of interpretation. Bodies "accessible to the senses" resemble questions that cannot di-vulge their rhetorical modes. Both are perceptible without being fully legible, as de Man claims in a passage so familiar that it is hard to read:

> Any question about the rhetorical mode of a literary text is always a rhe-torical question which does not even know whether it is really question-ing. The resulting pathos is an anxiety (or bliss, depending on one's mo-mentary mood or individual temperament) of ignorance, not an anxiety of reference—as becomes thematically clear in Proust's novel when read-ing is dramatized, in the relationship between Marcel and Albertine, not

as an emotive reaction to what language does, but as an emotive reaction to the impossibility of knowing what it might be up to. (AR 19)

De Man assumes not only that rhetoric must be received with uncertainty, but that that uncertainty will be channeled and transformed by an emotive reaction, a "resulting pathos." Particular emotive inflections reflect "momentary" or "individual" factors, but the general basis of "emotive reaction" can be traced to the "impossibility of knowing what [language] might be up to." That is not the end of de Man's narrative of emotion—emotions produce artifacts of interiority and subjectivity, break them down and build them back up anew—but it is the beginning, and the energy of this beginning is never exhausted. To "question . . . the rhetorical mode of a literary text"—a description of de Man's own enterprise, by any account—elicits pathos, but why? If we have emotions because we can't know what to believe (what texts and people are up to), as de Man suggests, then we have emotions even though we can't know which emotions we ought to have. If we truly *knew* which emotions we should have, we would no longer feel like having any. We are in no danger of being emotionless, though—nor is de Man's theory—since this "if" condition is never fulfilled.

CHAPTER THREE

A Parallel Philosophy

Productive and disruptive, active and passive, first- and second-order, rational and nonrational, emotions open the self-difference posited by poststructuralist theory, and complicate concepts of integrity and intentionality on which subjectivity depends. Despite these disadvantages, few philosophers are willing simply to denounce emotion; decisive antiemotionalism like Locke's remains rare. Rather, classical philosophy since Aristotle has attempted to fold emotion into unitary accounts of the mind. Because of emotion's multivalence and ubiquity, however, it's difficult to incorporate emotion fully into the mind without threatening subjectivity. The result is that in practice theories of emotion depict dilemmas in the philosophy of mind; emotion theory is the internal supplement to the history of that philosophy. Classical philosophy has not been wrong about emotion, but rather righter—and less classical—than it has cared to be. The nonclassical nature of the discourse of emotion indicates that emotion exerts pressure on theories of subjectivity; emotion engenders what Ronald de Sousa calls *"a kind of parallel philosophy"* (RE 3). There is, moreover, a secondary parallel between the parallel philosophy of emotion theory and the parallel philosophy of poststructuralist readings of Continental texts, in which defenses of subjective unity similarly describe self-difference.

This chapter examines four episodes within the recent philosophical discourse of emotion. Previous chapters have worked from inside theories; this one works from outside, for the texts I discuss have in common the fact that they are not *trying* to disconnect emotion from subjectivity. Rather, emotion's presumption of the death of the subject appears as a force with which they contend. The texts are ordered according to their increasing openness to nonsubjective emotion. First, I consider some Anglo-American philosophical writings on musical emotion. Most of these texts are transcendental in that they seek universals of experience; music seems to stimulate such searches. The texts tend to force apparently objectless musical emotions into subject-object schemes. The authors show the strength of the imperative to tie emotion to subjects, since in their work this imperative stands alone: in musical aesthetics, the expressive hypothesis has no objects to work with and no function except to sustain subjectivity. Hence, the philosophy of music offers a negative image of nonsubjective experience.

Ronald de Sousa's important *Rationality of Emotion* (1987)—a pervasively insightful book—affirms the heterarchy of living systems and stops just short of discarding the human subject. De Sousa defines the human subject by the singularity of its intentional objects—a definition so particular as to suggest that the subject is preserved for the sake of preserving singular reference. The length to which de Sousa is willing to go toward nonsubjective emotion, in other words, challenges the line he finally draws between iterable compulsion and singular emotion, nonhuman and human intentionality. His approach may be contrasted to Daniel Dennett's proposals about how one might conceive experience without subjects. Like the deconstructive texts in Chapters 1 and 2, Dennett's work recognizes the existence of fields outside experience but orients itself to interpretation. A high value on interpretation, I submit, is necessary to any theory of emotion. Like Derrida and de Man, Dennett asserts the possibility and the full operability of nonsubjective interpretation. Finally, two sections consider Deleuze's theory of affect as reflected in his early readings of Spinoza and in Deleuze and Guattari's *A Thousand Plateaus*. These sections examine what happens to emotion when a system widens its scope beyond experience. Deleuze's project is nonsubjective but ontological rather than experiential. While emotion thrives without a subject, it cannot survive the loss of any interpretive perspective whatsoever. In breaking through the restrictions of interpretive thought, Deleuze implicitly destroys a condition for emotion, which, unlike affect, relies on interpretation. This chapter, then, moves through the following philosophical combinations: the texts in musical aesthetics are transcendental, not interpretational; de Sousa's work is subjective and interpretational; Dennett's is nonsubjective and interpretational; and Deleuze's is nonsubjective and noninterpretational. The philosophers of music and de Sousa enact the difficulty of tying emotion to subjectivity through their efforts, to various degrees, to do so. Dennett's texts suggest that a system of micro-interpretations alone accounts for the experience that according to the classical story, only subjectivity can explain. And Deleuze shows—negatively, from the objective side—that while emotion exceeds subjectivity it does not exceed phenomenality. Deleuze makes it clear that there is a space between the nonsubjective and the objective. This space of nonsubjective interpretation is the terrain of emotion.

Nobody's Passion: Emotion and the Philosophy of Music

In language typical of musical aesthetics, Hegel writes that music "[finds] utterance in its tones for the heart with its whole gamut of feelings and passions."[1] It is no accident that Rousseau's *Essay on the Origin of Languages*—so often about emotions—also deals at length with music. The discourse of emotion is curiously saturated with musical metaphors, instruments figuring selves and music figuring feeling. Rilke's poem "Am Rande der Nacht," adduced by de Man in *Allegories of Reading,* is narrated by a voice which declares itself to be "a string / strung over wide, roaring resonances [*eine Saite, / über rauschende breite / Resonanzen gespannt*]" while "things" are the bodies of violins (quoted in AR 33–34). Associations of this sort flourish in literature after the eighteenth century; as Rosalind Picard observes, "the metaphor is one of subtle and powerful influence on our behavior."[2] Musical figuration has been examined a good deal in poststructuralist theory—by Barthes, Deleuze and Guattari, de Man, Derrida, Philippe Lacoue-Labarthe, and Cathérine Clément, for instance.[3] The poststructuralist analysis of music extends that of voice; like voice, music takes place irreducibly close up. It seems to fill space or even to emanate from within, unfurling feelings inside us. Music is all too transparent, a language so fine that no content can penetrate it. This leads to a peculiar dilemma: if particular emotions involve particular beliefs, how can music create such keen emotions without, usually, seeming to refer to anything nonmusical, anything not utterly formal?

There are three ways out: to decide that music doesn't arouse true emotion after all; to preserve subjective emotion without nonaesthetic beliefs and objects; or to reevaluate the ideology of emotion's reliance on subjectivity. Even more than in most areas of philosophy, "cognitive" accounts of emotion take priority in musical aesthetics, and so the third possibility is often eliminated at the outset. As I suggested in Chapter 1, emotion is rendered "cognitive" in order to brace expression and ultimately subjectivity. The philosophy of music plays this game with one hand tied behind its back, boxing musical emotion into the expressive hypothesis even though music seems to have no contents to express. In musical aesthetics, in other words, the content approach to emotion appears as a bare diagram, without the network of empirical beliefs and objects that often confer plausibility. Lifted from this network, the formal armature of the content approach can seem arbitrary, in search of significance, as the literature of musical aesthetics is well aware. The consequent convolution of arguments has set off a proliferation of corrective arguments and so on, so that the literature on musical emotion has grown a bit baroque. This body of work wants understandably to counter the perceived modernist disdain of affect and emotion. Although it now respects musical emotion, the philosophy of music remains perplexed, however, about how music can move anybody. Malcolm Budd's *Music and the Emotions* (1985) acknowledges the difficulty; surveying theories that dissociate musical aesthetics from emotion and those that link the two, Budd concludes that no available theory supports the relation *or* nonrelation of music to emotion.[4]

The philosophy of musical emotion tends to present ideas from other areas of philosophy, especially Susanne Langer's expressive aesthetics and Richard Wollheim's synthesis of psychological and concept-analytic methods.[5] Its patterns reflect what is at stake in those larger movements: the wish to retain programs of aesthetic value specific to subjectivity. Musical aesthetics openly declares why one would want an expressive hypothesis of emotion: to posit a subject of expression.

The debate between two prolific scholars in the field, Jerrold Levinson and Peter Kivy, gives an idea of the investments involved. Both

Levinson and Kivy hold that music is expressive and want to explain why. Levinson claims that "expressiveness in music, and perhaps in some other arts, is in essence *ready perceivability as personal expression*" (*Pleasures of Aesthetics,* 91);[6] Kivy, that music is expressive because it mimes conventional emotional mannerisms without referencing emotion.[7] Thus Stephen Davies, arguing from a position sympathetic to Kivy, terms Levinson's approach "hypothetical emotionalism" and Kivy's, "appearance emotionalism."[8]

Levinson contends that "music impresses us ultimately as if it were actually someone's expression of such-and-such emotion" (*Pleasures of Aesthetics,* 125). Even though we do not have to envision a particular person to feel the emotion, he believes, we cannot get the impression of expressiveness without imagining *some* expresser. Surveying rival approaches, he sets the following conditions for expressiveness:

1. Musical expressiveness should be seen as parallel or closely analogous to expression in its most literal sense, that is, the manifesting of psychological states through outward signs, most notably, behavior ("analogy" requirement).
2. Musical expressiveness should be seen to be related intelligibly to expressiveness in other arts. . . . ("extendibility" requirement).
3. Musical expressiveness should be seen to belong unequivocally to the music—to be a property or aspect thereof—and not to the listener or performer or composer ("externality" requirement).
4. Musical expressiveness should be something an attuned listener experiences or perceives immediately, rather than arrives at intellectually, through reasoning or weighing of evidence, at least in basic cases, i.e. ones of simple expression ("immediacy" requirement). (*Pleasures of Aesthetics,* 91–92)

Levinson also lays down a "generality" requirement of psychological familiarity, a "valuability" requirement that lends worth to musical pieces, and an "affectivity" requirement:

6. Musical expressiveness should be such that, when perceived or registered by a listener, evocation of feeling or affect, or the imagination of feeling, naturally, if not inevitably, ensues. (*Pleasures of Aesthetics,* 92)

Levinson draws up these conditions to confirm expression. Expressive unity among the arts, for example, is desirable because disunity inhibits the analogizing goals of expression itself (its insinuation of a

vast and profound unity). Expression must be structured like perception; expressiveness is "a property or aspect" in the external world,
"experience[d] or perceive[d] immediately." Intellection, introspec-
tion, and inference are disallowed, since they would hint that expressiveness may be projected, or as Levinson puts it, "ascribed": "the
state of mind associated with expressive music must be *heard in* it, not
just justifiably *ascribed to* it" (*Pleasures of Aesthetics*, 102, my italics). Maintaining the distinction between the "heard" and the "ascribed" leads to the demand that listeners *not* feel musical emotions
as their own. There is a contemporary theory, the "evocation" theory,
that argues that musical suggestions of emotion are the same emotions that listeners feel.[9] For Levinson, though, an account that fo-
cuses on listeners' emotions shows a "creeping narcissism" that trou-
bles him because it no longer makes strong statements about the
properties of the music, and thus unbalances the symmetry of insides
and outsides. To argue that it is implausible that listeners feel musical
emotions as their own, Levinson invokes the resemblance and distinction between expressed traits and expressed emotions:

> Music can express character or personality traits, such as nobility, sobri-
> ety, mischievousness, and aggressiveness, almost as easily as it can emo-
> tions, and in the same sense of "express." But it is doubtful one ever
> imagines that one's hearing of a passage of music constitutes an experi-
> ence of such a trait, for traits are not experienced: they are not states
> that one is in or that one feels. (*Pleasures of Aesthetics*, 95)

Traits and emotions are expressible "in the same sense of 'express.' "
But to Levinson this means automatically that emotions must be like
(and unlike) traits, not the other way around. It has to be this way:
otherwise, what we think are traits may be "states that one is in or
that one feels." Someone else's giantism, as Rousseau guesses, may be
a displaced image of one's fear. A further consequence of the possibility that traits may be experienced is that, if emotions and traits may be
expressed "in the same sense of 'express,' " then even expressiveness—the trait of having traits—may be a state that one is in or that
one feels. Levinson fends off this possibility by reifying expressiveness
through a proliferation of abstract nouns, as though it were in itself
recognizable. Why is it desirable to aver that "expressiveness," "perceivability," and "hearability-of-an-expressing-of emotion" are qualities of music? Because expression verifies subjectivity only by reflect-

ing objects. It's not enough that listeners find music expressive in that it causes them to feel emotions. Thus Levinson criticizes sensible Aaron Ridley for arguing that "expressive music expresses the particular affective condition of the listener": he sees this position as committing "the error of conflating what it is for a listener to experience music as expressive . . . with what it is for the music simply to be expressive" (*Pleasures of Aesthetics*, 97).[10] Rather, "part of the reason we have an emotional reaction to music is perception of a *corresponding* emotional quality in it" (*Music, Art, and Metaphysics*, 318; my italics). The purpose of expression—the whole outside-inside-outside game—is to posit insides, outsides, and a match between them confirmed by the alleged matchmaker, emotion. The attraction of objectivity is the flattering mirror it offers to subjectivity. The representation of music put forward here owes less to recent Anglo-American philosophy than it does to eighteenth-century and romantic ideologies of emotion.

Kivy criticizes Levinson from the perspective of a modernist, nonpathic formalism, maintaining that musical contours merely remind listeners of conventional emotional behaviors. "Works of music have expressive properties as part of their structure," but these properties do not "make up some emotive, semantic content." They wind up in the music as "the unintended result" of a composer's "other, intentional choices," namely formal choices.[11] They are not contents, but artifacts. Kivy holds—along the lines of Wimsatt and Beardsley's "Affective Fallacy" (1954)—that while people feel emotional over music, emotion neither produces musical value nor means that music itself expresses emotion: "in instrumental music, the pure musical parameters are always trump."[12] Kivy is interesting because, since he contends that music does not need emotional expressivity, but only universal nonemotive forms, he has an irritated sensitivity to other philosophers' unexamined fancy for emotive expression. Forgoing musical "aboutness" altogether, he can afford to point out that when Levinson has trouble establishing content for music he "gloms on to 'emotional content' and tries to make an argument for the view that music can be about the emotions it displays" ("Quest for Musical Profundity," 163). Kivy's complaint recalls the design of allegory: allegory—a text's appearing to be about its own undoing—emerges at the moment when a case for content collapses. Finding emotional content in music in the face of its general vacancy thus betrays a preexisting allegiance to the vehicle-content duality as such. As Kivy puts it, "the quest for sameness—the compulsion to see music as another example of literary or painterly values—drives the argument" ("Quest for Musical Profundity," 178).

De Man makes exactly this point: aesthetics assimilates music to emotion because there seems to be nothing else that music could communicate except " 'inward' patterns" of feeling. Reconceiving emotion as an object, eighteenth-century aesthetic theory contrives an analogy between music and painting:

> The power of the image reaches beyond duplication of sense data: the mimetic imagination is able to convey non-sensory, "inward" patterns of experience (feelings, emotions, passions) into objects of perception and can therefore represent as actual, concrete presences, experiences of consciousness devoid of objective existence. This possibility is often stressed as the main function of non-representational art forms such as music: they imitate by means of signs linked by natural right with the emotions which they signify. (BI 123–124)

Rather than admit the dearth of "actual, concrete presences" to which music can refer, de Man suggests, aestheticians fall back on supplementary "feelings, emotions, [and] passions," "experiences . . . devoid of objective existence" which music might express. Music can then be seen as outdoing representation rather than undermining the goals of representation. Like Husserlian expression, music would not "duplicat[e] . . . sense data" but "convey" "inward" phenomena outward.[13] "Linked by natural right with the emotions which they signify," musical structures can be regarded as uniquely direct forms, continuous extensions of what they represent.[14]

An alternative explanation of musical emotion is that it is because we don't know why these emotional-sounding signs are being made, or even what emotions they incite, that music is so intensely affecting. Schopenhauer writes that "music does not express this or that particular and definite pleasure, this or that affliction, pain, sorrow, horror, gaiety, merriment, or peace of mind. . . . *Hence* it arises that our imagination is so easily stirred by music, and tries to shape that invisible, yet vividly aroused, spirit-world that speaks to us directly, to clothe it with flesh and bone, and thus to embody it in an analogous example."[15] He finds uses for imagination that complement Rousseau's. While Rousseau's imagination interiorizes and idealizes particulars,

Schopenhauer's particularizes—shapes and embodies—idealities. Schopenhauer loves music because it grants rare access to generality; yet listeners react to this "spirit-world" by refacing it, clothing the abstract universal in "flesh and bone." Levinson's hypothetical expresser of emotions, too, is a figment of this desire literally to face the music. Aaron Ridley comes at the underdetermination of music from the opposite angle when he writes that musical emotion is "infinitely particular": "the melismatic gesture is unable to resemble behavior expressive of responses *to* persons, things, ideas or states of affairs. All that music can do is resemble, in an infinitely particular way, pieces of expressive behavior in isolation from the contexts in which what they express is fully distinctive—in which what they express is *this* passion rather than *that*" (*Music, Value, and the Passions,* 120). These comments suggest that whether music is seen as particular or abstract, what matters is that its gestures seem "infinitely" so, either way upsetting the balance required for expression. Musical power implies that for much the same reason that people are perturbed by the ability of dead subjects to feel, they are perturbed by music's ability to touch. An emotion that is not about something— and is not even "*this* passion rather than *that*"—seems as implausible as an emotion without a subject. Yet Ridley suggests that sounds that express no content are still "expressive of a passion" because "that passion does not need to be thought of as *someone's* passion" (*Music, Value, and the Passions* 73).

One might put this formulation together with Wollheim's usefully indeterminate location of psychic feelings:

> The claim that certain music is sad because of what the composer felt is sometimes equated—by its proponents as well as by its critics—with the claim that at the time the composer was suffering from a bout of gloom. Or, again, to say that a certain statue is terrifying because of the emotions it arouses in the spectators is sometimes interpreted as meaning that someone who looks at it will take fright. In other words, to establish that the composer was not on the verge of tears or that the average spectator exhibits no desire to run away, is thought to be enough to refute this whole conception of expression. But there are feelings that a man has of which he is not conscious, and there are ways of being in touch with those which he has other than experiencing them in a primary sense; and a more realistic statement . . . should not require more than that the state expressed by the work of art is among those states, conscious or unconscious, to which the artist and the spectator stand in some possessive relation. (*Art and Its Objects,* 29)

Wollheim notes that one can be "in touch" with feelings without "experiencing them in a primary sense"—feeling is not definitionally primary. To say this, as he observes, is to "enlarge the conception of human feelings" (30). It is in fact to enlarge it so much, and so effectively, that one wonders why Wollheim stops where he does, so that our relation to nonprimary feelings is still "some possessive relation." Willing not to know where these feelings are—and by this, implying that location questions are the wrong questions to ask about feelings—Wollheim nonetheless knows that wherever they are, we possess them. As the trajectory of Wollheim's thought hints, the puzzle of musical emotion is normative; puzzlement about emotion's sources defines emotional experience. "All passion is to some degree *passion inutile*," de Man remarks, "made gratuitous by the non-existence of an object or a cause" (BI 134). The dilemma of musical emotion reflects the dilemma of emotion as such: if emotion presumes a "dead" subject, music figures its surprising ability to speak.

Emotional Reference

Like musical aesthetics, other branches of philosophy grapple with the mystery of emotive cause. Ronald de Sousa's *Rationality of Emotion* is a perceptive exploration of those struggles, and one of the most poised treatments of emotion in recent philosophy. De Sousa considers the antinomies of emotion, as he calls them,[16] that question human subjectivity, and responds with a causal account of emotional motivation and justification. Although de Sousa discusses the extensive internal differentiality of emotional experience in ways consistent with poststructuralist theory, he calls on subjectivity to explain the capacity for singular reference—the discrimination of a unique object—that he sees as indispensable to emotion. Complementarily, however, it can seem as though de Sousa brings his system to bear on singular reference in order to be able to have something by which to define subjectivity.

Throughout his book, de Sousa emphasizes supplementarity. His "leading idea," in his own words, "is that in organisms sufficiently complex to exhibit intentionality, pure reason—cognitive or strategic—will need supplementation" (RE 172). Reason needs help controlling the economic intricacy of information retrieval; it can get "lost in computation, long past the time for action" (RE 193). "The insufficiency of strategic reason" (RE 194) shows in our inability quickly to decide rationally "how to make use of just what we need" of all our store of information "and how not to retrieve what we don't need" (RE 193):

> Emotions spare us the paralysis potentially induced by this predicament by controlling the salience of features of perception and reasoning. . . .

> For a variable but always limited time, an emotion limits the range of information that the organism will take into account, the inferences actually drawn from a potential infinity. (RE 172, 195)

The problem is that "we need to know whether a consequence will turn out to be relevant *before drawing it*" (RE 194). Emotions, as I mentioned earlier, are those gun-jumping responses that act on conclusions before they are drawn. In situations like the "giant" scene from Rousseau's *Essay*, emotions shape information by "imitating the encapsulation of perceptual modes" (RE 195). The sheer existence of emotion assumes a minimal deficiency in reason, a deficiency that the ideology of emotion displaces onto emotion itself. De Sousa notes that emotions guide attention at the cost of simplifying and to that extent falsifying information; the thought of this cost prompts anxiety that emotion may impede the intellect by, in Kant's words, "mak[ing] it difficult or impossible for us to determine our power of choice through principles" (*Critique of Judgment*, 132n39). Where emotion seems to curtail reasoning, it can look debilitating. All the same, emotions in de Sousa's narrative logically (only logically) *follow* rational judgments and, far from getting in reason's way, occur when its inadequacy is already clear: "we need emotion . . . to break a tie when reason is stuck" (RE 16). This circumstance does not confine emotions to emergencies—there are peaceful and routine emotions, and emotions that have no names.[17] Rather, it implies that rationality is insufficient for *any* situation. Unless, as de Sousa puts it, you are either an "angel" or an "ant," "some kind of Kantian monster . . . or else a Cartesian animal-machine" (RE 190).

To invoke supplementarity is automatically to engage cause-and-effect issues, and these, in turn, cue anxieties about intentionality. The sequence reason-emotion suggests the sequence emotion-reason: emotion is both rhetorical and a reaction to rhetoric. On the one hand, de Sousa writes, sophists get people to notice selected things by playing on their emotions; on the other, Iago gets Othello to feel jealous by steering his attention: "the order of causal accessibility of emotion and attention is not fixed" (RE 196). The difficulty of ordering emotional cause and effect creates concern since as long as cause and effect cannot be told apart, emotions might not be rational ends, but merely be rationalized after the fact.

De Sousa's reference points for the problem of cause are Plato's *Euthyphro,* which inquires "whether the gods love piety because it is pious, or whether they merely call pious whatever they love" (RE 9), and the story of Alcmene, "faithful wife of Amphitryon, whom Zeus was able to seduce only by taking the form of her husband":

> The man she loved that night was, by hypothesis, qualitatively the same as her husband, though not the same numerically. But wasn't it for his qualities that she loved her husband? I don't mean to imply that his qualities must have been lovable ones. What she loved about him might have been quite unworthy. Nevertheless, there must have been something that she loved about him, and whatever it was, Zeus had that. . . . if her love is rational only if it relates to Amphitryon's qualities, then love must be either irrational or fickle. (RE 8–9)

As Rousseau suspects, the very idealization that makes emotion "cognitive" generates "promiscuity." De Sousa poses the problem this way: "Either endorse high-minded promiscuity, loving whomever you have reason to love, or admit that your love is literally groundless" (RE 112).

Building on naturalistic treatments of cause from Hume to Davidson, de Sousa solves the problem by separating, then articulating cause and justification. Gradually, de Sousa's text layers a rational scheme onto an empirical one. This solution interests me because it necessitates—and calls into question—the subjectivity, not the rationality, of emotion, and pits rationality and subjectivity against one another. I would like to go slowly, therefore, through de Sousa's solution. It moves through the following stages: first, de Sousa distinguishes several kinds of emotional objects. Emotions refer to "targets," usually empirical things; targets cause emotions. Targets possess "focal properties"—"motivating aspects" to which emotions respond—and "formal objects," "second-order qualit[ies] that must be implicitly ascribed to the motivating aspect if the emotion is to be intelligible" (RE 336).[18] A target is to a focal property is to a formal object as cause is to motivation is to justification. When "something is frightening by virtue of being dangerous," for example, the formal object, the dangerousness, makes the fear intelligible (RE 122). "The formal object's very definition" in turn is anchored in "paradigm scenarios"—early childhood events that condition people to normative responses, "where normality is first a biological matter and then very quickly becomes a cultural one" (RE 182). While Aristotle roots the social normativity of preferred scenarios in human nature—his paradigms are paradigmatic because they're naturally normal—de Sousa gives sociality the power to assemble norms out of the genetic materials available, while making room for "individual normality" as well.[19]

The solution compresses the terms of the problem, internally repeating circles of cause and effect. As de Sousa knows, the distinction between focal property and formal object is tenuous. The formal object is a property of the focal property, suggesting a "threatening regress" (RE 131). If I flee from a stranger because he scares me, and he scares me because I think he's dangerous, how do I know he's dangerous? (Because he's a giant?) "Dangerous" can be just a way of saying "frightening" that asserts the justification of the fear; "dangerous" can be the literalization of the metaphor "frightening." Second, formal objects and paradigm scenarios, the elements of the plan that justify emotion rationally, reinforce its potential tropism, or lack of intentionality. De Sousa notes that the idea that in circumstances of type A, I feel an emotion in range A–B is consistent with a merely intermediate grade of intentionality where we don't yet have singular reference, but rather just "clusters of properties" (RE 78). The problem with "intermediate" intentionality, for de Sousa, is that it doesn't require a human subject.[20]

I would suggest that this is yet another antinomy of emotion, or perhaps a version of the antinomy of determinism: the inverse ratio of rationality to subjectivity. As one might expect, the target, the usually empirical thing that may quite contingently cause an emotion, needs to be connected to an idealization—normative dangerousness or pleasantness—in order for true emotion to occur. At the same time, the idealizable, repeatable qualities that justify the emotion rationally imply that the emotion is iterable *wherever* they are found, and so model emotion as the outcome of a set of organic circumstances rather than as the act of an intending subject.

Therefore, de Sousa stipulates that "what makes emotions fully mental and specifically human relates to their capacity for certain sorts of *intentionality* and in particular, at the highest level, for *singu-*

lar reference" (RE 80). Singular reference is the last stop for an intentionality that has developed grades and become difficult to situate in subjectivity. According to de Sousa, its target makes emotion "uniquely human" (RE 78). While the qualities explain the target, the target bounds the qualities and therefore frames an object fit for a subject.

De Sousa aptly illustrates this claim with the beautiful, *Amphitryon*-like plot of Stanislaw Lem's novel *Solaris* (1961).[21] In the novel, researchers travel to a planet on which they find sentient replicas of their dead relatives and lovers, discoveries that torture them with guilt and longing. Kris, the narrator, wrangles with the double of Rheya, a girlfriend whose suicide he may have provoked. De Sousa asserts that

> he is so horrified by the appearance of the döppelganger that—until he forms a *new* relationship with her—he tries to get rid of her by any means possible. Why? Why not instead welcome someone exactly like your long-lost lover or friend? The reason must be that Kris cares about the particular identity of that singular person, Rheya, more than he cares about her properties. The reason, in short, stems from Kris's capacity for singular reference, or nonfungible identification. (RE 100)

$Rheya_1$ is full at the level of quality but empty as a target; indistinguishable from Rheya, she may not exist at all. There is no explanation of what she is.

Can you love someone you know may not exist? De Man's answer, as we've seen, is that you cannot love someone whom you know exists absolutely. The object of love is necessarily a phenomenal object. The lover must believe it is possible that the object exists as she sees it but not know it does. Thus literature often portrays the love object as absent (like Isolde) or illusory (like Dulcinea, another of de Sousa's examples). De Sousa's answer, based on the organization of the object into target and focal properties, is that only Amphitryon, and not Zeus, is the historical cause of Alcmene's love and that the original Rheya is the cause of Kris's love. Not only the validity of Kris's feelings but his status as a human subject depends on this. The difference between Kris and a dog attached to its human friend, de Sousa asserts, is that Kris "can intend a logical distinction even between qualitatively indiscriminable individuals" (RE 100). A dog is a suitably tough competitor, because even if it doesn't possess the power of singular reference, it may be "attached to a particular as opposed to a mere bundle of qualities" (RE 98; this seems to be Hume's dog). The bundles may be maximally particular—the dog might require $Rheya_1$ to have the same DNA as Rheya, for example. To exhibit higher intentionality than the dog, Kris would have to resist seeing $Rheya_1$ as the cause of his love even if she did have the same DNA. It is hard to know who would be behaving in a more "human" fashion in this situation, Kris or the dog. Is it desirable, even if love is specific, to hinge its specificity on the capacity to intend logical distinctions between things that are experientially exactly alike?

Solaris can be read as a tale of nonsubjective love by taking $Rheya_1$ as a pattern for Rheya. Kris's colleague Snow, who invents a technology to "kill" the replicants, eventually kills $Rheya_1$, who wants to die. Her awareness of her own ontological enigma crops up in her suicide note: "She had crossed [it] out, but I could see that she had signed 'Rheya' " (Lem, *Solaris*, 198). Despite the apparent irreversibility of his second solitude, Kris continues to love "Rheya" without knowing what that means:

> I was waiting for something. Her return? How could I have been waiting for that? We all know that we are material creatures, subject to the laws of physiology and physics, and not even the power of all our feelings combined can defeat those laws. All we can do is detest them. The age-old faith of lovers and poets in the power of love, stronger than death, that *finis vitae sed non amoris*, is a lie, useless and not even funny. . . . I hoped for nothing. And yet I lived in expectation. Since she was gone, that was all that remained. I did not know what achievements, what mockery, even what tortures still awaited me. I knew nothing, and I persisted in the faith that the time of cruel miracles was not past. (Lem, *Solaris*, 211)

$Rheya_1$ is explicitly not a human subject, and it is impossible to say positively what she is. Lem implies that love projects itself across this barrier. Out of her very iterability, she achieves the value but not the status of the nonfungible object: because she can recognize that she is not a human subject, she is already as valuable as she would be if she were a human subject. De Sousa remarks that Kris "forms a *new* relationship" nonfungibly for $Rheya_1$, but I wonder about this: by the end of the novel, Kris seems to love a specific but not singular bundle of qualities—neither Rheya nor $Rheya_1$ but ~~Rheya~~.

De Sousa's array of targets, formal objects, and paradigm scenarios closes ranks around subjectivity. One of Western society's norms is that love is nonfungible; the suppositions that any justification of a formal object must be intentional and that the highest grade of intentionality depends on singular reference dovetail with that social regard for singular objects:

> The case of Alcmene poses the question, If it was Zeus in her bed in the guise of Amphitryon, why should she mind? In summary, the discussion of fungibility has led us to a partial answer in terms of logical form: she should mind, because not to would be a category mistake. But underlying this grammatical consideration are some natural metaphysical and psychological ones. The metaphysical answer . . . [is that] our attachments are to particulars, and if there are no particulars, or if we have the wrong one, then something has gone wrong with the ontological correlate of our emotion. The psychological answer, in brief, is that we are so wired as to acquire attachments in the course of our causal interaction with such individuals as are posited in our metaphysics. The fabric of our social and emotional life depends on our ability to transcend the original fungibility of all reactivity and transform it into nonfungible emotions. (RE 134)

Natural and social normality coincide, as in Aristotle. Logic dictates that we use our talent for singular reference; luckily, we are wired to do so, and (as a result?) the social fabric depends on it. To be intentionally subjective, emotions demand singular targets; the fact that we do conceive such targets is imputed to our being subjects, that is, our having "transcend[ed]" "the original fungibility of all reactivity."

Human subjectivity and singular reference thus seem to form de Sousa's answer to his own reformulation of rationality. That reformulation goes a long way. For de Sousa, emotion is not always rational only because *rationality* is not always rational. Seeing emotion as "cognitive" means that, in various ways, "the cognitive may turn out to be more like the emotional than we had assumed emotion could be like cognition" (RE 69). Accordingly, de Sousa affirms that life is an assortment of parallel processes. Much of life's activity, he writes, "is organized by the structure of our appetites, emotions, and short- or long-term goals. But it may not be organized in any unique *hierarchy*, with a single controlling system at the center of it all. Instead, each of us may comprise a radical *heterarchy*, in which many partial systems work in parallel, of which any one can take over control according to need. . . . In a heterarchic system there is no master program" (RE 74). Emotion evidences this absence of a "master program." But because it does so, it is just the thing to obscure the absence as well; because emotion supplements the absence, it becomes easy to say that subjectivity is not absent, since emotion, its content, is there. De Sousa performs this substitution in his reflection on one of those instances where "reason is stuck":

> The best candidate for the agency that plugs one argument over another into the motor system is emotion. The reason is this. It cannot be merely a physiological factor that is in itself arational, that is, beyond the reach of assessment for evaluative rationality. Otherwise . . . it becomes unclear whether the action is an intentional act of the subject's at all. On the other hand, the causal factor in question can be neither a desire nor a belief. The reason for this was expressed with characteristic pith (and uncharacteristic wit) by Aristotle himself: "When water chokes, what will you wash it down with?"[22] By hypothesis all the reasons, both cognitive and desiderative, are already in. So whatever tips the balance cannot be another reason. It must be something that, in some sense, acts on reasons. . . . Only emotions are left. (RE 200)

In order for the action to be "an intentional act of the subject's," it cannot be a twitch of "the motor system" nor the gesture of one of the rational processes just exhausted. Thus "only emotions are left" to fill the place of the "agency." Despite the agency's *being* the emotion at the beginning of the passage, three sentences later the act produced by emotion belongs to a subject. There seems to be a subject here because we define acts as determinations of subjects in the first place. According to Aristotle's proverb, it's hard to know what to do when reason (water) has not sufficed to wash a decision down; in de Sousa's reading, emotion can persuade where reason has failed and washes reason down when it becomes hard to swallow. Subjectivity does not seem to be doing anything here that emotion in a heterarchy cannot do by itself.

Why You Can't Make a Subject That Feels Pain

What is there to do the feeling if there are no subjects? While de Sousa is willing to state that persons are "heterarchic system[s]" (RE 74, 200) and that not all intentionality is subjective, Daniel Dennett goes further, arguing that nonsubjective interpretation alone explains experience. Dennett does not write directly about emotion; like Derrida, he addresses issues that underlie theories of emotion, most crucially the conditions for experience as such. In Dennett's "heterophe-nomenology," all phenomena of experience "can be observed, directly or indirectly, by anyone who wants to observe them and has the right equipment."[23] Heterophenomenology demonstrates why it doesn't matter that subjects don't exist. Phenomena and registration in sufficient density take care of the tasks of subjectivity. My own point is a little different: it matters to emotion, but inversely.

Dennett draws closest to emotion in his analyses of the philosophical debate about "qualia." "Qualia" is the term of art for "something that could not be more familiar to each of us: the *ways things seem to us*":

> Look at a glass of milk at sunset; *the way it looks to you*—the particular, personal, subjective visual quality of the glass of milk is the *quale* of your visual experience at the moment. The *way the milk tastes to you then* is another, gustatory *quale,* and *how it sounds to you* as you swallow is an auditory *quale*. These various "properties of conscious experience" are prime examples of *qualia*. Nothing, it seems, could you know more intimately than your own qualia; let the entire universe be some vast illusion, some mere figment of Descartes's evil demon, and yet what the figment is *made of* (for you) will be the *qualia* of your hallucinatory experiences.[24]

Qualia have a lot in common with expressivity, especially with expresseds figured by abstract nouns. Recall that for Dufrenne, for example, expressivity is the "primordial reality of affective quality," appearing in the "tenderness" that is "a quality of Mozart and of a Mozartian melody" (*Phenomenology of Aesthetic Experience,* 455). Similarly, in Levinson's consideration of qualities heard in music, expressiveness is "a property or aspect" in music (*Pleasures of Aesthetics,* 102). As Dennett points out, "the ancient philosophical conundrum" of qualia has been phrased in much the same way since the seventeenth century, for instance in Locke's definition of secondary qualities as "*powers of things* in the world . . . to produce or provoke certain things in the minds of normal observers" (*Consciousness Explained,* 371). Qualia are whatever exceeds the sum of the parts. A computer might understand every harmonic relationship in *The Magic Flute,* so the story goes, but can never understand the work's sweetness.

Dennett attacks the distinction between the quantity and quality of properties, whether or not those properties are in the mind—as in theories that find uniqueness in one's mental experience—or in things. There is an ideology of qualia: by preferring quality to quantity, experience to information, one falsely projects the *non*qualitative nature of quantity and information. Dennett, in contrast, maintains that observation of quantity produces the qualitative effect. It is the nature of "highly informative way[s] of thinking" to seem ineffable, "but what is inscrutable in a single glance, and somewhat ambiguous after limited testing, can come to be justifiably seen as the deliverance of a highly specific, reliable, and projectible property detector" ("Quining Qualia," 70). Dennett illustrates this point in *Consciousness Explained* through philosopher Frank Jackson's "much-discussed case of Mary, the color scientist who has never seen colors." According to Jackson, if Mary "acquires . . . all the physical information there is to obtain about what goes on when we see ripe tomatoes," then only later sees color for the first time, "it is inescapable that her previous knowledge was incomplete."[25] Dennett points out that "in any realistic, readily imaginable version" of the story, Mary "might know a lot, but she would not know everything physical"; it isn't fair to substitute this "readily imaginable" version of events for the one Jackson pretends to consider, that Mary literally has "all the physical information" there is (*Consciousness Explained*, 400). For Dennett, if Mary can really read her brain responses without vision, "she can leverage her way to complete advance knowledge, because she doesn't just know the *salient* reactions, she knows them all" (*Consciousness Explained*, 401).

Dennett reaches a similar conclusion regarding the loaded issue of pain in his great negative empirical article, "Why You Can't Make a Computer That Feels Pain."[26] Noting that "it has seemed important to many people to claim that computers cannot *in principle* duplicate various human feats, activities, happenings" (*Brainstorms*, 190), Dennett sets out to define pain, and then to imagine "writing a pain program" (*Brainstorms*, 191). Detailed inquiries into the gray areas of anesthesia, pain thresholds, and the complex location of pain in bodies show that "a great deal of the counterintuitiveness of the notion of robot pain no doubt derives from a dim appreciation of this side of our notion of pain" (*Brainstorms*, 197). "Well-entrenched intuitions" about the immediacy and awfulness of pain prove to be incompatible (*Brainstorms*, 226). In the end, Dennett argues, there is no standing theory of pain, which is why you can't make a robot to instantiate it:

The inability of a robot model to satisfy all our intuitive demands may be due not to any irredeemable mysteriousness about the phenomenon of pain, but to irredeemable incoherency in our ordinary concept of pain. . . . If and when a good physiological sub-personal theory of pain is developed, a robot could in principle be constructed to instantiate it. Such advances in science would probably bring in their train wide-scale changes in what we found intuitive about pain, so that the charge that our robot only suffered what we artificially *called* pain would lose its persuasiveness. In the meantime (if there were a cultural lag) thoughtful people would refrain from kicking such a robot. (*Brainstorms*, 228–229)

Since Dennett published this essay in 1978, people have constructed robots that breathe, cough, and contract pneumatic "muscles"; their sensitivity to their own malfunctions (measured against their own standard of efficiency), coupled with the stipulation that malfunction is a bad thing, should constitute discomfort. "Emotions are often said to be the last and impassable frontier of computationalist theories of mind," as de Sousa points out (RE 70); but models for computer emotion, too, have arrived.[27]

Heterophenomenology is nothing other than a very strong content approach to qualitative experience. As such, it challenges content approaches to emotion that also demand a subject to oversee the contents. It looks different from these approaches for the very reason that Dennett follows through, collapsing experience into information, feeling into thinking: "content" is the wrong metaphor because nothing is necessary besides content. The subject is revealed to be the personified correlative of qualia—a supplement to information. Dennett's nonsubjective account of interpretation "challenges a deeply held intuition: our sense that for *real* understanding to occur, there has to be *someone in there* to validate the proceedings, to *witness* the events whose happening constitutes the understanding." Dennett calls this "someone" the "central Witness"; characteristically, the central Witness is kept busy apprehending presentations and experiencing qualia. Qualia, Dennett makes clear, have served as "props" in the history of what he calls "the witness protection system": "These raw materials, whether they are called 'sense data' or 'sensations' or 'raw feels' or 'phenomenal properties of experience,' are props without which a Witness makes no sense. These props, held in place by various illusions, surround the idea of a central Witness with a nearly impenetrable barrier of intuitions" (*Consciousness Explained*, 322).

Qualitative states become hostages of the human subject: we hold on to the subject for the sake of qualitative states. Dennett remembers the philosopher Wilfrid Sellars protesting: "But Dan, qualia are what make life worth living!" (*Consciousness Explained*, 383). In Dennett's materialist philosophy, though, qualitative states live on. "The sort of difference that people imagine there to be between any machine and any human experiencer" does not exist; "there is no such sort of difference. There just seems to be" (*Consciousness Explained*, 375).[28] What remains consistent between the machine experiencer and the human experiencer is—of course—experience, the recursive registration of information. Dennett's heterophenomenology is interpretive in a manner consistent with his contention elsewhere that, to put it very broadly, patterns become describable from a stance.[29] An interpretive stance is the minimum stance—the stance of there being a stance. This is all that is required for qualitative experience to emerge. Conversely, of course, experience cannot emerge without a stance. This does not mean that states of affairs outside interpretation do not exist, even within ourselves. It does mean that these states of affairs cannot be experienced, hence cannot be emotional. To show how emotion fades with interpretation, I turn now to Deleuze's theory of affect.

From Affection to Affect

The idea that poststructuralist theory deals with impersonal affects as opposed to personal emotions, since that's what must happen if one doesn't believe in subjects, seems to have been derived from Deleuze's example. Perceptions of poststructuralism's minimization of emotion fit Deleuze better than Derrida or de Man. Like Spinoza, his main precursor in affect theory, Deleuze is mainly interested in what would in conventional terms be *nonaffective* affect. Neither "affect" nor "affection" "denotes a personal feeling (*sentiment* in Deleuze and Guattari)," Brian Massumi comments in his notes to his translation of *A Thousand Plateaus*.[30] In his solo texts and collaborations with Guattari, Deleuze redefines affection as an experience of a set of affairs and affect as a dynamic principle that passes through but also beyond personal feelings and indeed experience of any sort. Since Deleuze's projects mobilize his concept of affect against that of the subject, and by showing affect's extension beyond any experience

Deleuze necessarily demonstrates the limits of emotion as well, Deleuze's work can easily leave the impression that disclaiming subjectivity requires disclaiming any personal feeling. Always touching on the categories of feeling, but never resting content with them, Deleuze executes a turn from emotion to affect that has come to be thought poststructuralist. We can think creatively about Deleuze's predilection for affect, however, only after realizing that there are other poststructuralist approaches to emotion.

The polemical effect of Deleuze's theory of affect is to divide poststructuralisms according to positions on emotive experience. There has been less comparative discussion of Deleuze's relation to poststructuralism than one might expect, much of the commentary on Deleuze being celebratory in the mode of Deleuze and Guattari's *A Thousand Plateaus*. Michael Hardt, however, opens the question in this way:

> When we broaden our perspective beyond the specific questions of Spinoza interpretation, we can see that Deleuze's objectivist reading marks him as radically out of sync with the intellectual movements of his time, as sustaining a precariously minoritarian theoretical position. . . . The various *mots d'ordre* that sprang up from different camps throughout the French intellectual scene in this period all insist on the foundational role of the intellect, of the *ratio cognoscendi;* consider, for example, the importance of the widespread discourse on "vision," on the seen and the non-seen, or rather the focus on "interpretation" as a privileged field of investigation. Deleuze's proposition of an objectivist ontological speculation in Spinoza runs counter to this entire stream of thought. The general trend, in fact, seems to constitute a forceful attack on Deleuze's position.[31]

Unlike deconstructive criticisms of subjectivity, Deleuze's is braided with his dissatisfaction regarding interpretive thinking, as Hardt observes. Now, accentuating interpretation's restrictiveness necessarily has a consequence for emotion, because it means accentuating the restrictiveness of experience itself. Complementarily, deconstruction is textualist to the same degree that it is invested in experience, or phenomenality. The texts of Derrida and de Man show how emotion presumes the death of the subject; Deleuze does not rule out this conclusion, but, continually contextualizing the phenomenal within the ontological, does not highlight it either.

A significant element of Deleuze's objectivism is his taste for the idea of expression. In Spinoza's *Ethics,* Deleuze explains, expression connects the ontological and the phenomenal, or in seventeenth-century terms, essence, substance, and attributes: "The idea of expression . . . combines these three moments and gives them a systematic form."[32] In *The Logic of Sense* [1969] Deleuze adapts expression from Leibniz's monadology.[33] Expression takes many modern inflections, its lineage running to unexpected corners—to the linguistic theory of Louis Hjelmslev, for example ("the Danish Spinozist geologist," as Deleuze and Guattari call him) (TP 43).[34] Expression animates Deleuze and Guattari's thought in *A Thousand Plateaus* and *What Is Philosophy?* "Over the last few years, the names Gilles Deleuze and Félix Guattari have crescendoed in the classrooms and conference halls," writes Massumi; "but has it sunk in that Deleuze has always unabashedly characterized his thought as a philosophy of expression?"[35] Following this controversy, Alain Badiou isolates Deleuze from other 1960s theorists. Through his reading of Deleuzian expression, Badiou suggests that Deleuze is of the angels' party without knowing it, a philosopher of being and not, as Deleuze describes himself, of becoming.[36]

Whether or not one wants to go that far, Deleuze's penchant for expression is and ought to be contentious for anyone interested in emotion, for debates about expression always involve emotion. Probably Massumi calls Deleuze "unabashed" because he believes contemporary theory is hostile to objectivism (one might be abashed to be called objectivist). Although Deleuze's expression is objectivist, however, it transposes subjectivist formulations of the expressive hypothesis from the discourse of emotion. In Chapter 1, I referred to John McDowell's proposal that theories of representational content still evoke content as intuition; here a corresponding observation can be made, that objectivist theories of expression like Deleuze's have a common ancestor with the folkloric thesis that expression entails interiority and subjectivity, while emotion is *what* a subject expresses. Although Deleuze's theory of affect does not take up this thesis, it does invoke its underlying appeal to universality. Here, again, is the philosophical context in which we should place Deleuze's theory: Derrida and de Man reply to the expressive hypothesis of emotion by sifting emotion from expression, while classical philosophers maintain the expressive hypothesis because they sense that there is no reason to retain subjectivity if emotion—even emotion—persists without it. Thus the philosophy of music labors to hold musical emotion within an expressive subject even though musical emotion, according to its own descriptions, often seems neither to be expressed by someone nor to express something in particular. Deleuze does something different from either deconstruction or classical philosophy: he retains expression while dropping subjectivity. The high place he gives to nonpersonal affect is the result not simply of his nonsubjectivism, as one might think, but of his unique combination of nonsubjectivism with expressivism. In a sense, Deleuze thematizes the subjectless expression that the philosophy of music describes. His writings both beguile with musical associations (references to sounds and music suffuse his texts) and outstrip the metaphysical longings of musical aesthetics.[37] Expression without subjects is easier to sustain than the subjective expression without subjects that the philosophy of music tries to sustain. Rather than containing the oddity of musical expression, as philosophers of music do by driving it into a too narrow subjective model, Deleuze embraces it and does what it asks: he redefines affect as a structure that holds up without subjective aid.

To the same degree that Deleuze is not simply a nonsubjective philosopher, but a philosopher of expression, he is also a philosopher of affect opposed to emotion. Insofar as his philosophy surpasses interpretive thought, it surpasses emotion as well. This may be surprising if one views the interpretive contingency of emotion as incidental. But Deleuze demonstrates by counterexample that emotion is thoroughly signifying and interpretive. By criticizing the signification and interpretation (*signifiance* and *interprétance*) that organize the discourse of emotion, he reveals *that it is there,* despite the ideology of emotion's tendency to efface it in favor of expression.

The interdependence of interpretation and emotion makes semiotics an emotive field. Deleuze's investments regarding affect thus inform his early readings of Spinoza's theory of signs, *Expressionism in Philosophy: Spinoza* [1968] and *Spinoza: Practical Philosophy* [1970]. His theory of affect originates in competition with other thought about interpretation, especially Derrida's deconstruction of Husserl in *Speech and Phenomena. Expressionism in Philosophy* stands in Deleuze's career where Derrida's introduction to Husserl's *Origin of Geometry* does in his, constituting the historical half of Deleuze's doctoral work. Through Spinoza Deleuze, too, confronts Husserlian dilemmas of representation. He goes out of his way to elaborate a Spinozan theory of signs from a small number of passages, notably *The Ethics* II, P16–18 and P40–41. Again, "affection" and "affect" no longer bear the meanings with which we have grown familiar, but rather more archaic ones: an affection is an idea construed as an organic impression, and an affect is a transitive link between states of affairs. "Affection" in Deleuze's Spinoza takes over the role of merely empirical affect in Husserl; the opposition between affect and emotion in *Speech and Phenomena* moves backward into an opposition between affection and affect. But the grounds of the hierarchy remain: variable sense needs to be channeled into something universal. In Derrida's texts, Husserl's pursuit of transparency seems not only impossible, but strange. In Deleuze's Spinoza texts, it is pursuing transparency through subjectivity that seems strange, not the value placed on transparency. The question is how transparency can be conceived *most* transparently.

Deleuze's explication makes it clear that while Spinoza finds signification and interpretation problematic, he believes that their defects grow from experience itself. In *The Ethics* Spinoza hierarchizes knowledge from confused sensory experience; "from signs" or from hearsay; from "common notions" of reason and "adequate ideas," or ideas wholly explicable by autonomous logical principles; and "intuitive knowledge."[38] According to Deleuze, Spinoza holds the lowest order of knowledge to be the *"state of nature"* in which "I perceive objects through chance encounters, and by the effect they have on me" (EPS 289). Spinoza, Deleuze explains, thinks that "as conscious beings, we never apprehend anything but the *effects*" of relations between bodies.[39] Our ability to experience only effects, not causes, "condemn[s] us *to have only inadequate ideas*" (S 19). Defensively, we tend to introject causes: in Spinoza's illustration—one that agrees with Wordsworth's and de Man's notion that milk is the supreme internalizable substance—"the infant believes he freely wants the milk" (Spinoza, *Ethics*, 157, quoted in S 20). Experience itself dooms the infant to inadequacy, since it is casual, self-regarding, and chancy (S 75). Signs merely extend this inadequacy. They belong to knowledge of the lowest order, to which "pertain all those ideas which are inadequate and confused" (*Ethics*, 141). The imperative signs of the civil or religious state claim only "knowledge by *hearsay*" (EPS 289), and indeed no system of signs through which I communicate my clueless, idiosyncratic sensory experience expresses adequate ideas by virtue of its organization as a sign system per se. One needs "common notions" of reason—universalizable qualities and principles—to "enter . . . into the domain of *expression*," since "any common notion leads us to the idea of the God whose essence it expresses" (EPS 290–291).[40]

In Spinoza, the paired terms "image-affection" *(affectio)* and "feeling-affect" *(affectus)* transfer into feeling the low worth of sensory experience and language, on the one hand, and the high worth of intuition and logic, on the other. According to Deleuze, Spinoza's "image-affections" are "images or corporeal traces first of all" (S 48), like impressions.[41] Feeling-affects, the responses of affected bodies, are transitive links between the states of affairs formed by affections; they occupy the interval between affection and action. While feeling-affects are still passive, they have effects, and differ according to their ability to diminish or enlarge power, or pave the way to activity, and are accordingly "sad" or "joyful." Since affections are encounters with other bodies and the ideas they give us—"images or corporeal traces"—they *are* indicative signs, or writing: "When a fluid part of the human body is determined by an external body so that it frequently thrusts against a soft part [of the body], it changes its surface and, as it were, impresses on [the soft part] certain traces of the external body striking against [the fluid part]" (*Ethics,* 128). Literally impressions in the body, affections imply that encounters with other bodies, and, moreover, between parts of one's own body, are in themselves semiotic. They infect all of experience with interpretation, and thus are portrayed as corrupting; they are also in danger of infecting signification with corporeal opacity.

It is Deleuze who arranges Spinoza's thought about signs into a fundamental opposition between indication and expression with their modern connotations. Glossing *The Ethics* II, P16–17, Deleuze writes, "Images are the corporeal affections themselves [*affectio*], the traces of an external body on our body. Our ideas are therefore ideas of images or affections that represent a state of things, that is, by which we affirm the presence of the external body so long as our body remains affected in this way. . . . Such ideas are *signs;* they are not *explained* by our essence or power . . . but *indicate* the presence of this body and its effect on us" (S 73–74). At issue is the contingency of indication and its potential interference with knowledge:

In one sense, a sign is always the idea of an effect apprehended under conditions that separate it from its causes. Thus the effect of a body on ours is . . . apprehended . . . in terms of a momentary state of our variable constitution and a simple presence of the thing whose nature we do not know. . . . Such signs are *indicative*: they are *effects of mixture*. They indicate the state of our body primarily, and the presence of the external body secondarily. These indications form the basis of an entire order of conventional signs (language), which is already characterized by its equivocity, that is, by the variability of the associative chains into which the indications enter. (S 105–106)

Such knowledge is not knowledge at all, it is at best recognition. And from this there follow the characteristics of indication in general: the primary "thing indicated" is never our essence, but always a momentary state of our changing constitution; the secondary (or indirect) thing indicated is never the nature or essence of some external thing, but is rather an appearance that only allows us to recognize a thing by its effect, to rightly or wrongly assert its mere presence. The fruits of chance and of encounters, serving for recognition, purely indicative, the ideas we have are inexpressive, that is to say, inadequate. (EPS 147–148)

Affection in Spinoza elicits from Deleuze the full range of shady associations usually whispered of the indicative sign. Indication is mutable, unreliable, and inarticulate. The idea an affection gives of external bodies "indicate[s] the condition of our own body more than the nature of the external bodies" (*Ethics*, 129). Affections stretch memory, with all the risks that entails: "although the external bodies by which the human body has once been affected neither exist nor are present, the mind will still be able to regard them as if they were present"; this can happen because, contemplating the affection, we continue to infer the existence of the body that caused it, even as we fail to understand the "nature or essence" of that body. Worse, affections whet the imagination: "we see, therefore, how it can happen (as it often does) that we regard as present things which do not exist. . . . The affections of the human body whose ideas present external bodies as present to us, we shall call images of things. . . . And when the mind regards bodies in this way, we shall say that it imagines" (*Ethics*, 129–130). Like interior address in Husserl, affections are faintly onanistic: they lead down a supplementary slope to an imagination that may not realize it is imagining. All too temporary at the same time, a matter of one's own too "variable constitution," affections are only locally "apprehended . . . in terms of a momentary state," like involuntary stirrings deep in the body of an animal.

The disparagement of affection as indication is part of Spinoza's and Deleuze's disparagement of interpretation. For these mute affections "form the basis of an entire order" known as "language." As a system of contingent signs, language elaborates affection and only insufficiently idealizes it. Deleuze considers here a judgment on language harsher than Husserl's; Husserl at least imagines a medium for adequate ideas *within* signs—the expressive sign, phenomenological voice. Deleuze's Spinoza entertains no such possibility.

While Husserl aligns indicative signs with affects, affections are not affects, but sense impressions—ideas of what is happening, not necessarily feelings. Strikingly, however, it does not matter much to the general value system proposed by Spinoza and Husserl whether affects or affections are aligned with indication: what matters is the indication/expression axis. While Derrida complains that Husserl does not recognize that the expressive sign is a type of indicative sign, Spinoza does recognize this, and yet the values of indication and expression remain the same. Deleuze explains Spinoza's contrast between affections and affects in the following way:

> Image affections or ideas form a certain state [*constitutio*] of the affected body and mind, which implies more or less perfection than the preceding state. Therefore, from one state to another, from one image or idea to another, there are transitions, passages that are experienced, durations through which we pass to a greater or a lesser perfection. Furthermore, these states, these affections, images or ideas are not separable from the duration that attaches them to the preceding state and makes them tend toward the next state. These continual durations or variations of perfection are called "affects," or feelings [*affectus*]. . . . Hence there is a difference in nature between the *image affections* or *ideas* and the *feeling affects*, although the feeling affects may be presented as a particular type of ideas or affections. . . . It is certain that the affect implies an image or idea, and follows from the latter as from its cause. But it is not confined to the image or idea; it is of another nature, being purely transitive, and not indicative or representative, since it is experienced in a lived duration that involves the difference between two states. (S 48–49)

Even though Spinoza regards feeling affects as particular kinds of indications, they are *still* not confined to the inconvenient characteristics of indication.

The mission of the feeling affects is to encourage adequate ideas. Spinoza sets about explaining how adequate ideas could come to exist by building a kind of ladder out of the distinctions between affections and feeling affects, between kinds of feeling affects, and between all affects and adequate ideas.[42] Affect is heuristically important because it faces both in and out, and therefore clinches the univocity of expression. What is striking in the passage above, however, is the "difference in nature" within the "type of ideas or affections." Affect is "not separable" from affection and at the same time "not confined" to it, "being purely transitive." The ultimate difference between phenomenality and ontology, at the top of the ladder, trickles down to value not only affection and affect, but the entire intraphenomenal system. It begins to look like affect's power just is the power to reflect these fractures. As though for emphasis, refinements of transitivity are projected back into "greater or lesser" affections so that they are all more or less proto-affects. It's as though Deleuze's Spinoza needed to make sure affect exceeded affection. There is coexistence in principle but hierarchy in Deleuze's narrative practice between the ontological and the phenomenal. The presence of the ontological is not neutral: everything phenomenal flowers or withers in relation to it.

I have been lingering in Deleuze's presentation of Spinoza's theory of signs because it is provocative in its historical context. Intervening directly in debates of the 1960s, Deleuze's texts offer specific ripostes to Derrida's emotionally charged readings of indication and expression. In Derrida's texts, Husserl and Rousseau correlate indicative signs with mute affects and expressive signs with eloquent emotions that point to unities beyond language. In Deleuze's texts, Spinoza correlates indicative signs with mute affections and expressions with affects that are more than interpretive. I have argued that while emotions are real experiences, the expression that supposedly conveys them and the subject that supposedly expresses them are unnecessary angels parasitical on the phenomenon of emotion; that, rather, the domain of emotion is at once interpretive and nonsubjective. Thus, contrary to the belief that because anything interpretive needs to be "for something," "something" must be viewed as a subject, things appear to entities other than subjects. Deleuze takes a different position. Keith Ansell Pearson points out that in very late work Deleuze commits himself to "a transcendental field . . . to be distinguished from the realm of experience in that it involves no reference to an 'object' and does not belong to a 'subject.' It does, however, *appear* as an 'a-subjective current of consciousness' but this is a consciousness 'without self,' entirely impersonal and pre-reflexive."[43] Already, in the script

Deleuze writes for affection and affect—a heuristic narrative, not something that either Spinoza or Deleuze believes in as an actual chronology—affection appears, affect separates from it, climbs, is "expressed," and half of it falls back into phenomenality while the other half remains in ontology, a realm like that of Deleuze's later consciousness without experience. As in interpretive systems emotion is what is experienced, in this objective world affect is what is expressed.

While not everyone feels there is use in talking about things that, supposing they existed, could have no impact on experience, my point, instead, is only that it isn't *necessary* to deemphasize experience to think beyond subjectivity. There are nonsubjective phenomenal conditions for emotions. The minimal condition is an interpretive stance in a living system and the experience of self-difference that such a stance involves. Contrary to the idea that emotion provides ballast against the variability and regresses of interpretation, emotion and the interpretation of signs are codependent. Expression works on a scale that dwarfs emotion; emotion comes in an interpretive package. By cutting expression loose from personal feeling, Deleuze shows its non-necessity to feeling from its "dark," unaccustomed side.

The Regime of Affect

Within the limits of experience, Deleuze and Derrida have another, more local disagreement regarding Cartesian passion. As we've seen, Deleuze conceives personal feeling as a circumscribed realm lapped and surrounded by nonpersonal affect and expression. The texts of Derrida and de Man suggest that personal experience is not automatically subjective; indeed, emotion is the symptom that it is not. While Deleuze might agree, he asserts that there is at least one variety of personal feeling—passion—that does require subjectivity: passion, for him, is the specific feeling concept that reflects subjectification. For Derrida and de Man, passion does not instantiate subjectivity, hence emotion and passion are more continuous; for Deleuze, interpretive emotion and subjective passion are discrete, but reflect each other, so that neither escapes the other's influence, while only affect eludes their interlocking regimes.

As Deleuze's Spinoza books reply to Derrida's *Speech and Phenomena*, Deleuze and Guattari's discussion of subjectification in *A Thou-*

sand Plateaus replies to Derrida's "Cogito and the History of Madness." Both Derrida and Deleuze depict the cogito as passionate. For Derrida, the existence of Cartesian passion does not, according to Descartes's own descriptions, create or imply a subject, although Descartes affirms that his "I" is such a subject; rather, passion's claim to subjectivity consumes itself. Deleuze conceives Cartesian passion as a pathology of subjectivist thought—a "sad" affect. He views it as pejoratively as he does the idea of the subject itself, and does not disengage the two but rejects both. Condemning passion as an especially ideological mode of feeling helps Deleuze to set in shade the possibility of other personal feelings. In *A Thousand Plateaus*, these other personal feelings are implicitly interpretive emotions like those analyzed by Derrida and de Man.

Interpretive emotion and subjective passion structure "On Several Regimes of Signs," the fifth section of *A Thousand Plateaus*. As Derrida writes of Husserl, one needs a general theory of signs to articulate particular regimes of signs. Deleuze and Guattari possess such a general theory; they postulate that the existence of signs is prepared by "the cerebral-nervous milieu" (TP 64):

> There is a semiotic system . . . because the abstract machine has precisely that fully erect posture that permits it to "write," in other words to treat language and extract a *regime* of signs from it. But before it reaches that point, in so-called natural codings, the abstract machine remains enveloped in the strata: It does not write in any way and has no margin of latitude allowing it to recognize something as a sign (except in the strictly territorial sense of animal signs). After that point, the abstract machine develops on the plane of consistency and no longer has any way of making a categorical distinction between signs and particles; for example, it writes, but flush with the real, it inscribes directly upon the plane of consistency. It therefore seems reasonable to reserve the word "sign" in the strict sense for the last group of strata. . . . The question here is not whether there are signs on every stratum but whether all signs are signifiers, whether all signs are endowed with significance, whether the semiotic of signs is necessarily linked to a semiology of the signifier. (TP 65)

Revamping Deleuze's depreciation of the sign in the Spinoza books, Deleuze and Guattari accept signs but question signification. They propose a different debasement of the sign—the exaltation of signification over the sign by "signifier enthusiasts" (TP 66). "At the limit," such enthusiasts "can forgo the notion of the sign, for what is retained is . . . only the formal relation of sign to sign" (TP 112). A "regime of signs," then, may be composed of "any specific formalization of expression," for a regime of signs is larger than a regime of significations (TP 111). "A regime of signs is much more than a language," Deleuze and Guattari assert; regimes are "determining and selective agents" that shape languages (TP 63).

It follows that "the signifying regime" is only one of the regimes of signs. In *A Thousand Plateaus* Deleuze and Guattari list four: the signifying regime; the "countersignifying semiotic" of "arithmetic and numeration" (TP 118); the "*postsignifying* regime . . . defined by a unique procedure, that of 'subjectification' " (TP 119); and the "presignifying semiotic" of "collective" and "polyvocal" expression. I am concerned here with the first and third of these and the contrast between emotion and passion implied therein. Deleuze and Guattari begin their narrative with the signifying regime because it "testifies to the inadequacy of linguistic presuppositions, and in the very name of regimes of signs" (TP 112). They depict the signifying regime in terms often used by people—Foucault, for instance—unhappy about the reduction to textuality. In the signifying regime, they write, "signs form an infinite network" (TP 113) that makes the principle of signification itself a "center of signifiance" (TP 114). Deleuze and Guattari portray the network as "despotic" and "paranoid," with its endless demand for interpretation and cultivation of "priests" to meet and reproduce the demand. Although their sketch of the signifying regime is polemically disparaging, it is recognizable as a kind of poststructuralist topography. Although they do not assert this, their pairing of the interpretive regime with the passional one implies that passion is the counterpart of interpretation. Indeed, the domain of emotion is the explicitly nonsubjective field of personal feeling driven by différance; signification and interpretation create emotion the way an amplification system creates sound.

A clue to the emotive temper of this regime is its fascination with faces. According to Deleuze and Guattari the face is the "substance of expression" specific to signification:

It is like the body of the center of signifiance to which all of the deterritorialized signs affix themselves, and it marks the limit of their deterritorialization. The voice emanates from the face; that is why, how-

ever fundamentally important the writing machine is in the imperial bu-
reaucracy, what is written retains an oral or nonbook character. The face
is the Icon proper to the signifying regime, the reterritorialization internal to the system. . . . The face is what gives the signifier substance; it is
what fuels interpretation. . . . The signifier is always facialized. Faciality
reigns materially over that whole constellation of signifiances and interpretations (psychologists have written extensively on the baby's relations to the mother's face, and sociologists on the role of the face in mass
media and advertising). The despot-god has never hidden his face, far
from it: he makes himself one, or even several. . . . Conversely, when the
face is effaced, when the faciality traits disappear, we can be sure that
we have entered another regime, other zones infinitely muter and more
imperceptible where subterranean becomings-animal occur, becomings-
molecular, nocturnal deterritorializations overspilling the limits of the
signifying system. (TP 115)

As Derrida and de Man would concur, the face can seem to be both
the cause for and the circumference of interpretive events. Deleuze
and Guattari note the prominence of social regulators—psychologists
and sociologists—in the discourse of emotion. Expressions on the face
of a mother or despot must be interpreted—as mothers and despots
emphasize by turning themselves into faces. Such pedagogical face
mirrors the notion of face that appears in, for example, Rousseau's
anecdote about Alexander of Pheros, who worries that his visage
might be too readable. For Deleuze and Guattari the psychoanalyst is
such a mirror-despot, whose facial immobility regenerates signification and interpretation: "Although psychoanalysts have ceased to
speak, they interpret even more, or better yet, fuel interpretation on
the part of the subject" (TP 114). Social regulators' paeans to face fur-
nish evidence by association of psychoanalysts' face-centrism. The
economy of interpretation develops alongside the economy of pathos.
Correspondingly, the signifying regime begins to end with what overflows the face. Deleuze connects "sensation" to defiguration in his
Logique de sensation (1981), in which he argues that Francis Bacon's
paintings of disfigured bodies—especially faces—excite sensation.
While de Man allows emotion to participate in its reterritorialization,
however—and consequently the reterritorialization of emotion reproduces emotion—Deleuze bestows on affect an eternal aspect. Affect
"overspill[s]" the flowchart of the system, flying from the reterritorialization of subjective passion.[44]

At this point in Deleuze and Guattari's narrative, subjective passion apparently responds to the signifying regime—it is "postsignifying"—but instead, re-creates it. Initially, subjectification spins off from signification and interpretation, rather than accompanying interpretation (thus Deleuze and Guattari flout the convention that a subject must be in place already for interpretation to occur [TP 121]). In the ongoing pathic parallel, subjectification brings a different style of desire. To illustrate the specificity of passion, Deleuze and Guattari examine changes of the phrase "I love you": the same statement can be interpretive, passional, or belong to still other regimes (TP 147). Particular passions in turn "are effectuations of desire that differ according to the assemblage: it is not the same justice or the same cruelty, the same pity, etc." (TP 399). In the "postsignifying" regime of "passional subjectification," Deleuze and Guattari write, "relation with the outside . . . is expressed more as an emotion than an idea, and more as effort or action than imagination ('active delusion rather than ideational delusion')" (TP 120). For Deleuze and Guattari, a passion is an idea construed as an intentional act. Like actions in the Spinoza books, subjectification is "authoritarian" rather than "despotic." The performative prophet replaces the interpretive priest; the written sign gives way to the vocal sign, the book to the internalization of the book. Contemporary criticism would speak of performance; Foucault, of "discursive fact"; de Man, of "position." By coupling signifying and postsignifying regimes, Deleuze and Guattari make a critical comment about the former: while the signifying regime may seem like an alternative to subjectivity, they imply, it is actually just a less virulent version of it. Here Deleuze and Guattari clear space for themselves as poststructuralists who are not interpreters. Latent in the pairing is the notion that interpretation itself is allied with passion.

Passion for Deleuze and Guattari is thus Cartesian-Husserlian philosophy's fashion of feeling, and it is "even worse than the chant of the signifier" (TP 127).[45] Here comparison to "Cogito and the History of Madness" is again useful. Deleuze and Guattari concur with Derrida that "the subject of the statement is the union of the soul and the body, or feeling, guaranteed in a complex way by the cogito" (TP 128), and that what makes the subject seem to emerge is "the doubling of the two subjects, and the recoiling of one into the other" (TP 129). But they find Cartesian passion compulsive, much as Foucault finds Derrida's reading of Descartes panicky. The word "passion" here connotes the passive/active paradox that characterizes the death of the subject. In the enunciatory force of passion "a new form of slavery is invented, namely, being slave to oneself" or to the idea of being a free subject: "Is there anything more passional than pure reason? Is there a colder, more extreme, more self-interested passion than the cogito?" (TP 130). Deleuze and Guattari discard both interpretation and passion, rejecting both as sides of the same occlusion of immanence. Instead, they push personal feeling past its breaking point in affect that does not have to be referred to anything, on the black, ontological side of the cosmological register.

The transcendental status of affect, which Deleuze ventriloquizes through Spinoza in the 1960s and systematizes with Guattari in *A Thousand Plateaus,* is phrased in aesthetic terms in Deleuze's *Cinema* books and Deleuze and Guattari's *What Is Philosophy?* [1991]. In these works, art and affect are homologous, for both offer routes to ontology. The face's film shot, the close-up, measures affect's capacity to overflow particular regimes such as that of the face.[46] Close-ups deface. Thus the close-up is the paradigmatic "affection-image"—the counterpart to Spinoza's image-affection—and its mode is "expression" (*Cinema 1,* 98). Deleuze's sequence of kinds of images climaxes in affection-images expressed "without reference to anything else, independently of any question of their actualization" (*Cinema 1,* 98). The independence of affect reveals it as art, and vice versa. Deleuze and Guattari maintain in *What Is Philosophy?* that art instates the objective, while nonart remains interpretation-dependent. "Independent of the viewer or hearer," "what is preserved—the thing or the work of art—is a *bloc of sensations, that is to say, a compound of percepts and affects.*"[47]

Deleuze's aesthetic, in which affect and art are compounds that "stand up on their own" (*What Is Philosophy?* 165), amounts to a nonsubjective transcendentalism that satisfies some of the desires of humanist expression. That is, Deleuze's project reaches for aims shared by subjective and nonsubjective expression alike.[48] After all, the idea that there *is* something connecting the phenomenal and the ontological is precisely what both senses of expression are after. Deleuze's readers distinguish him from humanist subjectivism by dissociating Deleuze's expression from analogy—the inside/outside imagery of personal experience. Seeming to bridge an inside and an outside, and thus projecting both, is a hallmark of representational thinking. In such thinking insides and outsides are "defined through an eternalized third term" (Massumi, introduction to *A Thousand Plateaus,* xiii). Deleuze and Guattari mount extended attacks on analogy—a major trope of the ideology of emotion, as shown by de Man's analyses of Proust and Rousseau. Deleuze is against "gross resemblances and imaginary universals,"[49] his readers like to say. For Deleuze and Guattari, there is "no unity to serve as a pivot" (TP 8) between inside and outside, but rather "simultaneous unity and variety" (TP 46) expressed by affects. Yet Deleuzian expression—like other contemporary assaults on the very notion of a conceptual scheme—remains sympathetic to subjective expression in that both disparage media. In this sense, the widespread conclusion that "[Deleuze's] problems . . . are not the problems of phenomenology"[50] is not entirely true. The reason that Deleuze prefers expression to analogy is that unlike analogy, it does not fall back on merely an expert sort of mediation. Deleuze never attempts to make technical advancements in vehicles. The whole idea of transparency, Deleuze knows, is not transparent enough. Deleuzian expression is a white mythology that does not make the mistake of having so much color as to be white. It is because Deleuze does not simply repair resemblance but eliminates it altogether that any point is connected to any other in his cosmology, and the physical world independent of experience is described by Deleuze as a world of consciousness without even minimal obstruction—the regime of affect.

Deleuze brings us full circle from the philosophy of music, for musical aesthetics is influenced by traditional transcendentalism, while Deleuze inaugurates a transcendental materialism. Moving around this circle clarifies the nature of different positions on it, and outside it in the interpretive space of textuality. Two alternatives, I suggest, may stand here for the main choices within poststructuralism. The first, which might represent the stances of Deleuze, Guattari, and the Lyotard of *Libidinal Economy,* can be seen in a passage from Deleuze's *Foucault,* cited by Badiou at the end of his book as an especially radiant piece of Deleuze's prose. In this passage Deleuze quotes Foucault's reflection—discussed in relation to Derrida in Chapter 1— that phenomenology's "modern cogito" revisits unanswered questions raised by thought. Foucault organizes phenomenology's impulses into two areas linked by a conjunction: "the phenomenological project continually resolves itself, before our eyes, into a description—empirical despite itself—of actual experience, and into an ontology of the unthought that automatically short-circuits the primacy of the 'I think' " (*Order of Things,* 326). The two parts of Foucault's sentence on either side of the "and" represent two choices: description—including unwilling description—of experience, and metaphysics. Deleuze's reading of Foucault takes up two paragraphs later:

> Foucault senses the emergence of a strange and final figure: if the outside, farther away than any external world, is also closer than any internal world, is this not a sign that thought affects itself, by discovering the outside to be its own unthought element?
>
> It cannot discover the unthought [. . .] without immediately bringing the unthought nearer to itself—or even, perhaps, without pushing it further away, and in any case without causing man's own being to undergo a change by that very fact, since it is deployed in the distance between them. (*Order of Things,* 327)
>
> This auto-affection, this conversion of far and near, will assume more and more importance by constructing an *inside-space* that will be completely co-present with the outside space on the line of the fold. The problematical unthought gives way to a thinking being who problematizes himself, as an ethical subject.[51]

Deleuze's cogito resolves into a vision of auto-affection more "auto" than ever, folding inside and outside spaces in order to consume both along the fold. "Description . . . of actual experience" is consumed in the same move. The subject of the fold, a consciousness more immediate than that of experience, is not sovereign, since it has no outside to reign over. It's more: it's all there is.

Francisco Varela, himself no stranger to theories of auto-affection, describes instead the understandable personification of a chiasmus of organic forces in "the self as virtual person":

> The seeming paradox resides in a two-way movement between levels: "upward" with the emergence of properties from the constituting elements, and "downward" with the constraints imposed by global coherence on local interactions. The result (and the resolution of the paradox) is a nonsubstantial self that acts as if it were present, like a *virtual interface.*
>
> The more we see the selfless nature of our selves in various "regions" of the organism, the more we become suspicious of our feeling of "I" as a true center. Either we are unique in the living and natural world, or else our very immediate sense of a central, personal self is the same kind of illusion of a center, accountable by more of the same kind of analy-

sis as we have already performed on the basic sensorimotor cognitive selves.[52]

Like Deleuze, Varela works with a "conversion" of the feeling of opposed directions—not near and far, but "upward" and "downward." The simultaneity of upward and downward processes in a living being generates a "feeling of 'I' " (61). As Varela goes on to observe, the personal and social efficacy of that feeling are debatable. Acknowledging the feeling as a feeling, though, leads at the least to more feelings; at the most, perhaps to different and fresher ones.

CHAPTER FOUR

Psyche, Inc.:
Derridean Emotion after de Man

What emotions become the theorist? How do readers feel about theorists' feelings? As I mentioned in the introduction, Derrida's essays on de Man are often viewed as undermining deconstructive theories of mind with their displays of anguish and affection. Because de Man "came to epitomize the coldness of theory,"[1] Derrida's emotion on de Man's behalf looks like unassimilated material overflowing that theory; it looks like something outside the text. Jeffrey Mehlman, for example, intimates that Derrida's fervent tone toward de Man is unseemly because de Man's own work repels emotional response. Mehlman gives an example from *Memoires for Paul de Man* (1986), Derrida's quotation of a letter de Man had written him about their two interpretations of Rousseau. "The disparity between the professorial decorousness of de Man's early letter and the pathos of Derrida's commentary," Mehlman writes, "makes this particular prosopopoeia ring singularly false" ("Prosopopoeia Revisited," 138). John Guillory goes further, applying a similar logic to recent American deconstruction as a whole. De Man's colleagues and students observe in their eulogies for him that his reticence whetted their affection;[2] Guillory argues from their examples that deconstruction disseminates itself by repressing the social relation between teacher and student. Unable to confess their love for de Man the person, made wary by de Man's own theories of their love for him, his students transfer their transference from de Man to his theory, which they faithfully replicate.[3] According to Guillory, the emotions of de Man's students speak louder than their nonsubjectivist beliefs, circulating in anecdotes "*alongside* the doctrine . . . but not in immediate logical relation to that doctrine" (182).

But there is an immediate logical relation between deconstructive affection and deconstructive theories of life and language: it is deconstruction's account of emotion itself, manifest in its best-known texts, *Of Grammatology* and *Allegories of Reading*. Derrida's writings about de Man reflect this account. The asymmetry of affection that Mehlman and Guillory note occupies a prominent place in this group of texts, as it does in many older theories of emotion in which love is also paradigmatically unrequited.[4] De Man's name for this asymmetry is "prosopopoeia," as Mehlman points out ("Prosopopoeia Revisited," 137), and it was what he spent most of his time writing about. In this chapter we will see that Derrida's own writings about de Man both accept prosopopoeia as a figure for affection and attempt to progress beyond it.

In his memorial service address and in *Memoires for Paul de Man*, Derrida links emotional and intellectual difficulty, making his grief for de Man exemplify the sensation of thought.[5] In *Memoires for Paul de Man* and "Psyche: Inventions of the Other," an essay dedicated to de Man, he presents his own thought as the obverse of de Man's so that their two bodies of work are conjoined. Framing his work as part of his mourning for de Man, Derrida answers de Man's notion of prosopopoeia. According to de Man, prosopopoeia is an essentially arbitrary imposition of self on everything the self does not understand; Derrida envisions the corresponding figure of Psyche, an unknown exteriority on the far side of prosopopoeia. For Derrida, prosopopoeia does not merely block out that exteriority, but implies it and leads to its threshold. In the context of *Memoires*, Psyche also suggests the projected realm of Derrida's reunion with de Man. Thus Derrida's work fills a space in de Man's and vice versa; each supplies the ground for the other's figure, their texts composing a formal correlative of their friendship. Derrida's previous work leads retrospectively to his de Man–related writing, as if his affection for de Man had always shaped that work, while the friendship between Derrida and de Man verifies itself in the codependence of their texts.

Derrida's essay on de Man's wartime writings, "Like the Sound of the Sea Deep within a Shell: Paul de Man's War" (1988), and

"Biodegradables" (1989), his reply to replies to "Like the Sound of the Sea," continue to consider figures of meeting and address. The emotions that Derrida's violently polemical exchange with other critics represents and transmits—rage, suspicion, and indignation, for example—obviously differ greatly from the emotions that Derrida sends toward de Man. Yet they, too, circulate through fictive identification and address. Derrida's thoughts about the literal sense of "responsibility"—what it takes to be able to respond to something—extend to the genre of the scholarly reply. Reply and counter-reply rotate on the axis of their failure to hear one another. This remains true even though Derrida does not want to participate in this particular demonstration of deafness, even though he feels frustrated by it and wants to end it.

Finally, Derrida's texts about de Man suggest a kind of "psyche" that is neither monadic nor metaphysical. Both intrapersonal and interpersonal, it is also material and technological. In the last section of this chapter, I'll suggest a few philosophical ancestors for Derrida's psyche. Guillory's scenes of academic affection can be analyzed in the terms of the Derridean nonsubjective psyche when we see deconstruction as providing alternatives to classical concepts of transference and sublimation instead of simply lacking them. On this view, theoretical desire shows not the sublimation of affection into theory, but the emergence of affection in and as theory.

Hardly Thinking

"Pardonnez-moi de parler dans ma langue," begins Derrida's eulogy for de Man, the words he delivered at de Man's memorial service at Yale in 1984. *"Je n'ai pas le cœur aujourd'hui de traduire ces quelques mots."*[6] On the one hand, the phrase *"Pardonnez-moi"* introduces a speaker who speaks too much for himself—excess of self is what one apologizes for. But on the other, Derrida's words call attention to the way that grief simplifies its own utterance so that something less than a "self" seems to be speaking. Even Derrida's association between pain and verbal inadequacy is a stock element of the language of grief. *"Nous savons combien il est difficile de parler en un tel moment, quand une parole juste et décente devrait s'interdire de céder à aucun usage, toutes les conventions paraissant intolérables ou vaines* [we know with what difficulty one finds right and decent

words at such a moment when no recourse should be had to common usage since all conventions will seem either intolerable or vain]" (YFS 14, trans. 323), Derrida recalls. Yet he describes this very protest against the vanity of convention as conventional—something "we know." Intimacy and convention conventionally meet in bereavement.

Memoires for Paul de Man embeds the emotion that Derrida claims is his in a discussion of difficulty; and he posits an alliance between the difficulty of theory, deconstructive theory in particular, and the trouble of feeling. Language becomes difficult when emotion overtakes its speaker—as we know. But difficulty also links the vocabulary of emotion to that of thought. Intellectual problems are "difficult," and some answers to complex questions are "hard to say," as though an economic principle of information density inhibited speech. As with strong emotion, it belongs to thought in some sense to be difficult. It seems that intellectual difficulty is a nonaffective expression for affect—a philosophical name for the feeling of thought.

Derrida pursues the discussion of difficulty in *Memoires'* prefatory remarks, the few pages entitled "A PEINE."[7] Derrida read these remarks before presenting the three lectures that make up *Memoires* for the first time at Yale in 1984, a few months after de Man's death. The remarks pick up where the memorial service address leaves off, pondering the phrase "*à peine*" as an example of the impediments to translation. Derrida claims that the translation and, to the same extent, the understanding of the phrase "*à peine*" are a difficult matter—which is in effect to say that it's difficult to translate or understand difficulty. Indeed, the problem of emotional expression is often modeled after problems of verbal complexity or translation. Derrida embodies the coincidence of emotional and verbal problems by resisting self-translation when he must speak of emotion-saturated matters. In French, Derrida observes, glossing "*à peine*" as "*presque pas*" ("scarcely") blanches the "pain" from "*peine*," a narcosis not performed by the English "hardly":

> In the expression *à peine*, the French would hardly have heard the hard, the dash or the pain, the difficulty that there is or the trouble that one gives oneself. "Hardly" might be the best approximation. The French ear hardly perceives the sense of hardly.
>
> To be able hardly to say something, hardly to begin this evening, hardly to recommence, repeat, or continue means to be able only with

difficulty, with the pain of *à peine*—the affliction of hardly's hardship: hardly able, almost not to be able to, almost no longer able to say something, to begin, recommence and continue. This having trouble; with trouble, troubled and pained, it is hard even hardly to do, think or say that which however is said, thought, or done. Having trouble, being pained, as one would say in French, following.[8]

> Each time, beginning so many years ago, when I spoke here [Paul de Man] will have been there. And, for many among you, so many other times as well.
>
> And it is hard for me to think that henceforth it should be otherwise. I can hardly think and speak otherwise henceforth. (M iv)

Derrida makes difficulty sensible in this passage, sharpening the dulled pain in *"à peine."* He portrays himself as one who literally has trouble going on, repeating himself over and over as though to defy narrative. Resistance to narrative typically identifies the poetic text, which insists on repeating and remembering, even in its very returns to the left margin, its interruptions of narration by lineation. *Memoires'* first lecture, "Mnemosyne," also begins with a statement of incapacity, "I have never known how to tell a story" (M 3). But as Derrida repeats the phrase *"à peine,"* difficulty reveals itself as a vehicle as well as an obstacle. He thinks and speaks *hardly,* as one thinks dreamily or with concentration, and by means of hardship, which has become a catalyst. Hardness is hard to understand because its relation to facility ordinarily goes unnoticed. It appears finally as a prerequisite for continuance: one is "able only with difficulty." As Derrida remarks in a 1975 interview, "to work on mourning" is "first of all . . . the operation which would consist in working *on* mourning the way one says that something functions on such and such an energy source, or such and such a fuel—for example, to run on high octane."[9] In this sense, pain cooperates with representation: language works *on* mourning and speaks *with* pain.

Wherever Derrida mentions difficulty in *Memoires,* these topics converge: emotional difficulty, difficult thought, the death of Paul de Man. Their convergence colors "deconstruction in America," and indeed deconstruction as a whole, with difficulty of the emotive sort. "Deconstruction in America" was originally to be the theme of the lectures collected in *Memoires,* a theme supposedly abandoned after de Man's death. Noting that "the uncontrollable overdetermination of the phenomenon" makes this donnée a less than ideal lecture topic, Derrida asks, "Can we speak of 'deconstruction in America'?" (M 13–14). There are many reasons why the phrase in quotation marks might not be a speakable (or feasible) one.[10] At least one is emotional: Derrida feels uncomfortable now with the fact that the figure of Paul de Man personifies "deconstruction in America." The personification itself is natural enough; de Man was the literary theorist who gave deconstruction a plausible American inflection, bringing it into relation with traditions that American readers were likely to appreciate. "What would it have been without him? Nothing; or something entirely different—this is too evident for me to insist on" (M 20). But now, because de Man stands for "deconstruction in America," Derrida associates the unspeakability of the complex idea of "deconstruction in America" with the unbearability of speaking on rather than to de Man:

> After the death of Paul de Man on December 21, a necessity became clear to me: I would never manage to prepare these lectures, I would have neither the strength nor the desire to do so, unless they left or gave the last word to my friend. Or at least, since that had become literally impossible, to friendship, to the unique and incomparable friendship that ours was for me, thanks to him. I could only speak *in memory of him*. (M 19)

To announce after "A PEINE" that deconstruction in America can hardly be spoken is to place it among those difficult topics that break the voice. Derrida has always claimed that it is necessarily hard to say what deconstruction is; but he now projects a correspondence between deconstruction's intellectual complexity and emotional pain. It's hard to talk about deconstruction in America; it's hard to talk about rather than to de Man. The parallel suggests that deconstruction is *"plus d'une langue*—both more than a language and no more of *a* language" (M 15)—as grief itself is: it can only be spoken with pain.

Derrida's claim that he can hardly speak about his assigned topic indicates by the same token that he thinks about it. Rather than preparing for speech, thinking picks up where speech breaks off; conversely, speech is inherently broken, that thought might occur. It is useful to recall Derrida's quotation of Feuerbach in a footnote to "Force and Signification": "Philosophy . . . does not speak for the pleasure of speaking . . . but in order not to speak, in order to *think*"

(WD 303n23). Thinking and feeling, in other words, go together in a way that feeling and speaking do not. Derrida commends here for the first time the coupling of feeling to thought to which *Memoires* often returns, a coupling which encloses deconstruction in its embrace. As we'll see, de Man's and Derrida's works exemplify the couple: the textual entirety of their work repairs the broken circle of their friendship. No longer speaking together, they will think together in philosophy.

Psyche and Prosopopoeia

De Man's theory of prosopopoeia is relevant to Derrida's elegies for him because prosopopoeia, for de Man, describes the delusory tendency of human consciousness to animate the inanimate. "Identified with 'understanding' itself," as Cynthia Chase observes,[11] prosopopoeia arises in place of contact with the unknown, as a continual deferral of that meeting. Now, grief would seem to epitomize de Man's vision of "terrible solitude" (M 33): "speaking at the death of a friend, we declare that from now on everything will be situated, preserved or maintained in us, only 'in us,' and no longer on the other side, where there is nothing more" (M 32). The mourner's longing for the dead friend, his desire to know "the other as other" (M 38), is in part a struggle against prosopopoeia, a search for a relation to the friend that is not a self-serving hallucination. The mourner, like the lover, wants to penetrate the barrier between minds and yet live to tell the tale of their difference. Derrida phrases the question this way—"Is it possible, when one is in memory of the other, in bereaved memory of a friend, is it desirable to think of and to pass beyond this hallucination, beyond a prosopopoeia of a prosopopoeia?" (M 28). Derrida then sets out to answer himself. The situation is hyperappropriate: de Man's death speaks to Derrida of the loneliness of prosopopoeia, an idea de Man developed in life. Derrida, who misses conversing with his friend, who cannot bear the thought of merely speaking *about* de Man, speaks *to* de Man's notion of prosopopoeia with a complementary notion of his own. But in order really to respond to prosopopoeia, Derrida has to make de Man respond to him. He confides early on, as I noted above, that he "would never manage to prepare these lectures . . . unless they left or gave the last word to [his] friend," even though this has become "literally impossible" (M 19). Derrida has, in other words, to answer de Man in such a way that de Man will answer him; for in the game he is playing, he wins only if he induces de Man to say the last word, thereby proving that something does still come from the other side.[12] By making his work on mourning complement de Man's, Derrida also makes de Man's work reply proleptically to his. Their conversation will go on forever in the body of their texts, for Derrida has made a perpetual motion machine of it.

Derrida answers prosopopoeia with a figure he calls Psyche. It may be surprising that Derrida writes about Psyche at all, since Psyche is "the common name for the soul" (M 39). As such, she is the personification of immortality, the traditional *deus ex machina* of all metaphysical mourning-plays. Socrates invokes the psyche in this way when he claims that knowledge can only be recollection, yet we recollect more than we know; ergo, either we know what we don't know or "our souls had a previous existence."[13] In "Psyche" Derrida stands up for the alternative: we do know what we don't know; that, in fact, is all we know. Why, then, does Derrida too intone the name of Psyche? No figure would seem to be harder to rehabilitate or more vulnerable to de Manian irony than Psyche, the goddess of prosopopoeia.

In naming Psyche, Derrida raises at the outset the question of whether this figure is an "invention." Invention is itself a capacious concept, stirring connotations of discovery, fabulation, and technical progress. "Psyche" concerns itself with invention most of all, I think, because invention in one sense designates exactly what prosopopoeia isn't. Prosopopoeia reproduces more of the same, while an invention has to be new—one can't claim to "invent" something that already exists (RDR 60). In another sense, however, invention is a synonym for prosopopoeia. Pejoratively speaking, an invention is "*only* an invention, a mirage . . . an admirable mirror effect" or a "technical mechanism" (RDR 40). Although Derrida asks, "Is the Psyche an invention?" (RDR 40), he actually grants to begin with that the answer is yes, in both senses of the word "invention." The Psyche, that would really be something else—but it would be an invention. Suppose that Psyche is an invention, a prosopopoeia, suppose that Derrida's text is "presented as an invention" (RDR 27): What does that mean? Does it mean that Derrida ventriloquizes or orchestrates, that is, mechanically manipulates, the relation between his and de Man's texts in a way that only mirrors himself? If Psyche, invention, and prosopopoeia overlap, what does that tell us about all three?

First, Derrida assumes that prosopopoeia must have a counter-part—something it reacts to when it arises so protectively. What does prosopopoeia defend against? Prosopopoeia seems to imply that we see something without seeing it—namely, the "text as text," as de Man would put it, the "other as other." We seem conscious enough of these to know, at least, that we cannot know them. Derrida now introduces two psyches, one a proper and the other a common noun; one psyche or the other, or both, is the other of prosopopoeia. Psyche with a capital *P* is Derrida's revisionary version of the mythical goddess. A psyche with a small *p* in French, as Derrida explains, is "a large double mirror installed on a rotating stand" (RDR 38). In the essay "Psyche" Derrida uses Francis Ponge's poem "Fable" to model the relation of Psyche to psyche:

> Fable
>
> Par le mot *par* commence donc ce texte
> Dont la première ligne dit la vérité,
> Mais ce tain sous l'une et l'autre
>
> Peut-il être toléré?
> Cher lecteur déjà tu juges
> Là de nos difficultés . . .
>
> (APRÈS sept ans de malheurs
> Elle brisa son miror.)

> [By the word *by* then begins this text / Of which the first line speaks the truth, / But this silvering under the one and the other // Can it be tolerated? / Dear reader you judge already / There as to our difficulties . . . // (AFTER seven years of misfortune / She broke her mirror.)] (quoted in RDR 30; trans. modified)

"The she, in this fable, I shall call Psyche" (RDR 38), Derrida declares. In his interpretation of the poem, Psyche breaks her psyche. Breaking a mirror traditionally brings seven years of bad luck; but "in this case," Derrida writes, "the misfortune would be the mirror itself" (RDR 37). Derrida argues that bad luck inhabits "the specular play for which language provides," that speculation which divides the self—allegorically, in de Man's lexicon—into one and another, Psyche and her reflection. Thus "*Fable* tells of allegory, of one word's move to cross over to the other, to the other side of the mirror. Of the desperate effort of an unhappy speech to move beyond the specularity that it constitutes itself" (RDR 31). We should remember here that the essay "Psyche" is, again, dedicated "to the memory of Paul de Man," to the memory, as Derrida puts it, of "an unfailing friendship that was to be utterly cloudless and that will remain in my life, in me, one of the rarest and most precious rays of light" (RDR 26). "Cross[ing] over to the other . . . side of the mirror" describes the desire of mourning, in which one craves "the possibility of stating the other or speaking *to* the other," perhaps even to the point of dying to get to the other side of the mirror where dead people live. It is no accident that Derrida composes "Psyche" and "Mnemosyne" in fairly close succession,[14] and that the figure of Psyche is also mentioned in "Mnemosyne."[15] By breaking the glass Psyche makes a "desperate effort" to destroy the circuit of specularity. If she succeeded, there would indeed be only one Psyche, the immortal capital-P Psyche of myth, and she would be on the other side.[16]

Traditionally Psyche personifies the self capable of outlasting life. In classical metaphysics, "life" and "death" are categories that obscure the greater reality of the Psyche. Derrida, however, imagines Psyche feeling the obverse of what mortal beings feel. Her position mirrors that of mortal beings and vice versa, since in her perspective our side is the "other side." Psyche maintains a second circular relation with the instrument of her reflection. To phrase it another way, "Psyche" can most accurately be defined as the unstable compound of Psyche and psyche—not so much the other as "the relation of the same to the other" (RDR 40). There are always at least two psyches. That is why Psyche does not appear as a single figure in Derrida's text—in spite of her best efforts in Ponge's poem—but as an "it/her" (RDR 40). Derrida discusses several additional examples of same/other circuitry in the essay—notably, the performative circularity of Ponge's poem which "does what it says" so that "it is hard to distinguish [the] telling and the told faces" (RDR 32, 33). In the context of de Man's death, the "rotating" pairs in "Psyche" recall the "unfailing friendship" between Derrida and de Man—de Man after death having become Derrida's asymmetrical complement and muse. Derrida recognizes the complementarity of their friendship in the ending of "The Rhetoric of Temporality," in which de Man compares allegory and irony to a legendary pair of lovers:

This successful combination of allegory and irony also determines the thematic substance of the novel as a whole [*La Chartreuse de Parme*], the underlying *mythos* of the allegory. This novel tells the story of two

lovers who, like Eros and Psyche, are never allowed to come into full
contact with each other. . . . When they can touch, it has to be in a darkness imposed by a totally arbitrary and irrational decision, an act of the
gods. The myth is that of the unovercomable distance which must always prevail between the selves, and it thematizes the ironic distance
that Stendhal the writer always believed prevailed between his pseudon-
ymous and nominal identities. As such, it reaffirms Schlegel's definition
of irony as a "permanent parabasis" and singles out this novel as one of
the few novels of novels, as the allegory of irony. (BI 228; quoted in
RDR 39)

De Man's allegory and irony, Eros and Psyche, resemble the two sides
of Ponge's revolving mirror. According to de Man, irony is the "reversed mirror-image" of allegory and "the two modes . . . are the two
faces of the same fundamental experience of time" (BI 225, 226;
RDR 38). Further, de Man writes, the separation between allegory
and irony is generative, driving the plot of Stendhal's novel.

Derrida's reading of the Eros and Psyche story conveys not only the
relation of allegory to irony, or of the self to the other, but the structure of his friendship with de Man. In the myth, Eros prepares a place
for Psyche, then leaves the window open—in Keats's words, "to let
the warm Love in!" Derrida's language highlights the penetrating
eroticism of Psyche's entry:

> This invention of the entirely other is beyond any possible status; I still
> call it invention because one gets ready for it, one makes this step des-
> tined to let the other come, *come in*. The invention of the other, the in-
> coming *of* the other, certainly does not take the form of a subjective gen-
> itive, and just as assuredly not of an objective genitive either, even if the
> invention comes from the other—for this other is thenceforth neither
> subject nor object, neither a self nor a consciousness nor an uncon-
> scious. . . . To invent would then be to "know" how to say "come" and
> to answer the "come" of the other.[17] Does that ever come about? Of this
> event one is never sure. (RDR 56)

Derrida and de Man, allegory and irony, as couples, may be compared
to pairs of lovers, each of whom prepares for the other's pleasure—
which is distinct from making it happen or even being sure it has occurred. Derrida's reading of the end of "The Rhetoric of Temporality"
is literally and we might say autobiographically allegorical, for he and
de Man are allegory and irony. Derrida observes in his eulogy that
"Paul was irony itself":

As you know, Paul was irony itself and, among all the vivid thoughts he leaves with us and leaves alive in us, there is as well an enigmatic reflection on irony and even, in the words of Schlegel which he had occasion to cite, on "irony of irony." At the heart of my attachment to him, there has also always been a certain beyond-of-irony which cast on his own a softening, generous light, reflecting a smiling compassion on everything he illuminates with his tireless [*infaillible*] vigilance. His lucidity was sometimes overpowering [*terrible*], making no concession to weakness, but it never gave in to that negative assurance with which the ironic consciousness is sometimes too easily satisfied. (YFS 14, trans. 324)

This passage already shows the reasoning of "Psyche," proposing that de Man, Irony, brings along a silent partner, a "beyond-of-irony." The "generous light" is not de Man's own, but is reflected toward him by something beyond him; but, then, that is *his* beyond, which couldn't exist without him. The reader suspects that the generosity is Derrida's—but if so, the generosity still belongs to de Man's Derrida and hence to de Man again. The pattern of continuous reflection determines Derrida's astronomical metaphor, in which de Man is the sun and he is the moon. De Man's lucidity is *"terrible," "infaillible,"* while his counterpart sheds a compassionate light. If de Man is the sun, however, then the moon's poetic license is also his own, reflecting back on him. If, on the other hand, Derrida's fancies are to be understood as written *in* a psyche as Derrida suggests Ponge's "Fable" is, it is all the other way around. In either case, Derrida's writings after de Man's death practice a lover's method: they speak in such a way as to respond to de Man and to prepare and imply de Man's answer in turn.

It is not difficult to imagine how Irony would reply to "Psyche." Derrida's figure of Psyche is vulnerable to a de Manian riposte like this one: *Even if you imagine that you leave the ground "beyond prosopopoeia" undefined, calling it merely "the other" or "the new," these characterizations are as definitional and as hallucinatory as others. "Beyond prosopopoeia" you have placed prosopopoeia itself. In fact that's what prosopopoeia is in the first place—the idea that there's something "beyond prosopopoeia."* But to this Derrida could reply: *Yes, but listen to what you've said: prosopopoeia is the idea that there's something beyond prosopopoeia. Isn't that just what "Psyche" says?* Derrida's "Psyche" invites its deconstruction "in order to allow the other to come or to announce its coming in the opening of this dehiscence" (RDR 59–60). The deconstruction that "Psyche" solicits would have to deploy de Man's notion of prosopopoeia, giving the last word to de Man.[18] Derrida leaves a window open in the text for de Man, though he is beyond the grave. As in Ponge's poem, which not only does what it says, but "more than it says" (RDR 59), the result is to be more than the sum of de Man's and Derrida's two positions. The two positions form a plural psyche between them, constituted not of subjects but of a rotation of ideas, "a 'we' that does not find *itself* anywhere" (RDR 61).

This conclusion recalls, among other precedents, Descartes's *Passions of the Soul*. Descartes's treatise was strongly influenced by his correspondence with Princess Elisabeth of Bohemia; it is, like *Memoires for Paul de Man*, the fruit of what "scholars have variously characterized . . . as an *amour raisonnable* or an *amour intellectuel*."[19] Amélie Rorty points out that Descartes's *amour intellectuel* "can serve as a model for the role of the will in determining the character of the compound individual, composed of two independent entities."[20] Derrida's intellectual love for de Man is, as we've seen, asymmetrical, not quite requited, always opening itself up; it forms a complex assembly, but no unity. Still, Descartes, like Derrida, models the mind on an interpersonal relationship, and Derrida, like Descartes, "affirms a new entity" of plural selves (Rorty, "Cartesian Passions," 527). As Derrida phrases it, "the objects we invent in this way are institutions" (RDR 59)—virtual entities that appear by convention and agreement. On the basis of their mutual criticism and legitimation, Derrida and de Man form Psyche, Inc.

"The Theater of Petty Passions"

None of Derrida's writings lie so open to the charge of inappropriate emotion as his essays on de Man's *Le Soir* articles. "Like the Sound of the Sea Deep Within a Shell: Paul de Man's War" is perhaps Derrida's most controversial piece, sometimes characterized as an apology for de Man's collaboration. On publishing "Like the Sound of the Sea" in 1988, *Critical Inquiry* "received a great many unsolicited responses" to Derrida's essay (editors' note, 764).[21] The summer 1989 issue presents six of these responses and Derrida's counter-response, "Biodegradables: Seven Diary Fragments," which develops some of the logic of "Like the Sound of the Sea." Both pieces are strongly shaped by debate; by genre they are responses and do not stand alone. Derrida therefore uses these two pieces as occasions to define responsiveness, often in de Manian terms; Derrida seeks "a responsibility which would never be cancelled, but on the contrary provoked by the experience of prosopopoeia, such as de Man seems to understand it" (R 130). "Like the Sound of the Sea" and "Biodegradables" also afford an opportunity to trace the critical circulation of emotion; for Derrida's statements purvey and excite intense emotions.[22] The emotionality of the debate as a whole—while certainly warranted by the dimensions of the issues—is usually regretted by all sides as a distraction; Derrida laments its "petty passions."[23] But he also asserts a necessary relation between "disquieting meaning" and response as such. "A calm and assured responsibility," Derrida writes, "is never a responsibility" (B 837). A little later he adds, "to speak of [responsibility] calmly . . . is irresponsibility itself" (B 846). What, then, connects the question of responsiveness, the scholarly genre of response, and emotional upheaval?

Critical reactions to "Like the Sound of the Sea" emphasize the personal nature of Derrida's predicament. Indeed, Derrida recalls the personal elements of his situation several times; "I wanted to tell you what my own *feeling* is," Derrida says at the conference at which he first addresses the subject of de Man's past. He acknowledges the danger of intimate rhetoric by noting—in a further intimacy—"(May I be forgiven these 'self-centered' references; I will not overdo them)" (R 129). The "'self-centered' references" have several functions and effects. Derrida goes over the sequence of his reactions to de Man's wartime writings as though searching his emotions for explanatory clues: "My feelings were first of all that of a wound, a stupor, and a sadness that I want neither to dissimulate nor to exhibit" (R 132).[24] But is there such a thing as a feeling that one can neither dissimulate nor exhibit? Derrida's instructions about how the reader should take his self-descriptions point to his Rousseauistic dilemma. It is difficult for Derrida to claim a feeling here without either exhibiting it—that is, seeming to ask credit for it—or exhibiting the fact that he's not exhibiting it, and seeming to take credit for *that*. The problem doesn't rely simply on the fact that Derrida mentions his emotions: it would be impossible to assume that he read de Man's wartime articles and didn't feel a thing, and given that this is the case, it would be an "exhibit" of stoicism if he didn't mention them at all. It is as though

Derrida's feelings were inherently inappropriate in relation to his argument. Yet these feelings, rhetorically inconvenient as they are, also propel and limit the argument. As Derrida puts it, he has to think, "What was it . . . I could identify on a first reading, through all the sadness and consternation?" (R 134). Sadness and consternation serve as controls; they define the idea strong enough to stand up against them.

Emotions, and Derrida's emotions in particular, are also inappropriate in his opponents' arguments. Jon Wiener meets the question of propriety by actually suggesting what Derrida should have said "to fulfill the responsibilities of friendship" in "an honorable way" ("Responsibilities of Friendship," 797). W. Wolfgang Holdheim "sympathize[s] with Derrida's feelings" of compassion for de Man and agrees that de Man must have suffered, but disagrees about the sort of suffering it was.[25] These acknowledgments of Derrida's and de Man's emotions, accompanied by hints of the authors' emotions, raise questions about presentation. Like the faint praise that begins negative book reviews, they buy the right to lodge complaints. When John Brenkman and Jules David Law comment that "Derrida's historical-political analysis is interwoven with an often moving testimony of his personal and intellectual ties to de Man," this sentence leads to the next: "He does not, however, have control over the interaction of the two."[26] "Even when, here or there, someone makes a show of being moved by my sadness or my friendship for de Man," Derrida objects, "it is in order to get the better of me and suggest that I am inspired *only* by friendship" (B 820). For both Derrida and his opponents, the emotion of the circumstance looms within it as something that cannot argue.

Derrida's focus on conditions for responsiveness in "Like the Sound of the Sea," then, ironically inspires "a great many unsolicited responses"—most of them hostile, if *Critical Inquiry*'s selection is representative. "Biodegradables" registers Derrida's reaction to this situation in turn, and in it he tries to turn away from the escalating production of passions. He imagines saying, "Forget it, drop it, *all of this is biodegradable*" (B 873). The impulse to turn away does not appear very often in Derrida's work; insofar as it takes priority here, it arises from an exhaustion about responsiveness.

According to Derrida, in order to respond to de Man's situation for oneself "one must respond, answer to the other, about the other, *for the other*, not in his place but as if in the place of another 'proper self,' but *for* him" (R 151). Because de Man is dead and cannot answer for himself, it becomes particularly obvious that someone or something must answer for him (but this would also be true even if de Man were alive). In this morality play de Man personifies writing: as Derrida points out in *Dissemination,* Socrates mocks written words for their incapacity to answer questions. "If you ask them anything about what they say," Socrates pretends to complain, "they go on telling you just the same thing forever" (quoted in D 135–136). Since de Man is so definitionally irresponsible, whatever is happening, however one would like to characterize it, "is *happening to us.* I name thereby, in utter darkness, many people" (R 128). Yet, although the experience is ours alone, we cannot just speak for ourselves about it. The very phrase "speaking for myself," in English, suggests two selves, making me my own representative. In speaking for himself about de Man, Derrida speaks as a plural entity. It is the "compound individual"—the incorporated psyche—who is called to speak. The volume of *Responses* to de Man's wartime journalism and the *Critical Inquiry* issue devoted to "Like the Sound of the Sea" show vividly what it is like to read a debate among compound individuals: everyone argues on behalf of an institution, everyone is being "spoken through" by former arguments, like "fingers of the same hand" (B 825).

The entanglement of arguments is a kind of intimacy, though it may take either an empathetic or a prosecutorial form. Although responsiveness helps to elicit compassion for others, the prosecutorial mentality too is a sort of hyper-responsiveness, even a sort of love. Thus Derrida notes the eroticism of "Paul de Man's war," suggesting in "Like the Sound of the Sea" that to say "fear" and "hatred" in such a context "is to say sometimes love" (R 128), and in "Biodegradables" reporting the words of a friend: "I think deep down they love you. I mean, they don't want to let you go. This is a good opportunity; they want *to stay with you* [*rester avec toi*]. As long as possible. At all costs" (B 866).[27] The disturbing implication is that Derrida's responsiveness to and for de Man is reflected in his encounter with hostile readers who, in his worst dreams, seem prepared to hound him to the grave. As we've seen, Derrida strives to make his posthumous relationship with de Man self-restarting by writing to de Man's writings so that they write to his; but this complementarity is now complemented in turn by Derrida's nearly perfect noncommunication with antagonistic critics. The rotation of prosopopoeia and psyche does not necessarily generate friendship, but commits itself only to a mechanism of circuitry that, in overdrive, fosters paranoia.

A "bad" version of the *amour intellectuel* between Derrida and de Man occurs in Derrida's "confrontation" with John Searle in "Limited Inc a b c . . ." (1977), and it's useful to revisit this example. In *Limited Inc,* too, Derrida implies the eroticism of the altercation with Searle, noting that Searle casts him as J. L. Austin's illegitimate philosophical heir.[28] It is partly because the exchange with Searle carries both passion and animosity, I think, that Derrida wonders whether it should really be called a "confrontation." In one sense this group of writings doesn't deserve the name of "confrontation"; how can people who never manage to come face to face be said to confront one another?[29] Derrida honors the torsional movement of their pseudoconfrontation—like that of magnets' opposite poles—by addressing not Searle but "Sarl," his fictive "front" (*Limited Inc,* 37), "a Searle who is divided, multiplied, conjugated, shared" (*Limited Inc,* 31). At the same time, Derrida depicts the disagreement as so profoundly mistaken that the writings do not disagree at all. Searle's "Reply" to "Signature Event Context" does not work as a reply because it repeats the argument of the text it thinks it disagrees with. "I have occasionally had the feeling," Derrida notes, "of having almost '*dictated*' this reply" (*Limited Inc,* 31).[30] Derrida celebrates his and Searle's blind affinity by borrowing the idea of a "confrontation that never quite takes place" from Searle, who had applied it to Derrida's reading of Austin (*Limited Inc,* 35), and by citing almost every word of Searle's piece within his own. The extensive citation runs a circle around Searle's refusal of permission to reprint his "Reply" in *Limited Inc.* It also opens the Menardian possibility of a rebuttal that repeats its source text word for word. Derrida and Searle, then, are not only too far apart to disagree, but too intimate to converse.[31] As Barbara Herrnstein Smith concludes, the line between verbal and material discord is a fine one. Rivalries between epistemological relativists who seem self-contradicting to epistemological foundationalists and foundationalists who seem self-confirming to relativists, she finds, are predictably and perhaps inevitably circular; in extreme versions when "*absolute epistemic supremacy*" is at stake, "'wars of truth' become duels to the not always figurative death."[32]

Derrida's response texts on de Man mobilize this oddly aggressive tenor of the reply as a genre. Replies seem aggressive in ratio to their secondary status, their subordination to a source text. Because the source text coerces the reply, it also liberates its enmity. The reply's hostility belongs partly to its companion text; it can afford to spend aggression because the expense will be jointly shared. The reiterative operation of the reply offers a way of amplifying polemical passion. Thus Derrida underscores the dialogical character of his polemical pieces, in which, in his opinion, he always occupies the second place. To Holdheim's complaints about his "coquettishly long-winded" style ("Jacques Derrida's Apologia," 785), Derrida replies, "Who obliges him, what obliges him to read me?" (B 855); he remarks of Roger Scruton, "Nobody forces this professor . . . to read me" (*Points*, 405). He wonders how twenty philosophers who sent a letter to the London *Times* objecting to a plan to confer an honorary degree on him could attack someone "who in this particular case hadn't asked for anything and was not a candidate for anything" (*Points*, 403). "When I seem to 'defend' de Man," he writes in "Biodegradables," "and I never would have done it otherwise, it is always, as it is here once more, in the face of murderous caricatures, abusive simplifications" (B 839). Anticipating that "someone . . . is perhaps going to reproach *Critical Inquiry* for publishing [him] too often and at too great a length," Derrida "point[s] out that I myself never asked for anything. . . . I have never in my life taken the initiative of a polemic. Three or four times, and *always in response, and always because I was invited to do so,* I have simply tried to confront some manipulations that were too serious to ignore" (B 872). In such comments Derrida attributes argumentative force to the genre of the reply. Without disputing that, one can point out that the secondariness of his replies does not make them less incendiary, and that Derrida feeds the fire that burns him.

In sequence, "Like the Sound of the Sea" and "Biodegradables" disseminate themselves without diminishing themselves. The first essay considers the de Man debate in general, while in "Biodegradables," an answer, the controversy of de Man's *Le Soir* writings is not the topic of discussion, but rather the controversy of the controversy. Derrida argues from the outset of "Like the Sound of the Sea" that the earliest manifestations of the controversy had already substituted deconstruction and, implicitly, himself for de Man. His critics claim that he does not cite, but incites the exchange. The longer the argument goes on, the more it becomes its own subject, and the more contentious it is. It can be either comforting or frightening, as Derrida remarks in another mourning-text, that the supposedly "substitutive value" of representation can bring about "a re-gaining of force or a supplement of intensity in presence, and thus a sort of potency or potentialization of power" ("By Force of Mourning," 178). The detour of communication as it replies to itself acts as an emotional intensifier, regardless of content. The fractious round of argument about argument parodies the wedding-ring structure of Derrida's textual friendship with de Man, through which their affection had traveled. In *Memoires* the affirmation of memory had "the form of a ring or an *alliance*" (M 19); in "Biodegradables" Derrida declares, "I give notice right now that I am tired of this scene and that I will not get back into the ring, at least not this ring" (B 872). Even so, this new "ring," too, a circus or (more likely) a boxing ring, constitutes an alliance, even if it is a misalliance.

Derrida's conversation with the dead de Man is not different in kind, then, from his arguments with critics over de Man. Derrida's textual relationship with his friend claims entity but not unity; their conversation is infinite only because interlocking internal divisions turn each thesis toward its antithesis. De Man's irresponsibility in death, and the deafness Socrates charges to writing, are tokens of the division that ordinarily exists between and within minds and that is, for Derrida, the spine of dialogue. He makes this clear toward the end of *Memoires* in his interpretation of the term "aporia":

> The word "aporia" recurs often in Paul de Man's last texts. I believe that we would misunderstand it if we tried to hold it to its most literal meaning: an absence of path, a paralysis before road-blocks, the immobilization of thinking, the impossibility of advancing, a barrier blocking the future. On the contrary, it seems to me that the experience of the aporia, such as de Man deciphers it, gives or promises the thinking of the path, provokes the thinking of the very possibility of what still remains unthinkable or unthought, indeed, impossible. The figures of rationality are profiled and outlined in the madness of the aporetic. (M 132)

Gasché, explicating Derrida's thoughts on responsibility through a reading of "Ulysses Gramophone," stresses Derrida's sense of a structure of implicit consent "prior to all possible [specific] acts or engagements."[33] "Before the act or the word, the telephone," as Derrida puts it in "Ulysses Gramophone."[34] Address for Derrida "is not necessarily a dialogue or an interlocution, since it assumes neither voice nor symmetry, but [only] the haste, in advance, of a response that is already asking" ("Ulysses Gramophone," 299). As Gasché notes, the structure of consent "can also lend itself to acts of negation and denegation" (*Inventions of Difference,* 243). Nowhere in Derrida's work does the consent of telephones intervene so bleakly as it does in the *Critical Inquiry* exchange, where it is used almost entirely in the service of indignation. The phone just won't stop ringing, so to speak, even though Derrida advises the reader not to pay attention when he does answer it. He picks it up by deciding to "Telephone *C.I.*" (B 821), although he believes nothing interesting will come of it. But as Gasché also contends, the possibility of acts of negation "is not the symmetrical counterpart of the enabling fundamental structure in question. All negation or denegation . . . presupposes it" (*Inventions of Difference,* 243). The fact that Derrida does not enjoy his role in this ring does not mean it is not a ring—a ring, that is, the contract and promise of a group.

L'âme

In averring that the psyche is an "invention," Derrida proposes that it is "an apparatus that we can call technical in the broad sense . . . a relatively independent mechanical apparatus" (RDR 48). Similarly, discussing Schelling's idea that human inventions "complement" nature, Derrida describes the soul as a supplement:

> Invention manifests, it is the revelation of God, but it completes that revelation as it carries it out, it reflects revelation as it supplements it. Man is the *psyche* of God, but this mirror captures the whole only by supplying for a lack. A *psyche* is this total mirror that cannot be reduced to what is called a "soul supplement" [*un supplément d'âme*]; it is the soul as a supplement, the mirror of human invention as the desire of God, in the place where something is missing from God's truth, from his revelation. (RDR 59)

The soul as supplement is an invention in that a supplement is a structural and technical prop. As a supplement, the soul is an absence in God's world that materializes in the mirror of wishful thought as an extra presence. It makes God's world more than the sum of its parts and thereby makes it whole.[35] Happy to grant that the soul is a fiction, contemporary critics worry that for Derrida, the subject, too, may be constructed on the model of the psyche. Emotion, however, is not predicated on the subject any more than on the psyche. The technicity of the psyche does indeed imply the technicity of the self: but this implication strengthens rather than weakens the case of emotion.

To begin with, the technicity of the psyche is not a Derridean invention, but a poetic idea that has long competed with the equally poetic idea of psyche as quality. Recall the supplement-soul in Diderot's "Letter on the Blind for the Use of Those Who See" [1749], a favorite piece of de Man's about which he planned to write.[36] The premise of Diderot's piece is that deaf-mutes—and in a companion essay, blind people—resemble philosophers, who tend to speculate "upon things that, if they were to be properly understood, seemed to require the aid of an organ they did not have" (as God's world requires a soul, as Descartes's mind requires a pineal gland).[37] Diderot lampoons the convenience of such philosophical prostheses in the following fancy out of Rube Goldberg or Max Ernst:

> Think of man as an automaton, as a sort of walking clock; let the heart represent its mainspring, and the other organs inside his chest the other principal pieces of the movement. Imagine in his head a bell furnished with little hammers and from these hammers an infinite multitude of threads stretching out in every direction and terminating at points all over the case. Then place on top of this bell one of those little figures we use to ornament the tops of our clocks, and let it have its head bent a little to one side, like a musician listening to hear whether his instrument is properly tuned or no: that little figure will be the *soul* [*l'âme*]. (32)[38]

The *locus classicus* of psychic technicity can be found in the Pythagorean theory of attunement, summarized by Socrates as the idea that the soul is an arrangement as of "the strings of a musical instrument" (*Phaedo* §86). The attunement theory postulates that the soul possesses material elements to tune and thus that it is finite. Socrates therefore orders his student Simmias, "Make up your mind which theory you prefer—that learning is recollection, or that soul is an attunement" (*Phaedo* §92; Heidegger references the Pythagorean tradition in his theory of *Stimmung*).[39] The Platonic context is significant, since de Man has often been dressed in the costume of Socrates by his friends and students. The memorial tributes in *The Lesson of Paul de Man* repeatedly allude to Socratic attributes: de Man was "eminently the great questioner" (YFS 6), "his jokes . . . joking at his own expense" (8); he was "ironic toward discipleship" (10); "he took each institutional encounter away from the murky plane of the personal, and made it appear . . . in its proper light, as a practical question" (11); he was "one of those rare teachers who do not make their own limitations the limitations of the student" (13).[40] Derrida himself comes closest to actually naming Socrates when he says "Paul was irony itself"—since as Kierkegaard observes, "it is common knowledge, of course, that tradition has linked the word 'irony' to the existence of Socrates."[41] The resemblance between de Man and Socrates grows even stronger when his friends describe his death. In the most melodramatic of the memorial tributes, Shoshana Felman avows that de Man was "generous even with his own mortality. . . . on his deathbed, he became, thus, all the more a giver, all the more a teacher: transforming his own death into a life-lesson" (YFS 9). In his eulogy and in a footnote to *Memoires for Paul de Man* Derrida quotes de Man's last letter to him, in which de Man, again like Socrates, purports to find dying rewarding:

> All of this, as I was telling you [on the phone], seems prodigiously interesting to me and I'm enjoying myself a lot [*je m'amuse beaucoup*]. I knew it all along but it is being borne out: death gains a great deal, as they say, when one gets to know it close up—that "*peu profond ruisseau calomnié la mort*" [shallow stream calumniated as death]. (YFS 16, trans. 325; M 87n2)[42]

"I never knew," Derrida recalls, "to what extent he adopted this tone . . . so as to console and spare his friends in their anxiety or their despair" (YFS 325). Of course, it is precisely this situation that obtains in the *Phaedo:* the context for the discussion of attunement, and for Socrates' insistence that the soul outlives the body, is his friends' distress at his impending death.

But unlike Socrates, or like a counter-Socrates, de Man takes the opposite opinion on attunement. Derrida offers a strange glimpse of the de Manian psyche in a story he relates at the end of the memorial service address:

> On that particular night . . . we were driving through the streets of Chicago after a jazz concert. My older son, who had accompanied me, was talking with Paul about music, more precisely about musical instruments. This they were doing as the experts they both were, as techni-

cians who know how to call things by their name. It was then I realized that Paul had never told me he was an experienced musician [*avait une expérience d'instrumentiste*]. . . . The word that let me know this was the word *"âme"* [soul] when, hearing Pierre, my son, and Paul speak with familiarity of the violin's or the bass's soul, I learned that the "soul" is the name one gives in French to the small and fragile piece of wood—always very exposed, very vulnerable [*menacée*]—that is placed within the body of these instruments to support the bridge and assure the resonant communication of the two sounding boards. I didn't know why at that moment I was so strangely moved and unsettled [*obscurément bouleversé*] in some dim recess by the conversation I was listening to: no doubt it was due to the word "soul" which always speaks to us at the same time of life and of death and makes us dream of immortality, like the argument of the lyre in the *Phaedo*. (YFS 325–326)

The musical psyche that Paul and Pierre contemplate references the Pythagorean tradition. *"L'âme"* is a technical term for a device with a practical function; the soul is a "support" and a go-between, a thing that possesses only relational significance. Yet this relational role is crucial: "assur[ing] . . . resonant communication," it allows music to be produced. As part of a bridge it is, like Derrida's *"brisure,"* a kind of literalization of analogy or metaphor. It also figures the exemplary soul of deconstruction—that is, just the sort of thing that deconstruction seeks to discover: a small material crux that invisibly braces the edifice of interiority and the metaphysics of "gathering" and "recollection" that depends on it. Derrida singles out de Man's similar metaphor of allegory as "the defective cornerstone of [Hegel's] entire system" (AI 104, M 72):

We have here a figure of what some might be tempted to see as the dominant metaphorical register . . . of "deconstruction," a certain architectural rhetoric. One first locates, in an architectonics, in the art of the system, the "neglected corners" and the *"defective* cornerstone," that which, from the outset, threatens the coherence and the internal order of the construction. But it is a cornerstone! It is required by the architecture which it nevertheless, in advance, deconstructs from within. . . . As a cornerstone, it supports [the system], however rickety it may be, and brings together at a single point all its forces and tensions. It does not do this from a central commanding point, like a *keystone;* but it also does it, laterally, in its corner. (M 72, 74)

The violin's soul is a defective cornerstone because its material humility exposes the fiction of depth. It is revealed, in this psychic x-ray, behind the supplementary metaphysical soul, the image of what is missing in the human system. *L'âme* is the soul "within the body" of the violin-self, the mechanism that creates the soul-effect. Thus Derrida's remembrance of *"l'âme"* offers a picture of "interiority" appropriate to the posthumous subject of postclassical theory. There is nothing in interiority but a "small and fragile piece of wood," or, perhaps, the small and fragile *"word* 'soul.'" But in Derrida's anecdote that "nothing" is what generates emotion—Derrida's emotion, in this case, of being "strangely moved and unsettled." Derrida is moved, not in spite of the fact that the soul is a piece of wood, but because it is; the very absence of depth compels emotion. Far from being impossible without the subject, emotion is our recognition of the subject's "death."

Conclusion:
Night of the Human Subject

Although Rousseau has a way of putting things that makes them seem eccentric, his observations are often generalizable. The giant-naming scene of the *Essay* has become a recurrent reference in poststructuralist theory not because theorists have difficulty saying anything new but because it depicts a way of thinking that is significantly recurrent. In the theory of emotion giants and monsters are behind every tree.

This happens partly because fear makes a good exemplary emotion (a nice, clear emotion).[1] Sartre, for example, uses horror to argue that emotional experience comprises "an irrational synthesis of spontaneity and passivity."[2] Sartre paints a scene in which an unwanted face is forced upon the viewer—an overly strong prosopopoeia:

> Suddenly a grinning face appears flattened against the window pane; I feel invaded by terror. (*Emotions*, 82)

> There are two forms of emotion, according to whether it is we who constitute the magic of the world . . . or whether it is the world itself which abruptly reveals itself as being magical. In horror, for example, we suddenly perceive the upsetting of the deterministic barriers. That face which appears at the pane—we do not first take it as belonging to a man who might open the door and with a few steps come right up to us. On the contrary, he is given, passive as he is, as acting at a distance. He is in immediate connection, on the other side of the window, with our body; we live and undergo his signification, and it is with our own flesh that we establish it. But at the same time it obtrudes itself; it denies the

distance and enters into us. . . . The behavior which gives emotion its meaning is no longer *ours*. (*Emotions*, 85–86)

The distance is no longer perceived as distance, because it is no longer perceived as "that which must first be travelled." It is perceived as the unitary *basis* of the horrible. The window is no longer perceived as *"that which must first be opened."* It is perceived as the *frame* of the horrible face. . . . The horrible can appear only in the kind of world whose existants are magical by nature and whose possible recourse against the existants are magical. This is rather well shown in the universe of the dream where doors, locks, walls, and arms are not recourses against the menaces of the thief or the wild animal because they are perceived in a unitary act of horror. And as the act which disarms them is the same as the one which creates them, we see the murderers cross these walls and doors. (*Emotions*, 88–89)

Sartre claims that we can lapse from reason into "the original magic," a prerational emotional state (*Emotions*, 85). Like Rousseau's primitive man, we advance properties to things even though we don't perceive properties, only phenomena. This pattern is familiar from several strands of research: emotions are gun-jumping, for better and worse; in fear the incentive to jump shows itself. It may or may not be safer to see others as giants, but it is safer to see them as something— to take a guess at the riddle—than to delay decision. (This might have been evolutionarily right, as de Sousa contends, without being right today—not to mention philosophically right.) Thus some people who use fear as their emotional paradigm are instrumentalists invested in the idea that assigning emotion any lesser purpose would be unsafe.

Something remains unexplained in Sartre's scenario, though: why should a stranger's passivity drive one to terror? Sartre explicitly suspends the threat. The man who presses his face against the window "is given, passive as he is"; insofar as he acts at all, he acts "at a distance" and more is not required to terrorize. The horrible in this scene goes hand in hand with the baring of the mechanisms of ordinary perception. The grinning face not only presents itself; it presents the window as its frame and the glass as the medium of its perception. The face discloses the latent activity of the frame, the glass, and implicitly the eye, naturalized instruments of perception. The face grows monstrous by pressing against the glass, that is, by forcing the glass to show itself as something that limits as well as lets be. The face's suspension between activity and passivity is unbearable—but the fact that one's perception of any face is similarly suspended is even more unbearable. Only exposure of the "synthesis of spontaneity and passivity" in its general aspect, in the third of the three passages above, has the power to make or reveal the world to be "the kind of world whose existants are magical by nature." Defacement such as we see in Sartre's example comes through overfiguration. The effect of face is predicated on the effacement of the figuration that produces the effect; Derrida writes similarly of the Kantian "frame" that it creates form while denying itself as a form, having "as its traditional determination not that it stands out but that it disappears, buries itself, effaces itself."[3] Defacement, the self-unraveling of prosopopoeia, occurs by an overdoing that forces figuration to the foreground. Monstrosity is not so much what exceeds the frame as the possibility of glimpsing the frame as frame. The attribution of monstrosity to monsters rebounds upon us, in Sartre's illustration, when "we see the [idealized] murderers cross" our (idealized) barriers. The point is Rousseauvian—live by mental theater, die by mental theater—and may be elaborated from the monstrosity of monsters to the deadness of subjects.

When critics literalize the "death of the subject" they repeat the impulse of Rousseau's frightened man. The apparition is both dangerous and impossible: look out, here comes a dead subject, unable to make decisions or refute Nazis,[4] likely to praise bad poetry or rip your lungs out. The persistence of monstrous metaphors suggests that the nonsubject—the functional but self-differential being—needs to be seen as someone else. The device philosopher Robert Kirk uses to imagine a nonsubject is called GIANT, or Gigantic Information Acquisitor and Non-wheeled Transporter:

> It is big enough to house a lot of machinery and a lot of people. From the outside it looks to us much as Gulliver looked to the Lilliputians. Its operators ensure that it not only behaves like a gigantic human being but has all the behavioral dispositions of a human being—for they are fanatics.[5]

Not only is this plural self figured as something that would look monstrous from the outside (balanced as the figure is by the reference to Gulliver, a normal being), but Kirk's passing joke creates a second tier of monstrosities in the persons of the "fanatics" who would want to support such an creature. Not only are nonsubjects monstrous: the actual people who promote the illusion of them are, too.

Dennett observes that philosophy has been preoccupied with what it calls "zombies":

> According to common agreement among philosophers, a zombie is or would be a human being who exhibits perfectly natural, alert, loquacious, vivacious behavior but is in fact not conscious at all, but rather some sort of automaton. The whole point of the philosopher's notion of zombie is that you can't tell a zombie from a natural person by examining external behavior. Since that is all we ever get to see of our friends and neighbors, *some of your best friends may be zombies.* (*Consciousness Explained,* 73)[6]

Dennett angles "the zombie problem," not in the usual way, to prove that our friends can't be zombies, but to show that if there were zombies they would deserve our friendship. He contends that with "a control system that permits recursive self-representation," a zombie that "began to 'communicate' with others and with itself . . . would become equipped with the very sorts of states . . . that suffice for consciousness" even if there were no one else "in" the zombie to receive the representations (*Consciousness Explained,* 311, 313). Recourse to "the zombie problem" is wrong even when—especially when—it is used to arrive at the (preformed) conclusion that no one is a zombie. Dennett's point is that no one needs *not* to be a zombie: "Are zombies possible? They're not just possible, they're actual. We're all zombies. Nobody is conscious—not in the systematically mysterious way that supports such doctrines as epiphenomenalism" (*Consciousness Explained,* 406).

Dead subjects are the zombies of literature departments. Thus Steven Shaviro regards the walking dead in George Romero's films—ex-humans who seem to need and act affectlessly—as postmodern figures of capitalistic life-in-death. Shaviro's discussion recalls Jameson's reflections on postmodern selfhood as a posthumous condition:

> These strange beings, at once alive and dead, grotesquely literal and blatantly artificial, cannot be encompassed by any ordinary logic of representation. In their compulsive, wavering, deorganicized movements, the zombies are *allegorical.* . . . They are allegorical in the sense that allegory always implies the loss or death of its object.[7]

This passage again substitutes the image of the corpse for the concept of self-difference. Self-differential selves are dead only *as* subjects; they are not dead as self-differential selves. Their apparent deadness is an artifact of our imposition upon them of the impossible expectation of subjectivity, just as the philosophical possibility of zombies is an artifact of the impossible expectation of "Central Meaners" (*Consciousness Explained*, 238). To put it another way, the abundance of zombies and dead subjects in philosophy and theory could not exist without an equal abundance of pineal glands, sovereign powers, "Oval Office[s] of the brain" (*Consciousness Explained*, 106), and so on. The subject, like these other plenipotentiaries, is always someone else, someone pushed back across a regress. There would be no living dead if there were no "rational homunculi" (de Sousa's term for "simplified model[s] of rational agent[s]").[8] The executive mirrors the zombie as ideality in Husserl's phenomenology mirrors the "merely" empirical.

We can advance still further. A living system is self-differential; experience is experience of self-differentiality. The idea of emotion is as compelling as it is because in the honest moments of philosophy it has served as the name of that experience. On some level everyone knows that rationality may be where we want to be, but emotion is where we are. So when we want to get from where we are to where we want to be, emotion has got to come along. If we lose it along the way there is no continuity; self-differentiality will not have been convincingly resolved. That's why the living dead emblematize postmodern subjectivity: everyone knows that if there's one thing dead subjects don't have, it's emotion. Actually things are the other way around. Romero's living dead are notably undivided about their desires, or rather, because their desires are undivided, they are mere needs and compulsions. They waver physiologically—as though their nervous systems had trouble working—but not intentionally. They don't think twice about anything; they are pure intentionality, directional in one direction at a time. A living system is self-differential; only self-differential entities—"texts"—feel. Romero's zombies have no feelings *because they are subjects*. They do not represent the poststructuralist post-human; they represent the "death of the subject" in the strongly genitive sense, the sense in which if there were subjects, they would have to be dead. A well-known counterillustration is convenient here. Dennett's position on zombies resembles Philip K. Dick's treatment of "replicants." In the film *Bladerunner* the explicitly sentimental moment for the replicant played by Sean Young—the one time she cries—is the moment when she discovers she's a replicant, whose memories are not her own. We assume that she has had feelings before, but reserving the sight of her tears for this occasion dramatizes the fact that destroying the illusion of subjectivity does not destroy emotion, that on the contrary, emotion is the sign of the absence of that illusion. *Bladerunner* comes to the conclusion of the postmodern Cartesian narrative: the detective protagonist Deckert (Descartes) realizes that subjectivity must go and emotion must stay. Unlike replicants, zombies don't experience themselves as though they were someone else. It is perversely to such beings alone—to subjects—that we have ascribed emotion. Perhaps Rousseau's primitive man is panicked most of all by the idea that the stranger coming over the horizon may be, finally, a human subject—as he knows himself, being frightened, not to be. A real subject would be really frightening; if I thought I saw one coming, I too would run away.

Notes

Introduction

1. Fredric Jameson, *Postmodernism, or, the Logic of Late Capitalism* (Durham: Duke University Press, 1991), 10. Although poststructuralism and postmodernism are different concepts, Jameson's discussion of postmodernism here reflects the most widespread critical assumptions about poststructuralist emotion as well.
2. Manfred Frank, *What Is Neostructuralism?* [1984], trans. Sabine Wilke and Richard Gray (Minneapolis: University of Minnesota Press, 1989), 10.
3. Joseph Frank, "Dialogical Introduction" to the symposium "A Turn away from 'Language'?" *Common Knowledge* 4 (1995): 24.
4. Luc Ferry and Alain Renaut, *French Philosophy of the Sixties: An Essay on Antihumanism* [1985], trans. Mary H. S. Cattani (Amherst: University of Massachusetts Press, 1990), 29. Ferry and Renaut quote Althusser, "Sur le rapport de Marx et de Hegel," in *Lenine et la philosophie* (Paris: F. Maspero, 1969), 84–86.
5. Responding to Derrida's reflections upon the "torment" that de Man must have experienced, Jon Wiener remarks, "deconstruction is ill-suited to make such judgments about character and psychology" ("The Responsibilities of Friendship: Jacques Derrida on Paul de Man's Collaboration," *Critical Inquiry* 15 [1989]: 802). See also Jeffrey Mehlman, "Prosopopoeia Revisited," *Romanic Review* 81 (1990): 138. In her history of masculine political sentiment, Julie Ellison asserts that "during the heyday of poststructuralist speculation" emotion was "everywhere . . . except in the individual author, reader, or lyric speaker." She finds Derrida's interest in sentiment in the *Politics of Friendship* a contrast to his earlier interests: "In the nineties, even Derrida evokes the cultural history of masculine sensibility" *(Cato's Tears and the Making of Anglo-American Emotion* [Chicago: University of Chicago Press, 1999], 5).

6. Jerome J. McGann, *The Romantic Ideology: A Critical Investigation* (Chicago: University of Chicago Press, 1983); Terry Eagleton, *The Ideology of the Aesthetic* (Oxford: Blackwell, 1990).

7. See Robert M. Gordon, "The Passivity of Emotions," *Philosophical Review* 95 (1986): 371–392.

8. Among the philosophers who make such classifications are Descartes, Kant, and Spinoza, whose efforts will be discussed later; but grouping into passive and active emotions is common. Massimo Cacciari points out the biparite organization of emotions in Robert Musil's *Man without Qualities,* and reads it as "a sign of the unreconcilable and double" (*Posthumous People: Vienna at the Turning Point* [1980], trans. Rodger Friedman [Stanford: Stanford University Press, 1996], 199). For Cacciari, Musil's scheme resonates with Heidegger's theory of moods: "Emotions appear to Ulrich in two fundamental types: those that develop in an exterior sense and those of an interior sense." The former are goal-directed, the latter, "by contrast, inactive," yet the former "discharge their strength at their targets" while "the *Stimmung* that flows over every object" endures (196–197).

9. Paul Ricoeur, *Freedom and Nature: The Voluntary and the Involuntary* [1949], trans. Erazim V. Kohák (Evanston: Northwestern University Press, 1966), 21.

10. David S. Hiley, *Philosophy in Question: Essays on a Pyrrhonian Theme* (Chicago: University of Chicago Press, 1988), 25.

11. Paul de Man, *Allegories of Reading: Figural Language in Rousseau, Nietzsche, Rilke, and Proust* (New Haven: Yale University Press, 1979), 35. (Hereafter AR.)

12. Roland Barthes, *The Pleasure of the Text* [1973], trans. Richard Howard (New York: Farrar, Straus & Giroux, 1975), 25.

13. Lawrence Grossberg, *We Gotta Get Out of This Place: Popular Conservatism and Postmodern Culture* (New York: Routledge, 1992), 81.

14. Feminist literary studies include Nancy Armstrong, *Desire and Domestic Fiction: A Political History of the Novel* (Oxford: Oxford University Press, 1987); Elizabeth Barnes, *States of Sympathy: Seduction and Democracy in the American Novel* (New York: Columbia University Press, 1997); Ann Cvetkovich, *Mixed Feelings: Feminism, Mass Culture and Victorian Sensationalism* (New Brunswick, N.J.: Rutgers University Press, 1992); Ellison, *Cato's Tears and the Making of Anglo-American Emotion;* Julia Stern, *The Plight of Feeling: Sympathy and Dissent in the Early American Novel* (Chicago: University of Chicago Press, 1997); and Jane Tompkins, "Criticism and Feeling," *College English* 39 (1977): 169–178. Philosophical approaches include Sandra Harding and Merrill B. Hintikka, eds., *Discovering Reality: Feminist Perspectives on Epistemology, Metaphysics, Methodology, and Philosophy of Science* (Dordrecht: D. Reidel, 1983); Alison M. Jaggar, "Love and Knowledge: Emotion in Feminist Epistemology," in *Gender/Body/Knowledge: Feminist Reconstructions of Knowing and Being,* ed. Alison M.

Jaggar and Susan Bordo (New Brunswick, N.J.: Rutgers University Press, 1989); and Genevieve Lloyd, *The Man of Reason: "Male" and "Female" in Western Philosophy,* 2nd ed. (Minneapolis: University of Minnesota Press, 1993).

15. Erica Harth, *Cartesian Women: Versions and Subversions of Rational Discourse in the Old Regime* (Ithaca, N.Y.: Cornell University Press, 1992), 83. See also Susan Bordo, *The Flight to Objectivity: Essays on Cartesianism and Culture* (Albany: SUNY Press, 1987), and Catherine Clément, *Syncope: The Philosophy of Rapture* [1990], trans. Sally O'Driscoll and Deirdre M. Mahoney (Minneapolis: University of Minnesota Press, 1994), 34.

16. René Descartes, *The Passions of the Soul,* in *The Philosophical Writings of Descartes,* 3 vols., trans. John Cottingham, Robert Stoothoff, and Dugald Murdoch (Cambridge: Cambridge University Press, 1985), 1:335.

17. Ronald de Sousa, *The Rationality of Emotion* (Cambridge: MIT Press, 1987), 50. (Hereafter RE.)

18. See especially Catherine Gallagher, *Nobody's Story: The Vanishing Acts of Women Writers in the Literary Marketplace* (Berkeley and Los Angeles: University of California Press, 1994); Deidre Lynch, *The Economy of Character: Novels, Market Culture, and the Business of Inner Meaning* (Chicago: University of Chicago Press, 1998); Adela Pinch, *Strange Fits of Passion: Emotional Epistemologies from Hume to Austen* (Stanford: Stanford University Press, 1996); and Yopie Prins, *Victorian Sappho* (Princeton: Princeton University Press, 1999).

19. Note the double-edged effect of anxiety as relief and displeasure, warning of danger and paralysis in the face of danger, in Sigmund Freud, "Inhibitions, Symptoms, and Anxiety," *Standard Edition of the Complete Psychological Works,* ed. and trans. James Strachey, 24 vols. (London: Hogarth, 1953–1974), 19:87–172.

20. Sigmund Freud, "Negation," *Standard Edition,* 19:235–240.

21. Michel Foucault, *The History of Sexuality,* vol. 1: *An Introduction* [1976], trans. Robert Hurley (New York: Vintage, 1990), 11.

22. Slavoj Žižek, *The Ticklish Subject: The Absent Centre of Political Ontology* (London: Verso, 1999), 289. Žižek refers to Judith Butler's *Psychic Life of Power: Theories in Subjection* (Stanford: Stanford University Press, 1997).

23. Jacques Derrida, "'Eating Well': An Interview" with Jean-Luc Nancy, in *Who Comes after the Subject?,* ed. Eduardo Cadava, Peter Connor, and Jean-Luc Nancy (New York: Routledge, 1991), 103–104.

24. Thomas Keenan, *Fables of Responsibility: Aberrations and Predicaments in Ethics and Politics* (Stanford: Stanford University Press, 1997), 175.

25. James R. Averill, "Inner Feelings, Works of the Flesh, the Beast Within, Diseases of the Mind, Driving Force, and Putting on a Show: Six Metaphors of Emotion and Their Theoretical Extensions." In *Metaphors in the History of Psychology,* ed. David E. Leary (Cambridge: Cambridge University Press, 1990), 107.

26. Mikel Dufrenne, *The Phenomenology of Aesthetic Experience* [1953], trans. Edward S. Casey, Albert A. Anderson, Willis Domingo, and Leon Jacobson (Evanston: Northwestern University Press, 1973), 455.

27. Contemporary scholarship does not consider itself indebted to phenomenology any more than it considers itself reliant on expression. I do not see much evidence that scholarship's image of itself is accurate in this respect. In a recent book Stanley Corngold draws on Stephan Strasser's *Phenomenology of Feeling* (1977) to claim the union of intellect and feeling in literature. Corngold states that "the purpose of such a claim is not to restore to feeling the authority it allegedly lost to reason at the beginning of the social contract" (*Complex Pleasure: Forms of Feeling in German Literature* [Stanford: Stanford University Press, 1998], xiii). Rather, its explicit purpose is to disable criticisms of the human subject: "What I want to stress is the fecklessness of postulating any such thing as the 'inhuman' of literary language—we have no access to it!—and on the other hand, the necessity of conceiving interpretation as an imaginative correlation of affects" (9). Subjectivity and feeling pay each other under the table—or in this case, over the table—in the expressive hypothesis.

28. Paul de Man, *The Rhetoric of Romanticism* (New York: Columbia University Press, 1984), 255. (Hereafter RR.)

29. I'm particularly worried about insistence on intellectual pleasure at a time of tension and economic pressure. See Martha Banta's editor's column, "Mental Work, Metal Work," in *PMLA* 113 (1998): 199–211, and my response, "Passion and Mental Work," *PMLA* 114 (1999): 99. I'm grateful to Susan Rosenbaum for her conversation on this topic.

1. Cogito and the History of the Passions

1. See Corngold, *Complex Pleasure*, 12; Wiener, "The Responsibilities of Friendship," 802; Mehlman, "Prosopopoeia Revisited," 138. Charles Bernheimer notes the "lack of affective language in deconstructive discourse" (*Flaubert and Kafka: Studies in Psychopoetic Structure* [New Haven: Yale University Press, 1982], 4). Martha Nussbaum makes a similar point more dramatically: "'Of all that is written,' says Zarathrustra, 'I love only what a man has written with his blood.' After reading Derrida, and not Derrida alone, I feel a certain hunger for blood; for, that is, writing about literature that talks of human lives and choices as if they matter to us all" (*Love's Knowledge: Essays on Philosophy and Literature* [Oxford: Oxford University Press, 1990], 171).

2. Jacques Derrida, "White Mythology: Metaphor in the Text of Philosophy," in *Margins of Philosophy* [1972], trans. Alan Bass (Chicago: University of Chicago Press, 1982), 207–272.

3. A close analogue to this position is Kristeva's notion of the "*subject in process . . . as is the case in the practice of the text*" (*Revolution in Poetic*

Language [1974], trans. Margaret Waller [New York: Columbia University Press, 1984], 37).

4. I thank Arthemy Vladimirovich Magun for calling my attention to this passage and to the importance of puppets in philosophy.

5. Michael Stocker with Elizabeth Hegeman, *Valuing Emotions* (Cambridge: Cambridge University Press, 1996), 26.

6. Paul Griffiths, *What Emotions Really Are: The Problem of Psychological Categories* (Chicago: University of Chicago Press, 1997), 2.

7. Stanley Schacter and J. E. Singer, "Cognitive, Social, and Physiological Determinants of Emotional State," *Psychological Review* 69 (1962): 379–399.

8. Amélie Oksenberg Rorty, "Explaining Emotions," in *Explaining Emotions,* ed. Amélie Oksenberg Rorty (Berkeley and Los Angeles: University of California Press, 1980), 105.

9. Robert C. Solomon, "Emotions and Choice," in Rorty, ed., *Explaining Emotions,* 274. For a theory of emotions as combinations of affects and beliefs, see Patricia Greenspan, *Emotions and Reasons: An Inquiry into Emotional Justification* (New York: Routledge, 1984).

10. Helen Nissenbaum, *Emotion and Focus* (Stanford: Center for the Study of Language and Information, 1985), 8.

11. Edmund Husserl, *Logical Investigations,* 2nd ed. [1913–1921], 2 vols., trans. J. N. Findlay (New York: Humanities Press, 1970), Fifth Investigation, §15.

12. John McDowell, *Mind and World* (Cambridge: Harvard University Press, 1996), 4, 6.

13. R. B. Zajonc and Hazel Markus, "Affect and Cognition: The Hard Interface," in *Emotions, Cognition, and Behavior,* ed. Carroll E. Izard, Jerome Kagan, and Robert B. Zajonc (Cambridge: Cambridge University Press, 1984), 73.

14. The discourse of emotion suggests that affective information "must be encoded and processed . . . in very much the same way as any other information that comes through the senses" (ibid., 76).

15. Kendall Walton, for example, argues that fictional objects are not the targets of the emotions fiction inspires (*Mimesis as Make-Believe: On the Foundations of the Representational Arts* [Cambridge: Harvard University Press, 1990]).

16. Adela Pinch locates a similar topos in Hume's *A Treatise of Human Nature,* arguing that "the lesson about the relationship between persons and passions in the *Treatise* is that feeling may always be vicarious, something we generate in attributing it to another figure" (*Strange Fits of Passion,* 43–44). Derrida's implication is that I myself am one of those other figures.

17. See Michel Foucault, *The Order of Things: An Archaeology of the Human Sciences* [1966], trans. Alan Sheridan (New York: Vintage, 1994), 322–328; Jean-Luc Nancy, "Dum Scribo," trans. Ian MacLeod, *Oxford Literary Review* 3 (1978): 6–21; and post-poststructuralist Slavoj Žižek, "The Cartesian

Subject versus the Cartesian Theater," in *Cogito and the Unconscious,* ed. Slavoj Žižek (Durham: Duke University Press, 1998), 247–274. Claudia Brodsky Lacour argues that Descartes conceives thought as the non-representational activity of drawing a line, the pure extension of the "I," but that this drawing must also "take place by way of discourse, writing which conceals its own status as line in its intelligibility as representation" (*Lines of Thought: Discourse, Architectonics, and the Origin of Modern Philosophy* [Durham, N.C.: Duke University Press, 1996], 8).

18. Husserl's *Cartesian Meditations* are unusual in that they often strive to unfold subjectivity from the phenomenology of the cogito; thus Husserl recapitulates Cartesian paradoxes.

19. Jacques Derrida, "Cogito and the History of Madness," in *Writing and Difference* [1967], trans. Alan Bass (Chicago: University of Chicago Press, 1978), 45, 55.

20. Many have noted that the ego of the cogito is a mere grammatical placeholder, an empty subject that logically precedes experience. This topos is prominent in *Who Comes after the Subject?,* a collection of essays generated by Jean-Luc Nancy's title question. Nancy writes that "what is posed here as the question of an 'after' (in history) is just as much a question of the 'before' (in the logic of being)" (introduction to *Who Comes after the Subject?,* ed. Eduardo Cadava, Peter Connor, and Jean-Luc Nancy [New York: Routledge, 1991], 6).

21. René Descartes, *Discourse on Method* [1637], in *Philosophical Writings of Descartes,* 1:127.

22. Vincent Descombes, "Apropos of the 'Critique of the Subject' and of the Critique of this Critique," in Cadava, Connor, and Nancy, *Who Comes after the Subject?* 125.

23. Arthur Danto, "Historical Language and Historical Reality," *Review of Metaphysics* 27 (1973): 219–259, quoted in Hiley, *Philosophy in Question,* 129.

24. Foucault's conclusion here is closer to Derrida's criticism of *Madness and Civilization* than to the reading of Descartes that appears in his response to Derrida's criticism.

25. Foucault registers Derrida's immersion in emotion by implying in his counter-response that Derrida's Descartes "behaves . . . like a madman in a panic at universal error," while his own behaves like a "cunning adversary, always alert, constantly rational" ("My Body, This Paper, This Fire" [1972], trans. Geoffrey Bennington, *Oxford Literary Review* 4 [1979]: 26).

26. Jean-Luc Marion, *Cartesian Questions* (Chicago: University of Chicago Press, 1999), 105–117.

27. Friedrich Nietzsche, *The Twilight of the Idols* [1889], trans. R. J. Hollingdale, 2nd ed. (Harmondsworth: Penguin Books, 1990), 47.

28. Jacques Derrida, *Speech and Phenomena and Other Essays on Husserl's Theory of Signs* [1967], trans. David B. Allison (Evanston: Northwestern University Press, 1973), 14. (Hereafter SP.)

29. Edmund Husserl, *The Phenomenology of Internal Time-Consciousness* [1905], ed. Martin Heidegger, trans. James S. Churchill (Bloomington: Indiana University Press, 1964), 131, quoted in SP 83. See also Martin Heidegger, *Being and Time* [1927–1957], trans. John Macquarrie and Edward Robinson (New York: Harper & Row, 1962), 195.

30. On Husserl's view of emotion, and for a comparison between Husserl and existential philosophers on this point, see W. George Turski, *Toward a Rationality of Emotions: An Essay in the Philosophy of Mind* (Athens: Ohio University Press, 1994), 30–34.

31. Rodolphe Gasché, *The Tain of the Mirror* (Cambridge: Harvard University Press, 1987), 231.

32. Jacques Derrida, *Of Grammatology* [1967], trans. Gayatri Chakravorty Spivak (Baltimore: Johns Hopkins University Press, 1976), 165–166. (Hereafter G.)

33. The erotic undercurrent in talk about expression brings to mind a gendered explanation for the dominance of the expressive hypothesis. In this light Derrida's critique of Husserl enacts the violent finale of a competitive sexual drama.

34. Husserl's example echoes moralist notions of inner speech in which interior address is not exceptional, but typical. Žižek notes that Dennett's "brief account of the evolutionary emergence of self-consciousness" in *Consciousness Explained* similarly "relies on G. H. Mead's famous account [of] how Self emerges from social interaction (from acts of imagining how I appear to another subject and from 'internalizing' the other's view: in my 'conscience,' I perform imaginatively, in 'silent inner speech,' the possible reproaches that others may voice against my acts, etc.)" ("Cartesian Subject versus the Cartesian Theater," 264–265). See also Butler's thoughts on reflexivity and "self-beratement" (*Psychic Life of Power*, 186, 188–189).

35. Ludwig Wittgenstein, *Philosophical Investigations*, 3rd ed., trans. G. E. M. Anscombe (New York: Macmillan, 1958), 191. Wittgenstein's reasoning—that having to collect information on oneself is madness—is common. Thus schizophrenia seems to be the maddest madness of all. Dennett and Kathleen A. Akins, responding wittily to an article on schizophrenia, cite its statement that "goals concurrent with verbal imagery do not seem to be communication goals (unless we must for some reason communicate with ourselves)." Dennett and Akins suggest that "there is in fact a lot to be said for the hypothesis that much of what is called thinking is a sort of verbal communicating to oneself, or, more provocatively, a form of communicating within oneself." "When *normal* people have verbal imagery, they form (self)-communicative goals," but "when schizophrenics attempt to engage in this familiar practice" they execute their own goals poorly enough that "the discordance . . . cannot be interpreted away as an accident or a slip, a low-level malfunction. . . . Indeed, because the images are voices, they are interpreted as speech acts; they are irresistibly interpreted as intended. And if I don't intend to say these things, then someone else must. The result: one 'hears

voices.'" Dennett and Akins assert the irresistibility of intentional ascription, but also imply that if we didn't have such a deep predilection to believe that *intentions are voiced and voices must be intentional,* we would not experience discordance in our own mental language as "hear[ing] voices" ("Who May I Say Is Calling?" *Behavioral and Brain Sciences* 9 [1986]: 517–518).

36. Edmund Husserl, *Ideas: General Introduction to Pure Phenomenology* [1922], 2 vols., trans. W. R. Boyce Gibson (London: Allen and Unwin, 1931), I §7, quoted in SP 70.

37. J. L. Austin, *How to Do Things with Words,* 2nd ed., ed. J. O. Urmson and Marina Sbisà (Cambridge: Harvard University Press, 1975), 22.

38. As Robert Smith observes, Derrida links this figure to the inner ear (*Derrida and Autobiography* [Cambridge: Cambridge University Press, 1995], 95).

39. The formulation is redundant: there can be no experience of the perfectly transparent.

40. Henry Staten, "Derrida and the Affect of Self," *Western Humanities Review* 50 (1997): 351. My thanks to David Wayne Thomas for this reference.

41. Immanuel Kant, *Critique of Judgment* [1790], trans. Werner S. Pluhar (Indianapolis: Hackett, 1987), 109. Kant invokes the distinction between affects and emotions on the one hand and excessive, compulsive passions on the other, barring passions, but not affects, from sublimity: "for while in an affect the mind's freedom is *impeded,* in passion it is abolished" (*Critique of Judgment,* 132n39). I will return to this passage in the next chapter.

42. Neil Hertz, "Dr. Johnson's Forgetfulness, Descartes's Piece of Wax," *Eighteenth-Century Life* 16 (1992): 174.

43. In a footnote to *Speech and Phenomena* Derrida explains that to make his argument easier to follow, he has "generally abstained from comparisons, reconciliations, or oppositions which seem to impose themselves . . . between Husserl's phenomenology and other theories, ancient or modern, of signification" (SP 4n2). We are now in a position to infer what some of those unwritten "comparisons" might have been.

44. Jean-Jacques Rousseau, *Oeuvres complètes,* ed. Bernard Gagnebin and Marcel Raymond (Paris: Gallimard, 1959), 1:109, quoted in G 151. Henceforward the *Oeuvres complètes* are cited as OCR, followed by volume and page number. When quoting Spivak's translation of *Of Grammatology,* as here, I quote the various English translations of Rousseau that she uses. Because these are many and various, however, I continue to cite page numbers of the *Oeuvres complètes.* The relevant English translations are listed in the bibliography.

45. Michael Fried, *Absorption and Theatricality: Painting and Beholder in the Age of Diderot* (Berkeley and Los Angeles: University of California Press, 1980), 167–168. David Marshall agrees that "the issue for Rousseau finally is not whether *a* theater should be established but whether theater (in its many manifestations) can be avoided at all" (*The Surprising Effects of Sympathy: Marivaux, Diderot, Rousseau, and Mary Shelley* [Chicago: University of Chicago Press, 1988], 136).

46. This is not to say that Husserl thinks what Rousseau thinks of imagination; see SP 52–55.

47. "So little does poetry depend for its effect on the power of raising sensible images, that I am convinced it would lose a very considerable part of its energy, if this were the necessary result of all description. Because that union of affecting words which is the most powerful of all poetical instruments, would frequently lose its force along with its propriety and consistency, if the sensible images were always excited" (Edmund Burke, *A Philosophical Enquiry into the Origin of Our Ideas of the Sublime and Beautiful* [1759] [Oxford: Oxford University Press, 1990], 155).

48. Winfried Menninghaus, *In Praise of Nonsense: Kant and Bluebeard* [1995], trans. Henry Pickford (Stanford: Stanford University Press, 1999), 2.

49. On this point see Derrida's *Dissemination* [1972], trans. Barbara Johnson (Chicago: University of Chicago Press, 1981), 198, 219n31, 233–234, 324–329. (Hereafter D.)

50. Aristotle, *The Art of Rhetoric*, trans. H. C. Lawson-Tancred (Harmondsworth: Penguin, 1991), §2.8. See also the *Poetics*, trans. Richard Janko (Indianapolis: Hackett, 1987), §4.1.2, which contrasts pity, a possibly aesthetic emotion, to shock, mere visceral reaction.

51. "Without imagination," as Derrida puts it, "pity does not awaken of itself in humanity, is not accessible to passion, language, and representation" (G 185).

52. Rousseau also claims that emotion follows the development of language. Imagination is a language that "speaks" to civilized but not to "savage hearts." While feeling is silent, emotion speaks and can only speak: "It is neither hunger nor thirst but love, hatred, pity, anger, which drew from [us] the first words," Rousseau writes in the *Essay* (OCR 5:380). Thus in Derrida "passion, language, and representation" go together (G 185); "language is born of the imagination which arouses or at any rate excites sentiment or passion" (G 183), while *"only the spoken word has the power of expressing or exciting passion"* (G 239; my italics). This striking restriction, this "only," sounds radical but makes sense in Rousseau's parabolic civilization, which climbs from animal affect to a peak of civilization, emotion, and speech, then slides down a slope of passion and writing. Rousseau illustrates this parabola with a hierarchy of aesthetic media in which verbal and sonic arts outdo the merely visual on the one side and the written on the other (G 239). As we know, something untouched by imagination—like thoughtlessly graphic dramaturgy—affects but doesn't move to emotion. The "only" is achieved along the arc of Rousseau's historical logic: a phenomenon that has followed imagination and hence emotion to their summit but not over it will move us through the spoken word. Rousseau's imagination "surmounts animality and arouses human passion only by opening the scene and space of theatrical representation" (G 185).

Foucault argues for a similar economy of pathos in *The History of Sexuality:* sex is not regulated simply through the prohibition of sexual discourse;

policing power "entail[s] effects that may be those of refusal, blockage, and invalidation, but also incitement and intensification" (*History of Sexuality,* 1:11). Foucault points out that ideality and formality—the values of civilizing language and emotion over instinctual affect—are brought to support love for boys in classical Greece and Rome: the "main argument against love for women is that it is nothing more than a natural inclination" (*History of Sexuality,* vol. 3: *The Care of the Self* [1984], trans. Robert Hurley [New York: Vintage, 1986], 199).

53. Paul de Man, *Blindness and Insight: Essays in the Rhetoric of Contemporary Criticism* [1971, 1983], 2nd ed. (Minneapolis: University of Minnesota Press, 1983), 132. (Hereafter BI.)

54. The point is not that in the theater, Alexander feels freer to reveal his emotions—if he felt easy about showing his feelings, he would dare to go to plays. He seems rather to worry that in the theater he is more likely to feel emotions in the first place, or at least to feel them more intensely and so have more to suppress, for the very reason that he knows those emotions are imaginative: "if theatrical imitations draw forth more tears than would the presence of the objects imitated, it is less because the emotions are feebler and do not reach the level of pain . . . than because they are pure and without mixture of anxiety for ourselves" (OCR 5:23).

55. David Marshall, *The Figure of Theater: Shaftesbury, Defoe, Adam Smith, and George Eliot* (New York: Columbia University Press, 1986), 38.

56. Daniel C. Dennett, *Consciousness Explained* (Boston: Little, Brown, 1991), 132.

57. Jerrold Levinson, *The Pleasures of Aesthetics: Philosophical Essays* (Ithaca, N.Y.: Cornell University Press, 1996), 115.

58. E. M. Dadlez, *What's Hecuba to Him? Fictional Events and Actual Emotions* (University Park: Pennsylvania State University Press, 1997), 3, 22.

59. The reception of Kendall Walton's *Mimesis as Make-Believe* (1990) reveals the extent to which philosophers perceive a conflict between imagination and the rest of life. As Walton notes in an interesting postscript to his book, commentators "concentrated on [his] negative claim that it is not literally true . . . that appreciators fear, fear for, pity, grieve for, or admire purely fictitious characters" ("Spelunking, Simulation, and Slime: On Being Moved by Fiction," in *Emotion and the Arts,* ed. Mette Hjort and Sue Laver [Oxford: Oxford University Press, 1997], 38). Because Walton wrote that these emotions were imaginary and called them "quasi," his readers assumed he meant that they were not genuine, not fully affective, and confined to aesthetic experience; the many who protested did so because they thought that everyday nonfactual emotions would now have to be "quasi" as well. Walton replies, "My make-believe theory was designed to help explain our emotional responses to fiction, not to call their very existence into question. My negative claim is *only* that our genuine emotional responses to works of fiction do not involve, literally, fearing, grieving-for, admiring fictional characters"

("Spelunking," 38). Rather like Rousseau, in fact, Walton contends that "our responses to works of fiction are, not uncommonly, more highly charged emotionally than our reactions to actual situations" ("Spelunking," 38) and that his theory "allows us to see fiction as continuous with the rest of life" ("Spelunking," 46). Walton's audience missed the point that his imaginary emotions were also genuine because they were so invested in believing that nonaesthetic experiences are not imaginary.

60. Richard Moran, "The Expression of Feeling in Imagination," *Philosophical Review* 103 (1994): 93.

61. To put it another way, the signifier of the passion is literal, but not of the passion.

62. Geoffrey Bennington, "Derridabase," in Jacques Derrida and Geoffrey Bennington, *Jacques Derrida* [1991], trans. Geoffrey Bennington (Chicago: University of Chicago Press, 1993), 65. Bennington illustrates emotion that may be mistaken with the example of embarrassment: embarrassment seems to be both the emotion mistaken and the emotion that would result from making a mistake—as though the mistake were already proleptically made. Emotion's gun-jumping character will return in Chapters 2 and 3.

63. A parallel passage appears in *Speech and Phenomena*: "While it cannot be doubted that, for Husserl, writing is *indicative* in its own sphere, it poses a formidable problem. . . . For in supposing that writing is indicative in the sense that he gives to the term, it has a strange privilege which endangers all the essential distinctions: in phonetic writing . . . what it would 'indicate' would be an 'expression,' whereas in nonphonetic writing it would take the place of expressive discourse and immediately connect with the 'meaning'" (SP 27n1).

64. Ludwig Wittgenstein, *Tractatus Logico-Philosophicus* [1921], trans. D. F. Pears and B. F. McGuinness (London: Routledge & Kegan Paul, 1961), §4.1212.

65. Jacques Derrida, *The Post Card: From Socrates to Freud and Beyond* [1980], trans. Alan Bass (Chicago: University of Chicago Press, 1987), 12.

66. Jacques Derrida, "Passions: An Oblique Offering," trans. David Wood, in *Derrida: A Critical Reader,* ed. David Wood (Oxford: Blackwell, 1992), 21. For further thoughts on passion and différance, see two readings of Derrida's 1967 essay "Ellipsis": Richard Klein, "The Blindness of Hyperboles: The Ellipses of Insight," *Diacritics* 3 (1974): 33–44, and Jean-Luc Nancy, "Elliptical Sense," trans. Peter Connor, in *Derrida: A Critical Reader,* ed. David Wood (Oxford: Blackwell, 1992), 36–51.

67. Philosophical studies frequently acknowledge that we can't say what we mean by "emotion" and that "emotion" may not exist as a proper category. See RE 19; Rorty, "Explaining Emotions," 1 and 3; Griffiths, *What Emotions Really Are,* 171–201; and Leslie Brothers, *Friday's Footprint: How Society Shapes the Human Mind* (Oxford: Oxford University Press, 1997), 111–125.

68. Butler seems to argue for such a reconception when she asserts that "subjectivity consists precisely" in a "fundamental dependency on a discourse we never chose but that, paradoxically, initiates and sustains our agency" (*Psychic Life of Power*, 2). Butler may mean that subjectivity and agency always only begin to be instituted, that subjectivity consists in its emergence (see also Etienne Balibar, "Subjection and Subjectivation," in *Supposing the Subject*, ed. Joan Copjec [London: Verso, 1994], 1–15). This is not what I mean to suggest when I write that "being Cartesian consists in practice in trying to be Cartesian" (and the like). I mean that because this is so, we have never been Cartesian.

69. Dianne F. Sadoff, review of Cathy Caruth, *Unclaimed Experience: Trauma, Narrative, and History* and John O'Neill, ed., *Freud and the Passions*, *South Atlantic Review* 62 (1992): 107.

70. I quote Richard Wolin's reasoning regarding Derrida's ideas of "otherness, heterogeneity, alterity, and the like" (*The Terms of Cultural Criticism: The Frankfurt School, Existentialism, Poststructuralism* [New York: Columbia University Press, 1992], 205).

2. Pathos (Allegories of Emotion)

1. De Man's fame as a "cold" theorist makes him particularly resistant to the thesis that emotion bears out poststructuralist theories of experience. One could argue that if *his* work yields to such an emotive scheme, the same may easily be true for other theorists.

2. Eric Santner, *Stranded Objects: Mourning, Memory, and Film in Postwar Germany* (Ithaca, N.Y.: Cornell University Press, 1990), 26–29.

3. References to de Man's supposed emotionlessness are voluminous. Alice Kaplan charges that de Man failed his students by burying the emotional basis of his own scholarship (*French Lessons: A Memoir* [Chicago: University of Chicago Press, 1993]). William Flesch writes that "beyond the limit of the human de Man describes a kind of crystalline purity of intentionless, affectless language" ("Ancestral Voices: De Man and His Defenders," in *Responses: On Paul de Man's Wartime Journalism*, ed. Werner Hamacher, Neil Hertz, and Thomas Keenan [Lincoln: University of Nebraska Press, 1989], 175; hereafter R). Gary Wihl believes that de Man uses emotional terminology "only if it can be purged of any affective overtones with regard to the human subject" (*The Contingency of Theory: Pragmatism, Expressivism, and Deconstruction* [New Haven: Yale University Press, 1994], 161).

4. Lindsay Waters, "Professah de Man—He Dead," *American Literary History* 7 (1995): 292. Waters revises his view of de Manian emotion in "On Paul de Man's Effort to Re-Anchor a True Aesthetics in Our Feelings," *Boundary 2* 26 (1999): 133–156.

5. A similar but less skeptical thesis is developed by Algirdas Julien Greimas and Jacques Fontanille, *The Semiotics of Passions: From States of Affairs to States of Feelings* [1991], trans. Paul Perron and Frank Collins (Minneapolis:

University of Minnesota Press, 1993). Greimas and Fontanille contend that in feeling, "the subject . . . reorganizes [the world] figuratively in his own way." This motive "explains . . . the unfolding of figurativity, the 'representational' character of all passional manifestation" (xxv).

6. Brian Caraher, "*Allegories of Reading:* Positing a Rhetoric of Romanticism; or, Paul de Man's Critique of Pure Figural Anteriority," *Pre/Text* 4 (1985): 21.

7. Charles Darwin, *The Expression of Emotions in Man and Animals* [1872] (Chicago: University of Chicago Press, 1965). For a psychological approach, see Silvan Tomkins, "The Primary Site of the Affects: The Face," in *Affect, Imagery, Consciousness,* vol. 1: *The Positive Affects* (New York: Springer Publishing Company, 1962), 204–242. A summary of the various strands of anthropological research on facial expression can be found in Griffiths, *What Emotions Really Are,* 50–55, and an analysis of seventeenth- and eighteenth-century conceptions of facial characterology in Deidre Lynch, *The Economy of Character: Novels, Market Culture, and the Business of Inner Meaning* (Chicago: University of Chicago Press, 1998), 33–38. The study of face recognition (and lack thereof) also links Antonio Damasio's research on brain lesions and his focus on the emotive brain. See Antonio Damasio, Hanna Damasio, and Gary W. Van Hoesen, "Prosopagnosia: Anatomic Basis and Behavioral Mechanisms," *Neurology* 21 (1982): 331–341.

8. Emmanuel Levinas, *Totality and Infinity* [1961], trans. Alphonso Lingis (Pittsburgh: Duquesne University Press, 1985), 50.

9. Jill Robbins, *Altered Reading: Levinas and Literature* (Chicago: University of Chicago Press, 1999), p. 9. As Robbins notes, Levinas's emphasis on the face's expressivity is antirepresentational, thus anti-aesthetic (132–134).

10. Cathy Caruth, *Empirical Truths and Critical Fictions: Locke, Wordsworth, Kant, Freud* (Baltimore: Johns Hopkins University Press, 1991), 50; see also de Man's treatment of Proust's links between love and voyage (AR 70). The *locus postclassicus* for discussions of passion as emergent writing—more narrowly construed than the emergence of language in the texts above—is Derrida's "Force and Signification" [1963], in *Writing and Difference,* trans. Alan Bass (Chicago: University of Chicago Press, 1978), 3–30.

11. Neil Hertz places de Man's association between "seeing and sucking" within a network of similar associations in both Wordsworth and de Man. Hertz argues that de Man "endors[es] whatever it was that led Wordsworth to substitute 'eye' for 'breast,'" even as the force of that endorsement participates in an open system of shifting positions "haunted by the pathos of intimacy and loss" ("Lurid Figures," in *Reading de Man Reading,* ed. Lindsay Waters and Wlad Godzich [Minneapolis: University of Minnesota Press, 1989] [hereafter RDR]), 98–99. See also Cynthia Chase, "Primary Narcissism and the Giving of Figure: Kristeva with Hertz and de Man," in *Abjection, Melancholia, and Love: The Work of Julia Kristeva,* ed. John Fletcher and Andrew Benjamin (New York: Routledge, 1990), 124–136.

12. Serge Leclaire writes that "whereas the object of need may easily be con-

ceived on the model of salt that allows the rechloridation of a dehydrated or-
ganism, or of sugar that puts an end to hypoglycemic coma, the object of desire must be conceived in an altogether different manner" (*Psychoanalyzing:
On the Order of the Unconscious and the Practice of the Letter* [1968],
trans. Peggy Kamuf [Stanford: Stanford University Press, 1998], 43). De
Man's recurrent point is that we nonetheless force objects of desire into physical models (AR 107–108). These treatments of milk recall Rousseau's association between passion and water in the *Essay on the Origin of Languages*.

13. Quoted in AR 149. Since in this chapter I deal only with portions of Rousseau texts cited directly by de Man, I will use de Man's translations of his citations and provide a reference to Rousseau's *Oeuvres complètes* in brackets.

14. Although I don't agree with de Man's reading of Derrida, Derrida does not
maximize the possibility of emotion as difference within his own text, so
there is warrant for de Man's conclusion. For more appraisal of de Man's
construction of Derrida's treatment of metaphor, see Robert Bernasconi, "No
More Stories, Good or Bad: de Man's Criticisms of Derrida on Rousseau," in
Derrida: A Critical Reader, ed. David Wood (Oxford: Blackwell, 1992), 150–
151; and Judith Still, "The Disfigured Savage: Rousseau and de Man," *Nottingham French Studies* 24 (1985): 1–14, esp. 2–6. For other reflections on
Rousseau's import for both Derrida and de Man, see Irene E. Harvey, "Doubling the Space of Existence: Exemplarity in Derrida—the Case of Rous-
seau," in *Deconstruction and Philosophy: The Texts of Jacques Derrida*, ed.
John Sallis (Chicago: University of Chicago Press, 1987), 60–70, and Hans-
Jost Frey, "Undecidability," *Yale French Studies* 69 (1985): 124–133.

15. Suzanne Gearhart argues that de Man "oversimplifies Derrida's interpretation" of the relationship between need and passion: "in fact, Derrida argues
that in the *Essay*, need and passion are *both* origins of language . . . the theory
of language as originating in passion and the theory of language as originating in need point to an origin which is irreducibly double, and which, as such,
predetermines any opposition which could be made between presence and
absence, between passion and need. This Derrida calls 'the law of the supplement'" ("Philosophy *before* Literature: Deconstruction, Historicity, and the
Work of Paul de Man," *Diacritics* 13 [1983]: 78).

16. De Man's phrase here recalls the earlier moment in "The Rhetoric of Blindness" in which he claims that in centering the *Essay* on fear, Rousseau chose
the wrong example. The outrageousness of this moment has often been
noted. Gearhart, for example, finds it "curious and highly significant" that
de Man "disputes [Derrida's reading] not because he considers that Derrida
has misread Rousseau, at least in the usual sense, but because Rousseau himself was 'wrong' at this point" ("Philosophy *before* Literature," 76). This
Gearhart terms an "extremely active and deliberate intervention in the text"
(77). And so it is. But the echo of "The Rhetoric of Blindness" suggests what
might have prompted de Man's intervention. Much as "giant" has a proper
meaning (fear) but "this meaning is not really proper," Derrida's reading of

Rousseau has a proper meaning (Rousseau does say what Derrida says he says), but this meaning is not really proper: in choosing the example of fear, Rousseau actually *reenacts* the emotionally hasty misrecognition of the scared man he writes about.

17. Carol Kay, "Hobbesian Fear: Richardson, de Man, Rousseau, and Burke," in *Critical Conditions: Regarding the Historical Moment,* ed. Michael Hays (Minneapolis: University of Minnesota Press, 1992), 106–107. Kay cites Part One, Chapter 13 of *Leviathan.* Kay compares the early de Man—as early as the wartime writings—to Burke and the later de Man to Hobbes, arguing persuasively that de Man moves from the belief that literature (or literary qualities such as the hypothetical nature of fear) might "disarm revolutionary challenges" to a darker admission that fictive delays can contribute to violent effects. I agree with Kay that "of all . . . Burkean elaborations on Hobbes, it is the Burkean view of literature that the later de Man was tempted to retain" (110, 111). De Man is indeed attracted to the idea of safe haven in fictive suspension, however brief the reprieve must finally be. Only very late, in "Kant and Schiller," does he expose the possible destructiveness of fictive refuge.

18. De Man is perhaps remembering some lines about memory from Valéry's "La Jeune Parque":

> Souvenir, ô bûcher, dont le vent d'or m'affronte,
> Souffle au masque la pourpre imprégnant le refus
> D'être en moi-même en flamme une autre que je fus . . .
> Viens, mon sang, viens rougir la pâle circonstance
> Qu'ennoblissait l'azur de la sainte distance,
> Et l'insensible iris du temps que j'adorai!

[Memory, bonfire whose gold wind assaults me, / Breathe and empurple my masque with the refusal / To be, in myself aflame, another than I was . . . / Come, my blood, come redden the circumstantial pallor / Ennobled by the blue of holy distance, / And the infinite slow iris of the time I loved!] (*Paul Valéry: An Anthology,* ed. and trans. James R. Lawler [Princeton: Princeton University Press, 1956], trans. modified).

19. Marc Redfield, "De Man, Schiller, and the Politics of Reception," *Diacritics* 23 (1990): 62. For other considerations of de Man's interest in feelings, see Minae Mizumura, "Renunciation," *Yale French Studies* 69 (1985): 81–97; Hertz, "Lurid Figures," in RDR 82–105, and "More Lurid Figures," *Diacritics* 20 (1990), 2–49; and Waters, "On Paul de Man's Effort to Re-Anchor a True Aesthetics in Our Feelings."

20. Paul de Man, *Aesthetic Ideology,* ed. Andrzej Warminski (Minneapolis: University of Minnesota Press, 1996), 142. (Hereafter AI.)

21. That is, de Man's oceanic metaphor recalls his discussion of the product of interpretive power in *The Prelude,* that "sea of infinite distinctions in which we risk to drown" (RR 92).

22. J. C. F. Schiller, "On the Sublime (Toward the Further Development of Some Kantian Ideas)" [1801], in *Essays,* trans. Daniel O. Dahlstrom, ed. Walter Hinderer and Daniel O. Dahlstrom (New York: Continuum, 1993), 35. De Man's loose translation, AI 146.

23. Fear occupies a nearly unique place in theories of emotion because of its crude social requirements and distinct physical correlations; it is one of the affectively stronger emotions (Griffiths, *What Emotions Really Are,* 80–99). As a result, fear makes a good object for the study of affect as distinct from emotion. Brian Massumi all but identifies fear with affect: "Fear is the direct perception of the contemporary condition of possibility of being-human . . . fear is the inherence in the body of the ungraspable multicausal matrix of the syndrome recognizable as late capitalist human existence (its *affect*)" ("Everywhere You Want to Be: Introduction to Fear," in *The Politics of Everyday Fear,* ed. Brian Massumi [Minneapolis: University of Minnesota Press, 1993], 12).

24. Friedrich Nietzsche, *The Gay Science* [1887], trans. Walter Kaufmann (New York: Vintage, 1974), §317. Nietzsche reinforces the emotive connotations of this passage by comparing pathos to a "painful and bold music."

25. Friedrich Nietzsche, *The Birth of Tragedy* [1872], ed. and trans. Walter Kaufmann (New York: Vintage, 1967), 130.

26. Ruben Berezdivin, "Drawing: (An) Affecting Nietzsche: With Derrida," in *Derrida and Deconstruction,* ed. Hugh J. Silverman (London: Routledge, 1989), 92–107. As Berezdivin points out, "affective will becomes aware of its presence only retroactively" (94). Once we do become aware of our feelings, though, they can be "dwelt on again and again" (95)—the convenience of all ideal objects, as we've seen.

27. Werner Hamacher, "'Lectio': de Man's Imperative." In *Premises: Essays on Philosophy and Literature from Kant to Celan,* trans. Peter Fenves (Cambridge: Harvard University Press, 1996), 193, 195.

28. See Hertz, "Lurid Figures" and "More Lurid Figures," and Robert L. Caserio, "'A Pathos of Uncertain Agency': Paul de Man and Narrative," *Journal of Narrative Technique* 20 (1990): 195–209. Again, it is common to attribute pathos to compensation. In John Guillory's reading of de Man's pedagogical relations, "the affect of the countertransference is turned around" in de Man's "Resistance to Theory" "into its opposite, the signature affect or 'pathos' of serene resignation to the triumphant or tragic circumstance that theory is the resistance to theory (that is, the transference onto theory)" (*Cultural Capital: The Problem of Literary Canon Formation* [Chicago: University of Chicago Press, 1993], 199).

29. Jane Marie Todd, "Framing the *Second Discourse,*" *Comparative Literature* 38 (1986): 316.

30. Anita Sokolsky, "The Resistance to Sentimentality: Yeats, de Man, and the Aesthetic Education," *Yale Journal of Criticism* 1 (1987): 67.

31. Stanley Cavell perhaps wants philosophy to be sentimental when he argues

that skepticism is melodramatic when it responds in a violently embarrassed way to the domestic, inherited, banality of existence: "If some image of human intimacy, call it marriage, or domestication, is the fictional equivalent of what the philosophers of ordinary language understand as the ordinary, call this the image of the everyday as the domestic, then the threat to the ordinary that philosophy names skepticism should show up in fiction's favorite threats to forms of marriage, namely, in forms of melodrama and tragedy" (*In Quest of the Ordinary: Lines of Skepticism and Romanticism* [Chicago: University of Chicago Press, 1988], 176). Cavell's version of events has the advantage of not having to the defend the idea that epistemological or subjective austerity entails emotional deprivation; rather, he opposes two kinds of emotionality, and hints, by characterizing skeptical procedures as melodramatic, that he might like skeptics to calm down. (Wittgenstein seems *hysterically* desirous that skeptics calm down.) Addressing the necessary emotionality of both sides of the debate produces more convincing formulations of the disagreements involved.

32. In a parallel argument in the Rilke chapter, de Man asserts that explaining literary figures by reference to authorial emotions posits a false unity between consciousness and its objects. Thus the exegesis of a Rilke commentator "implies that language is entirely ancillary in its relation to a fundamental experience (the pain and pathos of being)" to which "it is also entirely truthful" (AR 26). According to de Man, this kind of reading also appears within Rilke's poems (see AR 29ff.).

33. In her study of Stoic emotion theory, Martha Nussbaum remarks that "it seems in no way strange to say that it is reason itself that reaches out and takes that appearance to itself, saying, so to speak, 'Yes, that's the one I'll have. That's the way things are'" (*The Therapy of Desire: Theory and Practice in Hellenistic Ethics* [Princeton: Princeton University Press, 1994], 374–375). She provides an example Rousseau would enjoy: "The ancient commentator Michael of Ephesus analyzes the *De Motu*'s sexual case in a similar way, using the Stoic terminology of assent: the alluring object appears, and appears alluring: but, being a temperate man, the person in the example does not 'assent to' the suggestion that this particular object is in fact alluring. He refuses it, and so we get just momentary arousal (an 'involuntary erection,' Michael writes), not emotion and not action" (*Therapy of Desire*, 84–85).

34. This conclusion leads de Man to the thought that Rousseau's "*Profession de foi* may well be a pre-Kantian rather than a neo-Cartesian text. . . . The problem now becomes, not how to construe an interpretation of existence by means of a rule of inner assent, but to account, by a critical act of judgment, for the occurrence of such an assent and to establish its epistemological status" (AR 229).

35. The presence of this possibility also defines "language" for de Man: "To the extent that judgment is a structure of relationships capable of error, it is also language. . . . What is then called 'language' clearly has to extend well

beyond what is empirically understood as articulated verbal utterance and subsumes, for instance, what is traditionally referred to as perception" (AR 234).

36. UCLA students will recognize here the bizarre logic of Engineering 11 (Patterns of Problem Solving), a popular physical science course which provided formulae that balance the advantages and disadvantages of decision outcomes, thus prescribing the right solution to your personally designed problem. First, unfortunately, each advantage and disadvantage had to be assigned an *intuitive* numerical weight. Usually the only way to make the formula solve the (ethical, practical, romantic) problem was to start with the desired outcome and work backward.

37. For a critical reading of this passage, see Mark Conroy, "De Man on *The Social Contract*: Reading Rousseau's Fine Print," *Criticism* 31 (1989): 53–73. Conroy believes that de Man's re-creation of Rousseau encourages quietism.

38. De Man may mean the *Essay,* not the *Second Discourse:* he supplies a note here which refers us to a previous note (AR 153n29) about the word "giant" in the *Essay.*

39. Paul Youngquist connects Kant's nervousness about substance abuse to De Quincey's and Coleridge's in "De Quincey's Crazy Body," *PMLA* 114 (1999): 346–358.

40. It cannot "be denied," Kant writes, "that all presentations in us, no matter whether their object is merely sensible or instead wholly intellectual, can in the subject still be connected with gratification or pain, however unnoticeable these may be (because all of them affect the feeling of life, and none of them can be indifferent insofar as it is a modification of the subject)" (*Critique of Judgment,* 139).

41. For a dissent from de Man's interpretation of *Augenschein,* see Rodolphe Gasché, "On Mere Sight: A Response to Paul de Man," in *The Textual Sublime: Deconstruction and Its Differences,* ed. Hugh J. Silverman and Gary E. Aylesworth (Albany: SUNY Press, 1990), 109–115.

42. Rodolphe Gasché, *The Wild Card of Reading: On Paul de Man* (Cambridge: Harvard University Press, 1998), 95.

43. Crucial stretches of Gasché's case lean on the verb "to be": "The singular that apathetic rhetoric centers on is so left to itself, is so insoluble and absolute, that it escapes that dialectic of the universal altogether. For the same reason, it cannot be called 'irrational' either. Or to put it differently, the apathetic linguistic atoms are singular to such a degree that their singularity no longer expresses singularity. Nor does it, in its very apathy, convey any negative pathos. There cannot be any pathos of apathy" (*Wild Card,* 110).

44. Steven Bruhm, analyzing the literal and metaphoric history of anesthesia, traces its slide from absence to bliss in the revolutionary era: while "too much feeling often creates too little," and, in particular, one blacks out from too much pain, there are two directions on this road: "In the early 1700s, 'anaesthesia' had meant a defect of lack of feeling, following its direct trans-

lation 'without feeling' *(OED)*. However, by the end of the century, 'anaesthetic' became a positive medical relieving of feeling, a blessing rather than a defect" ("Aesthetics and Anaesthetics at the Revolution," *Studies in Romanticism* 32 [1993]:407, 404).

3. A Parallel Philosophy

1. G. W. F. Hegel, *Introductory Lectures on Aesthetics* [1842], trans. Bernard Bosanquet, ed. Michael Inwood (Harmondsworth: Penguin, 1993), 95.
2. Rosalind Picard, *Affective Computing* (Cambridge: MIT Press, 1997), 4.
3. See Roland Barthes, *The Responsibility of Forms: Critical Essays on Music, Art, and Representation* [1982], trans. Richard Howard (New York: Hill and Wang, 1985); de Man, BI 124–133, AR 33–39, RR 239–262; Derrida, G 195–200, 210–216, 249; Philippe Lacoue-Labarthe, *Typography: Mimesis, Philosophy, Politics,* trans. Eugenio Donato, ed. Christopher Fynsk (Cambridge: Harvard University Press, 1989); and Clément, *Syncope.*
4. Malcolm Budd, *Music and the Emotions: The Philosophical Theories* (London: Routledge & Kegan Paul, 1985), xiii. Budd writes early in the chronology of literature I refer to.
5. See Susanne K. Langer, *Feeling and Form: A Theory of Art Developed from Philosophy in a New Key* (New York: Charles Scribner's Sons, 1953), and Richard Wollheim, *Art and Its Objects,* 2nd ed. (Cambridge: Cambridge University Press, 1980). In some intramusical debates, "expression theory" refers to the idea that the emotions of music are expressed by the composer. I continue to mean something broader by "expression."
6. Levinson classes his own account along with Kivy's among "*appearance-of-expression*-based views" and believes that "its difference from its close competitors" emerges only after detailed comparison (*Pleasures of Aesthetics,* 93). Levinson's appearance of expression is intrinsic to music, Kivy's incidental. Because Levinson sees appearance capacities as intrinsic, it really doesn't matter to him whether responses are emotions or feelings, proper emotions or only like proper emotions, emotions induced or emotions recalled. In the course of one page and its note Levinson suggests that a response to music is a feeling split from "cognitive elements" and "an experience produced in a listener which is *at least* the characteristic feeling of some emotion, but which is short of a complete emotion" (*Music, Art, and Metaphysics: Essays in Philosophical Aesthetics* [Ithaca, N.Y.: Cornell University Press, 1990], 314). "All that need ultimately be conveyed," he writes, "is at most the *idea* or *impression* of having an object. . . . What need *not* be conveyed, in the domain of musical expression, is either the specific *object* of the emotion, or the *subject* of the emotion, or the concrete *material context* of the emotion—which is just as well, since these are all literally absent in such situations" (*Music, Art, and Metaphysics,* 348; by "subject" Levinson means a particular subject). This remarkable process of elimination preserves the one idea for which

Levinson works, the preconception he started out with: the necessity of the expressive hypothesis.

7. Peter Kivy, *The Corded Shell: Reflections on Musical Expression* (Princeton: Princeton University Press, 1980).

8. Stephen Davies, "Contra the Hypothetical Persona in Music," in *Emotion and the Arts,* ed. Mette Hjort and Sue Laver (Oxford: Oxford University Press, 1997), 96–97.

9. Derek Matravers, *Art and Emotion* (Oxford: Oxford University Press, 1998). The idea that musical emotions are the listener's also occurs in Rousseau: "The sounds in a melody do not only affect us as sounds, but as signs of our emotions, of our feelings. This is how they produce within us the responses they express and how we recognize the image of our emotions in them" (*Essay,* 57; de Man's translation, BI 125). How can sounds signify "*our* feelings" when we can't feel these emotions until the music is playing? The commonsensical reading that would take Rousseau to be referring not to the particular current feelings of listeners but merely to the sorts of things we usually feel will be hard pressed to deal with his assertion that musical signs "produce within us the responses they express." In what otherworldly chronology would this be possible? It seems to be possible because there is no lag between music and its reception; the vague emotional script sketched by the music actualizes itself in real time in listeners. In Rousseau's account, we are not so much feeling sympathetic emotions toward "painted passions" as having the passions painted on us.

10. Levinson paraphrases Aaron Ridley, "Musical Sympathies: The Experience of Expressive Music," *Journal of Aesthetics and Art Criticism* 54 (1995): 49–57; see also Ridley's *Music, Value, and the Passions* (Ithaca, N.Y.: Cornell University Press, 1995).

11. Peter Kivy, "The Quest for Musical Profundity," in *Philosophies of Arts: An Essay in Differences* (Cambridge: Cambridge University Press, 1997), 165, 164. Kivy's article responds to Levinson's "Musical Profundity Misplaced," *Journal of Aesthetics and Art Criticism* 50 (1992).

12. Kivy believes in compositional intentionality; but because he defines music by its content-freedom, a composer's intention to evoke emotion "must be, on [his] view, a failed intention" ("Quest for Musical Profundity," 166).

13. De Man's reading of *The Birth of Tragedy* targets Nietzsche's Schopenhauerian claim that "music is the unmediated image of the will" (*Birth of Tragedy,* 102). Henry Staten defends Nietzsche from de Man's criticism, in part by pointing out that "when Schopenhauer declares that music is 'immediately' the image of the Will . . . he means simply that music is, unlike the other arts, not a *representation at two removes,* not a representation of the Platonic or species-ideas, but a representation of the original which the Platonic ideas also copy." Since as I understand him, de Man objects primarily to the idea that music fulfills representation's obligations to subjectivity more deeply than representation can, I am not much moved by this defense. As

Staten notes, "Nietzsche says that the Dionysian musician is 'pure primordial pain and its primordial re-echoing' (*Birth of Tragedy,* 50), and this state, which is what Nietzsche calls, in Schiller's phrase, the 'musical mood' (*Birth of Tragedy,* 49), is what is 'copied' in the form of music" (Staten, "*The Birth of Tragedy* Reconstructed," *Studies in Romanticism* 29 [1990]: 21, 30). De Man resists Nietzsche's notion of "copying," however, *because* it no longer corresponds to the mere representation of external objects, and therefore seems unusually powerful. In Deleuze's terms, such direct expression is no longer analogically representational but is for that reason subjective. On the allegorical dimensions of de Man's aesthetics of music, see Christopher Norris, "Utopian Deconstruction: Ernst Bloch, Paul de Man, and the Politics of Music," *Paragraph* 11 (1988): 24–57.

14. In a similarly allegorical move, Dubos, in a passage analyzed by de Man, asserts that music imitates the "means" (the language) by which "feelings and emotions" are conveyed without giving any idea why these emotions are occurring. Dubos converts nonrepresentational musical features into direct natural signs that are more efficient than representations, incorporating musical abstraction into the expressive hypothesis: "Just as the painter imitates the lines and colors of nature, the musician imitates the tone, the stresses, the pauses, the voice-inflections, in short all the sounds by means of which nature itself expresses its feelings and emotions. . . . they are the signs of passion instituted by nature itself. They receive their strength directly from nature, whereas articulated words are merely the arbitrary signs of the passions. . . . These natural signs have an amazing power in awakening emotions in those who hear them. They receive this power from nature itself" (*Réflexions critiques sur la poésie et sur la peinture* [Paris, 1740], 1:435–436, 438; trans. de Man, BI 124).

   At the outset Dubos suggests that musicians imitate only the nonsemantic aspects of speech. Effects in the margins of communicative content—"the stresses, the pauses, the voice-inflections"—float free from the denotations they inflect. For all his insistence on "nature," then, Dubos does not bring up imitative instances of language such as onomatopoeia. The absence of imitation is strategic; knowing in the first place that music usually doesn't imitate anything, Dubos needs a nonimitative kind of naturalness instead. The properties he selects are not imitative but rather *as natural as* imitation, "instituted by nature itself"; they are what remains of nature inside the arbitrary signs of speech. Dubos appeals to something within language that is not of the same order as words. Yet rather than seeing this other quality in language as nonrepresentational, or indirectly or arbitrarily representational, he sees it as *super*-representational—as directly expressive. And so Dubos testifies to de Man's claim that eighteenth-century aesthetic theory insists suspiciously upon expression. "The possibility of making the invisible visible, of giving presence to what can only be imagined," is indeed "stated as the main function of art" as de Man contends (BI 124).

Kant calls the alternative order of music "tone" [*Ton*] in a comparable passage: "Every linguistic expression has in its context a tone appropriate to its meaning. This tone indicates, more or less, an affect of the speaker and in turn induces the same affect in the listener too, where it then conversely arouses the idea which in language we express in that tone. And just as modulation is, as it were, a universal [*allgemein*] language of sensations that every human being can understand, so the art of music [*Tonkunst*] employs this language all by itself in its full force, namely, as a language of affects" (*Critique of Judgment*, 198–199).

According to Kant, we do not react to music as we would if we were spoken to *by* someone in a particular tone. We do not take up the posture of an actual listener. We do recognize "an affect of the speaker," but instead of feeling an answering affect, act "in turn" as though *we* were feeling the affect corresponding to the tone. This circularity suggests the atopia of musical emotion, but Dubos fends off a similar conclusion by declaring that musical signs "receive [their] power from nature itself" (quoted in BI 124). Peter Fenves observes that "the 'emotions' that correspond to these vibrations [of tone] are themselves tonal; they are the various *Stimmungen*, the moods or dispositions, that respond to a sometimes silent but always vibrant voice [*Stimme*]" ("The Topicality of Tone," in *Raising the Tone of Philosophy: Late Essays by Immanuel Kant, Transformative Critique by Jacques Derrida*, ed. Peter Fenves [Baltimore: Johns Hopkins University Press, 1993], 4). The tonalism of emotion formalizes the expressive circularity of emotion and music. Fenves goes on to note that in early and late Kant, "the chronic vibrations to which the human mind is exposed make themselves known with the greatest clarity . . . at the precise moment that cognitive discourse—'mathematical' language in a broad sense—exhausts itself" (4–5).

15. Arthur Schopenhauer, *The World as Will and Representation* [1859], 2 vols., trans. E. F. J. Payne (New York: Dover, 1969), 1:261. Schopenhauer does not explicitly connect heightening imagination to heightened emotion as Rousseau does, but implies the connection: "The inexpressive depth of all music . . . is due to the fact that it reproduces all the emotions of our innermost being, but entirely without reality" (1:264).

16. De Sousa identifies emotional antinomies regarding rationality (emotions are reasonable and unreasonable); objectivity (they are objective and subjective); activity and passivity; integrity ("which one, the spontaneous or the deliberate self, is the real self?"); and determinism ("the classic argument according to which neither determinism nor indeterminism is compatible with free will") (RE 1–2).

17. On emotion's continuity, see Antonio Damasio, *Descartes' Error: Emotion, Reason, and the Human Brain* (New York: G. P. Putnam's Sons, 1994), and Stocker, *Valuing Emotions*.

18. As de Sousa believes that emotions do not form a natural class, their formal objects are irreducible to one type for all emotions (RE 20). Emotions are not

"merely compounded of beliefs and wants," but are *sui generis* forms of experience; thus their formal objects are not beliefs' and wants' formal objects (truth and satisfaction), but *sui generis* as well.

19. I take de Sousa to mean that individuals help to form paradigm scenarios and experience them variously, and that the idiosyncrasies produced by biological and social individuality are legitimate parts of normality (RE 202–203, 260, 270, 295–296).

20. De Sousa establishes an intermediate level of intentionality by requiring emotions to be teleological, on the assumption that "the assessment of rationality of any [intentional] act or belief looks both forward to consequences . . . and backward to origins" (RE 162). Here de Sousa draws on Donald Davidson's notion that all actions have teleological structures; see Davidson, *Essays on Actions and Events* (Oxford: Clarendon Press, 1990).

21. Stanislaw Lem, *Solaris* [1961], trans. Joanna Kilmartin and Steve Cox (New York: Berkley Publishing Corporation, 1970). The story of Alcmene and Amphitryon has attracted various skeptics about identity and phenomena. It is dramatized in Kleist's *Amphitryon* (1807) and Jean-Luc Godard's *Hélas pour moi* (1994); *Solaris* is also a haunting film by Andrei Tarkovsky (1972). De Man briefly compares Kleist's *Amphitryon* to Rousseau's *Pygmalion*: "[Galathea's] statement after touching Pygmalion is as ambiguous as Alcmene's famous 'Ach!' at the end of Kleist's play *Amphitryon*: 'Galathea goes in his direction and looks at him. He rises precipitously, stretches out his arms toward her and looks at her ecstatically. She touches him with one of her hands: he trembles, takes her hand, presses it against his heart, then covers it with kisses. *Galathea* (with a sigh): Ah! *encore moi*' [OCR 1:1230–31]. . . . The line 'Ah! *encore moi*' spoken with a sigh that suggests disappointment rather than satisfaction can also mean '*de nouveau moi*' ('me again'), a persisting, repeated distinction between the general Self and the self as other" (AR 186). For interpretation of this passage of *Allegories*, see Carol Jacobs, *Telling Time: Lévi-Strauss, Ford, Lessing, Benjamin, de Man, Wordsworth, Rilke* (Baltimore: Johns Hopkins University Press, 1993), 147ff.

22. Aristotle, *Nicomachean Ethics*, trans. Terence Irwin (Indianapolis: Hackett, 1985), §7.3.

23. Daniel C. Dennett, "Back from the Drawing Board," in *Dennett and His Critics: Demystifying Mind*, ed. Bo Dahlbohm (Oxford: Blackwell, 1993), 211.

24. Daniel C. Dennett, "Quining Qualia," in *Consciousness in Contemporary Science*, ed. A. J. Marcel and E. Bisiach (Oxford: Clarendon Press, 1988), 42. Once again milk stands for the irreducibility of personal experience.

25. Frank Jackson, "Epiphenomenal Qualia," *Philosophical Quarterly* 32 (1982): 128.

26. Daniel C. Dennett, "Why You Can't Make a Computer That Feels Pain," in *Brainstorms: Philosophical Essays on Mind and Psychology* [1978] (Cambridge: MIT Press, 1981), 190–229.

27. Picard has recently assessed the ongoing research in *Affective Computing*.
28. Here some humanists might be willing to extend subjectivity to nonhumans. Such humanists would have come a very long way from classical humanism.
29. For Dennett, "real but (potentially) noisy patterns abound . . . there for the picking up if only you are lucky or clever enough to hit on the right perspective. They are not *visual* patterns but, you might say, *intellectual* patterns. Squinting or twisting your head in front of the computer screen is not apt to help, whereas posing fanciful interpretations (or what Quine would call 'analytical hypotheses') may uncover a gold mine." Possible intellectual perspectives Dennett discusses include the physical stance, the design stance, and the "intentional or folk-psychological stance" (*Darwin's Dangerous Idea: Evolution and the Meanings of Life* [New York: Simon & Schuster, 1995], 237). His earlier *Intentional Stance* contends that the hypothesis of intentionality is unavoidable "with regard to oneself and one's fellow intelligent beings" (*Intentional Stance* [Cambridge: MIT Press, 1987], 27). In an appendix to *Consciousness Explained* Dennett has an imaginary interlocutor ask a very good question: "There seems, however, to be a tension—if not an outright contradiction—between the two halves of your theory. The intentional stance presupposes (or fosters) the rationality, and hence the unity, of the agent—the intentional system—while the Multiple Drafts [parallel processes] model opposes this central unity all the way. Which, according to your view, is the right way to conceive of a mind?" Dennett responds, "It all depends on how far away you are. The closer you get, the more the disunity, multiplicity, and competitiveness stand out as important" (458, italics omitted). The intentional half of Dennett's philosophy is its classical half, but the other half, as he remarks, qualifies it considerably.
30. Gilles Deleuze and Félix Guattari, *A Thousand Plateaus: Capitalism and Schizophrenia*, vol. 2 [1980], trans. Brian Massumi (Minneapolis: University of Minnesota Press, 1987), hereafter TP; notes on the translation, p. xvi.
31. Michael Hardt, *Gilles Deleuze: An Apprenticeship in Philosophy* (Minneapolis: University of Minnesota Press, 1993), 76–77.
32. Gilles Deleuze, *Expressionism in Philosophy: Spinoza* [1968], trans. Martin Joughin (New York: Zone Books, 1998), 44. (Hereafter EPS.)
33. Gilles Deleuze, *The Logic of Sense* [1969], ed. Constantin V. Boundas, trans. Mark Lester with Charles Stivale (New York: Columbia University Press, 1990), pp. 110–111.
34. Here "a stratum always has a dimension of the expressible or of expression serving as the basis for a relative invariance" (TP 43).
35. Brian Massumi, "Deleuze, Guattari, and the Philosophy of Expression," *Canadian Review of Comparative Literature/Revue Canadienne de Littérature Comparée* (1997): 745. This is a special issue devoted to expression in Deleuze.
36. Alain Badiou, *Deleuze: The Clamor of Being* [1977] (Minneapolis: University of Minnesota Press, 1999).

37. See especially the discussion of harmony in Gilles Deleuze, *The Fold: Leibniz, or the Baroque* [1988], trans. Tom Conley (Minneapolis: University of Minnesota Press, 1993).

38. Benedict [Baruch] de Spinoza, *The Ethics* [1677], in *A Spinoza Reader: The Ethics and Other Works*, ed. and trans. Edwin Curley (Princeton: Princeton University Press, 1994), 141.

39. Gilles Deleuze, *Spinoza: Practical Philosophy* [1970], trans. Robert Hurley (San Francisco: City Lights Books, 1981), p. 19. (Hereafter S.)

40. Spinoza's suspicion of indication has roots in his criticism of biblical revelation and prophecy and of traditional proofs of God. Spinoza contrasts the necessary "attributes" of God to his *propria*, "which indeed belong to a thing, but never explain what it is. For though *existing of itself, being the cause of all things, the greatest good, eternal*, and *immutable*, and so on, are proper to God alone, nevertheless through those *propria* we can know neither what the being to which these *propria* belong is, nor what attributes it has" ("From a Non-Geometric Draft of the *Ethics*," in *Spinoza Reader*, 56). Deleuze glosses this passage: "*Propria* are not properly speaking attributes, precisely because they are not *expressive*. Rather they are like 'impressed notions,' like characters imprinted, either in all attributes, or in some one or other of them" (EPS 50).

   Spinoza is loath to bank on the contingency of a sign's meaning, on one hand, and the arbitrary nature of cogito-like position on the other. One of his quarrels with "the whole of prophetic certainty" is that prophecy is founded on signs, which can never "follow from the necessity of the perception of the thing perceived or seen," but rely on "the opinions and capacity of the prophet, in such a way that a sign which would render one prophet certain of his prophecy could not convince at all another, who was imbued with different opinions" (*Spinoza Reader*, 17–18). The result is that rather than penetrating appearance, interpretations demonstrate only that the prophet thinks he perceives something.

41. Compare Deleuze's treatment of impressions in Hume in *Empiricism and Subjectivity: An Essay on Hume's Theory of Human Nature* [1953], trans. Constantin V. Boundas (New York: Columbia University Press, 1991), 113–120.

42. Greimas and Fontanille complain that in Spinoza's theory of affect "only the modality of *being-able* seems to be involved" (*Semiotics of Passion*, 60). Antonio Negri puts it this way: "The great couples 'joy-sadness' and 'love-hate' [one could also speak in a utilitarian way of pleasure and pain—RT] make their appearance here as signals, keys to the reading of the constitutive process of the world of the affects: For now that is what they are, constructive, formal elements of a scheme of ontological projection" (*The Savage Anomaly: The Power of Spinoza's Metaphysics and Politics* [1981], trans. Michael Hardt [Minneapolis: University of Minnesota Press, 1991], 147).

43. Keith Ansell Pearson, *Germinal Life: The Difference and Repetition of*

Deleuze (New York: Routledge, 1999), 135. Ansell Pearson cites Deleuze, "Immanence: A Life . . . ," trans. N. Millett, *Theory, Culture, and Society* 14 (1997): 3.

44. Dana Polan discusses Deleuze's "quest for defiguration": "in a sense, Deleuze argues, the logic of sensation of the figure can only go so far, can achieve only a limited defiguration: insofar as the figure constitutes a given against which permutations are measured, there is always the danger that representation makes a reappearance and turns the figure into a stable meaning" ("Francis Bacon: The Logic of Sensation," in *Gilles Deleuze and the Theater of Philosophy*, ed. Constantin V. Boundas and Dorothea Olkowski [New York: Routledge, 1994], 243).

45. Lacan perhaps accepts this description but values it positively: in the Kantian manner, feeling compelled is the height of ethics.

46. Gilles Deleuze, *Cinema 1: The Movement-Image* [1983], trans. Hugh Tomlinson and Barbara Habberjam (Minneapolis: University of Minnesota Press, 1986), 59.

47. Gilles Deleuze and Félix Guattari, *What Is Philosophy?* [1991], trans. Hugh Tomlinson and Graham Burchell (New York: Columbia University Press, 1994), 164. See also Brian Massumi, "The Autonomy of Affect," *Cultural Critique* 31 (1995): 83–109. Paul Trembath traces Deleuze's development of aesthetics as sense in "Aesthetics without Art or Culture: Toward an Alternative Sense of Materialist Agency," *Strategies* 9/10 (1996): 122–151.

48. Paul Bains reads Deleuze as endowing subjectlessness with the values of subjectivity. See his "Subjectless Subjectivities," *Canadian Review of Comparative Literature / Revue Canadienne de Littérature Comparée* (1997): 512–528. James Morrison notes that "Deleuze's rhetoric of absolutes, of essences, of infinites, of the spiritual and eternal, makes sense as the thematization of something like a 'sublime subject' which has escaped or gone beyond the 'regime of signs'" ("Deleuze and Film Semiotics," *Semiotica* 88 [1992]: 288).

49. Aurelia Armstrong, "Some Reflections on Deleuze's Spinoza: Composition and Agency," in *Deleuze and Philosophy: The Difference Engineer*, ed. Keith Ansell Pearson (London: Routledge, 1977), 56.

50. Timothy S. Murphy, "Quantum Ontology: A Virtual Mechanics of Becoming," in *Deleuze and Guattari: New Mappings in Politics, Philosophy, and Culture*, ed. Eleanor Kaufman and Kevin Jon Heller (Minneapolis: University of Minnesota Press, 1998), 212. Murphy compares Deleuze's thought to that of "contemporary physicists, including Roger Penrose, J. S. Bell, and David Bohm," realists who contest the representation-centered Copenhagen interpretation of quantum mechanics (213).

Foucault asserts that "*The Logic of Sense* can be read as the most alien book imaginable from *The Phenomenology of Perception*" ("Theatrum Philosophicum" [1970], in *Language, Counter-Memory, Practice: Selected Essays and Interviews*, ed. Donald F. Bouchard, trans. Donald F. Bouchard and Sherry Simon [Ithaca, N.Y.: Cornell University Press, 1977], 170). Compare

Badiou: "It is exactly because it is the same Being that occurs and that is said that there is no intentional relation *between* things and words—those actualizations of the Same. . . . in assuming that there is an intentional relation between nomination and the thing, or between consciousness and the object, one necessarily breaks with the expressive sovereignty of the One" (*Deleuze: The Clamor of Being,* 22).

51. Gilles Deleuze, *Foucault* [1986], trans. Seán Hand (Minneapolis: University of Minnesota Press, 1988), 119, quoted in Badiou, *Deleuze: The Clamor of Being,* 129, trans. modified by Badiou.

52. Francisco Varela, *Ethical Know-How: Action, Wisdom, and Cognition* (Stanford: Stanford University Press, 1999), 61.

4. Psyche, Inc.

1. Waters, "Professah de Man—He Dead," 290.

2. Peter Brooks, Shoshana Felman, and J. Hillis Miller, eds., *Yale French Studies* 69 [*The Lesson of Paul de Man*] (1985): 9–12. (Hereafter YFS.)

3. Guillory, *Cultural Capital,* 190–207. In this model the *apatheia* of deconstruction (which comes from its critique of classical subjectivity) and its addictiveness therefore work together, symbiotically. For Guillory this phenomenon shows "the failure of de Manian theory (and theory in general) to function as anything other than an interim, imaginary solution to the new conditions of intellectual labor" (181).

4. Surveys of this topic appear in Giorgio Agamben, *Stanzas: Word and Phantasm in Western Culture* [1977], trans. Ronald L. Martinez (Minneapolis: University of Minnesota Press, 1993), and Niklas Luhmann, *Love as Passion: The Codification of Intimacy* [1982], trans. Jeremy Gaines and Doris L. Jones (Stanford: Stanford University Press, 1998).

5. These texts have received relatively little critical attention. Robert Smith discusses *Memoires* in the context of Derrida's theory of "life" (*Derrida and Autobiography,* 166–171); Dominick LaCapra assesses Derrida's use of de Man's ideas about Hegelian *Gedächtnis* and *Erinnerung* (*Soundings in Critical Theory* [Ithaca, N.Y.: Cornell University Press, 1989], 186–189). See also Juliet Flower MacCannell, "Portrait: de Man," *Genre* 17 (1984): 51–74, and R. D. Ackerman's review of *Memoires for Paul de Man, Philosophy and Literature* 11 (1987): 171–181.

6. Derrida's tribute may be found in YFS 13–14; trans. Kevin Newmark, YFS 323–324.

7. *Memoires for Paul de Man* actually has two introductions, a "Preface" and the introductory remarks to which I refer.

8. Jacques Derrida, *Memoires for Paul de Man,* trans. Cecile Lindsay, Jonathan Culler, and Eduardo Cadava (New York: Columbia University Press, 1986), iii–iv. (Hereafter M.)

9. Jacques Derrida, *Points . . . Interviews, 1974–1994,* ed. Elisabeth Weber,

trans. Peggy Kamuf et al. (Stanford: Stanford University Press, 1995), 48. See also Derrida, "By Force of Mourning" [1993], trans. Pascale-Anne Brault and Michael Nass, *Critical Inquiry* 22 (1996): 171–192.

10. This question is addressed again by Derrida and others in a collection of conference papers, *Deconstruction is/in America: A New Sense of the Political,* ed. Anselm Haverkamp (New York: New York University Press, 1995).

11. Cynthia Chase, *Decomposing Figures: Rhetorical Readings in the Romantic Tradition* (Baltimore: Johns Hopkins University Press, 1986), 82.

12. As Tobin Siebers notes, Derrida's and de Man's contest of one-downsmanship dates back to "The Rhetoric of Blindness," "where de Man outmaneuvers Derrida at his own game by giving away the game to Rousseau" ("Mourning Becomes Paul de Man," in R 365).

13. *Phaedo,* in The *Collected Dialogues of Plato,* ed. Edith Hamilton and Huntington Cairns, various trans. (Princeton: Princeton University Press, 1961), §76c. According to Socrates, "we must have had some previous knowledge of equality before the time when we first saw equal things and realized that they were striving after equality, but fell short of it" (*Phaedo* §75).

14. William R. Schultz and Lewis L. B. Fried note that "Psyche" was "first presented at Cornell University in 1984" (*Jacques Derrida: An Annotated Primary and Secondary Bibliography* [New York: Garland Publishing, 1992], 104).

15. Derrida introduces Psyche in "Mnemosyne" this way: "The death of the other, if we can say this, is also situated on our side at the very moment when it comes to us from an altogether other side. Its *Erinnerung* becomes as inevitable as it is unliveable: it finds there its origin and its limit, its conditions of possibility and impossibility. In another context, I have called this Psyche: Psyche, the proper name of an allegory; Psyche, the common name for the soul; and Psyche, in French, the name of a revolving mirror." Jacques Derrida, *Memoires for Paul de Man,* trans. Cecile Lindsay, Jonathan Culler, and Eduardo Cadava (New York: Columbia University Press, 1986), 39.

16. We can tell that Psyche does not really break her mirror because "Fable" itself seems to be written in a mirror, in mirror-logic—thus, "it is *after* seven years of misfortune that she breaks the mirror." As Derrida points out, the poem is formally the mirror image of a fable as well: "A fable of La Fontaine's usually does just the opposite: there is a narrative, then a moral in the form of a maxim or aphorism. But reading the narrative we get here in parentheses and in conclusion, in the place of the 'moral,' we do not know where to locate the inverted time to which it refers" (RDR 36).

17. See also Jacques Derrida, "On a Newly Arisen Apocalyptic Tone in Philosophy" [1981], trans. John Leavey, Jr., in *Raising the Tone of Philosophy: Late Essays by Immanuel Kant, Transformative Critique by Jacques Derrida,* ed. Peter Fenves (Baltimore: Johns Hopkins University Press, 1993), 117–171.

18. Siebers comments that "the future of de Man's theories depends on whether

the present 'loss' [Derrida's deferral to de Man in *Memoires*] can be construed as a 'win'" ("Mourning Becomes Paul de Man," R 366). The answer to this can only be "yes and no"; yes because Derrida's deferral is precarious and overdone, no because this reaction, too, has been invited.

19. Harth, *Cartesian Women*, 71.

20. Amélie Oksenberg Rorty, "Cartesian Passions and the Union of Mind and Body," in *Essays on Descartes' Meditations,* ed. Amélie Oksenberg Rorty (Berkeley and Los Angeles: University of California Press, 1986), 527.

21. Editors' note, *Critical Inquiry* 15 (1989): 764. Page numbers for "Like the Sound of the Sea" refer to the essay as reprinted in R 127–164.

22. Niall Lucy uses Derrida's heated exchanges with others to present "the double form of a 'Derrida' who is both a subject and an object of debate" (*Debating Derrida* [Victoria: Melbourne University Press, 1995], xi). Lucy notes that "feeling around 'Derrida' can run very high" (xi) and that, in the case of Derrida's debate with Rob Nixon and Anne McClintock, "the text of Derrida's complaint—the unkind, infantalizing terms of his reply—should not be separated from the strong feelings he has about apartheid. . . . For how could feelings be in 'here,' with texts outside over 'there'? How could *this* be 'semiotic,' and *that* 'sentimental'?" (20).

23. Derrida contrasts "the theater of petty passions" to "rational arguments," yet he is not uninterested in the melodrama: "some of [its] mechanisms and old rhetorical tricks I really must try to describe" ("Biodegradables: Seven Diary Fragments," *Critical Inquiry* 15 [1989]: 838). (Hereafter B.)

24. In a later phrase, Derrida calls the feeling "of a wound" that he had in this period by a slightly more direct name, "hurt" (R 156).

25. W. Wolfgang Holdheim, "Jacques Derrida's Apologia," *Critical Inquiry* 15 (1989): 792.

26. John Brenkman and Jules David Law, "Resetting the Agenda," *Critical Inquiry* 15 (1989): 805.

27. This last phrase implies that some critics are attached to Derrida in the sense that they are parasites seeking fifteen minutes of professional fame, writing "with the sole aim of provoking a response that will make them stand out" (B 822). The theme of the "biodegradable" suggests the kind of writing professional self-interest produces—disposable prose, perhaps. Derrida also asks how he should respond to this genre of writing: "What would you be doing by responding 'no' to someone who says to you 'beat me so at least people see me or hear me crying and don't forget me'?" (B 822).

28. Jacques Derrida, *Limited Inc* [1972, 1977, 1988], trans. Samuel Weber and Jeffrey Mehlman, ed. Gerald Graff (Evanston: Northwestern University Press, 1988), 94. Believing himself the executor of Austin's philosophical will, Searle claims to develop a general theory of speech acts that Austin did not live to finish. Derrida remarks, "I sincerely regret that 'Austin did not live long enough,' and my regret is as sincere as anyone else's is, for there are surely many of us who mourn his loss. It is unfortunate, even infelicitous. But

through my tears I still smile at the argument of a 'development' (a word sufficiently ambiguous to mean both produce, formulate, *as well as* continue, so as to reach those 'detailed answers') that a longer life might have led to a successful conclusion" (*Limited Inc*, 94–95).

29. Derrida asks the same question of an interviewer in 1992, after the public commotion regarding his proposed honorary degree: "Can one speak of a debate when newspapers and television seem only to have offered . . . a stereotyped presentation?" (*Points*, 399).

30. See Jacques Derrida, "But, beyond . . . (Open Letter to Anne McClintock and Rob Nixon)," trans. Peggy Kamuf, in *"Race," Writing, and Difference*, ed. Henry Louis Gates, Jr. (Chicago: University of Chicago Press, 1986), 354.

31. Derrida portrays Richard Wolin and Thomas Sheehan in a similar way: "I find Wolin and Sheehan, in the end, more eloquent than I am. I even believe that, in the eyes of a vigilant reader, they say more or less everything" (*Points*, 424). Wolin and Sheehan exchanged letters with Derrida in the *New York Review of Books* after Wolin reprinted an interview with Derrida without Derrida's permission. Sheehan charged that Derrida did not want the interview reproduced because he was embarrassed by its contents, dealing with Heidegger's affiliations with Nazism.

32. Barbara Herrnstein Smith, *Belief and Resistance: Dynamics of Contemporary Intellectual Controversy* (Cambridge: Harvard University Press, 1997), 149.

33. Rodolphe Gasché, *Inventions of Difference: On Jacques Derrida* (Cambridge: Harvard University Press, 1994), 243.

34. Jacques Derrida, "Ulysses Gramophone: Hear Say Yes in Joyce" [1987], trans. Tina Kendall and Shari Benstock, in *Acts of Literature*, ed. Derek Attridge (New York: Routledge, 1992), 270.

35. Nicolas Abraham finds a similar supplementation in the "phantom," which he also terms "an invention": "the phantom is meant to objectify . . . the gap produced in us by the concealment of some part of a love object's life" ("Notes on the Phantom: A Complement to Freud's Metapsychology," in Nicolas Abraham and Maria Torok, *The Shell and the Kernel*, vol. 1 [1987], ed. and trans. Nicholas Rand [Chicago: University of Chicago Press, 1994], 171, quoted in Robert Smith, *Derrida and Autobiography*, 145n18).

36. Waters quotes an outline of a projected work "on aesthetics, rhetoric and ideology" that de Man sent him in August 1983 referring to an essay in progress on "Diderot's Battle of the Faculties" ("Paul de Man: Life and Works," introduction to *Critical Writings, 1953–1978*, lxx). De Man mentions that Kant's "faculties of reason and of imagination are personified, or anthropomorphized, like the five squabbling faculties hilariously staged by Diderot in the *Lettre sur les sourds et les muets*" (AI 86); he also cites Diderot's companion piece *Lettre sur les aveugles, à l'usage de ceux qui voient* in "Aesthetic Formalization in Kleist" (RR 289).

37. Denis Diderot, "Letter on the Blind for the Use of Those Who See" [1749], in

Selected Writings, trans. Derek Coltman, ed. Lester G. Crocker (New York: Macmillan, 1966), 32.

38. Averill notes that "during the sixteenth century, spring mechanisms came into widespread use as the motive power for clocks; by analogy, human motives came to be viewed as 'springs of action'" ("Inner Feelings, Works of the Flesh," 111).

39. See the etymological note of Heidegger's English translators, Macquarrie and Robinson, *Being and Time,* 172n3.

40. The above remarks are made by Peter Brooks, Shoshana Felman, Barbara Johnson, E. S. Burt, and Andrzej Warminski respectively.

41. Søren Kierkegaard, *The Concept of Irony, with Continual Reference to Socrates* [1841], ed. and trans. Howard V. Hong and Edna H. Hong (Princeton: Princeton University Press, 1989), 11.

42. De Man quotes Mallarmé's "Tombeau" (*Oeuvres complètes,* ed. Henri Mondor and G. Jean-Aubry [Paris: Gallimard, 1945], 71). De Man thus cites a testament to friendship in his parting letter to his friend. De Man offers an extended reading of this poem in "Lyric and Modernity" (BI 176–182). There he notes that the Verlaine elegy is "chronologically though not stylistically perhaps Mallarmé's last text" (BI 174–175), and concludes that "death for Mallarmé means precisely the discontinuity between the personal self and the voice that speaks in the poetry from the other bank of the river, beyond death" (BI 181).

Conclusion

1. Brothers asks us to "imagine a continuum of subjective experience, which ranges from your experience of an abstract idea, your experience of a word, or your experience of a color on one end, to your experience of the approach of someone who is about to tear you limb from limb on the other" (*Friday's Footprint,* 117). He also points out that empirical research has not managed to expand the clarity of fear to other emotional states (114–115).

2. Jean-Paul Sartre, *The Emotions: Outline of a Theory* [1948], trans. Bernard Frechtman (New York: Philosophical Library, 1948), 84.

3. Jacques Derrida, *The Truth in Painting* [1978], trans. Geoff Bennington and Ian McLeod (Chicago: University of Chicago Press, 1987), 61. Derrida's text is explicitly concerned with monstrosity and giantism in "the colossal," as in Goya's painting "The Colossus" or "Panic" (141).

4. See Barbara Herrnstein Smith, *Contingencies of Value: Alternative Perspectives for Critical Theory* (Cambridge: Harvard University Press, 1988), 154–155.

5. Robert Kirk, *Raw Feeling: A Philosophical Account of the Essence of Consciousness* (Oxford: Oxford University Press, 1994), 117–118.

6. "Some of your [or my] best friends . . ." alludes to the racist cliché, suggesting that the fear of dead subjects extends the fear that different people are differ-

ent in kind. The fact that real "zombies" are Haitian, as Dennett also points out, supports this connection (during colonialism people called them "automata"). Dennett is wholly explicit about racism's part in philosophical zombiemania: "It echoes the sort of utterly unmotivated prejudices that have denied full personhood to people on the basis of the color of their skin. It is time to recognize the idea of the possibility of zombies for what it is: not a serious philosophical idea but a preposterous and ignoble relic of ancient prejudices. Maybe women aren't really conscious! Maybe Jews!" (*Consciousness Explained*, 405–406). Maybe animals, too (*pace Consciousness Explained*, 442–451).

7. Steven Shaviro, *The Cinematic Body* (Minneapolis: University of Minnesota Press, 1993), 86–87.

8. Ronald de Sousa, "Rational Homunculi," in *The Identities of Persons*, ed. Amélie Oksenberg Rorty (Berkeley and Los Angeles: University of California Press, 1976), 218.

References

Abraham, Nicolas. "Notes on the Phantom: A Complement to Freud's Metapsychology." In Nicolas Abraham and Maria Torok, *The Shell and the Kernel*, vol. 1 [1987], ed. and trans. Nicholas Rand, 171–176. Chicago: University of Chicago Press, 1994.

Ackerman, R. D. Review of *Memoires for Paul de Man. Philosophy and Literature* 11 (1987): 171–181.

Agamben, Giorgio. *Stanzas: Word and Phantasm in Western Culture* [1977], trans. Ronald L. Martinez. Minneapolis: University of Minnesota Press, 1993.

Althusser, Louis. "Sur le rapport de Marx et de Hegel." In *Lenine et la philosophie*, 84–86. Paris: F. Maspero, 1969.

Ansell Pearson, Keith. *Germinal Life: The Difference and Repetition of Deleuze*. London: Routledge, 1999.

Aristotle. *The Art of Rhetoric*, trans. H. C. Lawson-Tancred. Harmondsworth: Penguin, 1991.

——— *Nicomachean Ethics*, trans. Terence Irwin. Indianapolis: Hackett, 1985.

——— *Poetics*, trans. Richard Janko. Indianapolis: Hackett, 1987.

Armstrong, Aurelia. "Some Reflections on Deleuze's Spinoza: Composition and Agency." In *Deleuze and Philosophy: The Difference Engineer*, ed. Keith Ansell Pearson, 44–57. London: Routledge, 1977.

Armstrong, Nancy. *Desire and Domestic Fiction: A Political History of the Novel*. Oxford: Oxford University Press, 1987.

Austin, J. L. *How to Do Things with Words*, 2nd ed., ed. J. O. Urmson and Marina Sbisà. Cambridge: Harvard University Press, 1975.

Averill, James R. "Inner Feelings, Works of the Flesh, the Beast Within, Diseases of the Mind, Driving Force, and Putting on a Show: Six Metaphors of Emotion and Their Theoretical Extensions." In *Metaphors in the History of Psy-*

chology, ed. David E. Leary, 104–132. Cambridge: Cambridge University Press, 1990.

Badiou, Alain. *Deleuze: The Clamor of Being* [1977]. Minneapolis: University of Minnesota Press, 1999.

Bains, Paul. "Subjectless Subjectivities." *Canadian Review of Comparative Literature/Revue Canadienne de Littérature Comparée* (1997): 512–528.

Balibar, Etienne. "Subjection and Subjectivation." In *Supposing the Subject,* ed. Joan Copjec, 1–15. London: Verso, 1994.

Banta, Martha. "Mental Work, Metal Work." *PMLA* 113 (1998): 199–211.

Barnes, Elizabeth. *States of Sympathy: Seduction and Democracy in the American Novel.* New York: Columbia University Press, 1997.

Barthes, Roland. *The Pleasure of the Text* [1973], trans. Richard Howard. New York: Farrar, Straus & Giroux, 1975.

——— *The Responsibility of Forms: Critical Essays on Music, Art, and Representation* [1982], trans. Richard Howard. New York: Hill & Wang, 1985.

Bennington, Geoffrey. "Derridabase." In Jacques Derrida and Geoffrey Bennington, *Jacques Derrida* [1991], trans. Geoffrey Bennington. Chicago: University of Chicago Press, 1993.

Berezdivin, Ruben. "Drawing: (An) Affecting Nietzsche: With Derrida." In *Derrida and Deconstruction,* ed. Hugh J. Silverman, 92–107. London: Routledge, 1989.

Bernasconi, Robert. "No More Stories, Good or Bad: de Man's Criticisms of Derrida on Rousseau." In *Derrida: A Critical Reader,* ed. David Wood, 137–166. Oxford: Blackwell, 1992.

Bernheimer, Charles. *Flaubert and Kafka: Studies in Psychopoetic Structure.* New Haven: Yale University Press, 1982.

Bordo, Susan. *The Flight to Objectivity: Essays on Cartesianism and Culture.* Albany: SUNY Press, 1987.

Brenkman, John, and Jules David Law. "Resetting the Agenda." *Critical Inquiry* 15 (1989): 804–811.

Brooks, Peter, Shoshana Felman, and J. Hillis Miller, eds. *The Lesson of Paul de Man. Yale French Studies* 69 (1985).

Brothers, Leslie. *Friday's Footprint: How Society Shapes the Human Mind.* Oxford: Oxford University Press, 1997.

Bruhm, Steven. "Aesthetics and Anaesthetics at the Revolution." *Studies in Romanticism* 32 (1993): 399–424.

Budd, Malcolm. *Music and the Emotions: The Philosophical Theories.* London: Routledge & Kegan Paul, 1985.

Burke, Edmund. *A Philosophical Enquiry into the Origin of Our Ideas of the Sublime and Beautiful* [1759]. Oxford: Oxford University Press, 1990.

Butler, Judith. *The Psychic Life of Power: Theories in Subjection.* Stanford: Stanford University Press, 1997.

Cacciari, Massimo. *Posthumous People: Vienna at the Turning Point* [1980], trans. Rodger Friedman. Stanford: Stanford University Press, 1996.

Cadava, Eduardo, Peter Connor, and Jean-Luc Nancy, eds. *Who Comes after the Subject?* New York: Routledge, 1991.

Caraher, Brian. "*Allegories of Reading:* Positing a Rhetoric of Romanticism; or, Paul de Man's Critique of Pure Figural Anteriority." *Pre/Text* 4 (1985).

Caruth, Cathy. *Empirical Truths and Critical Fictions: Locke, Wordsworth, Kant, Freud.* Baltimore: Johns Hopkins University Press, 1991.

Caserio, Robert L. "'A Pathos of Uncertain Agency': Paul de Man and Narrative," *Journal of Narrative Technique* 20 (1990): 195–209.

Cavell, Stanley. *In Quest of the Ordinary: Lines of Skepticism and Romanticism.* Chicago: University of Chicago Press, 1988.

Chase, Cynthia. *Decomposing Figures: Rhetorical Readings in the Romantic Tradition.* Baltimore: Johns Hopkins University Press, 1986.

——— "Primary Narcissism and the Giving of Figure: Kristeva with Hertz and de Man." In *Abjection, Melancholia, and Love: The Work of Julia Kristeva,* ed. John Fletcher and Andrew Benjamin, 124–136. New York: Routledge, 1990.

Clément, Catherine. *Syncope: The Philosophy of Rapture* [1990], trans. Sally O'Driscoll and Deirdre M. Mahoney. Minneapolis: University of Minnesota Press, 1994.

Conroy, Mark. "De Man on *The Social Contract:* Reading Rousseau's Fine Print." *Criticism* 31 (1989): 53–73.

Corngold, Stanley. *Complex Pleasure: Forms of Feeling in German Literature.* Stanford: Stanford University Press, 1998.

Cvetkovich, Ann. *Mixed Feelings: Feminism, Mass Culture, and Victorian Sensationalism.* New Brunswick: Rutgers University Press, 1992.

Dadlez, E. M. *What's Hecuba to Him? Fictional Events and Actual Emotions.* University Park: Pennsylvania State University Press, 1997.

Dahlbohm, Bo, ed. *Dennett and His Critics: Demystifying Mind.* Oxford: Blackwell, 1993.

Damasio, Antonio. *Descartes' Error: Emotion, Reason, and the Human Brain.* New York: G. P. Putnam's Sons, 1994.

Damasio, Antonio, Hanna Damasio, and Gary W. Van Hoesen. "Prosopagnosia: Anatomic Basis and Behavioral Mechanisms." *Neurology* 21 (1982): 331–341.

Danto, Arthur. "Historical Language and Historical Reality." *Review of Metaphysics* 27 (1973): 219–259.

Darwin, Charles. *The Expression of Emotions in Man and Animals* [1872]. Chicago: University of Chicago Press, 1965.

Davidson, Donald. *Essays on Actions and Events.* Oxford: Clarendon Press, 1990.

Davies, Stephen. "Contra the Hypothetical Persona in Music." In *Emotion and the Arts,* ed. Mette Hjort and Sue Laver, 95–109. Oxford: Oxford University Press, 1997.

Deleuze, Gilles. *Cinema 1: The Movement-Image* [1983], trans. Hugh Tomlinson and Barbara Habberjam. Minneapolis: University of Minnesota Press, 1986.

———— *Empiricism and Subjectivity: An Essay on Hume's Theory of Human Nature* [1953], trans. Constantin V. Boundas. New York: Columbia University Press, 1991.

———— *Expressionism in Philosophy: Spinoza* [1968], trans. Martin Joughin. New York: Zone Books, 1998.

———— *The Fold: Leibniz, or the Baroque* [1988], trans. Tom Conley. Minneapolis: University of Minnesota Press, 1993.

———— *Foucault* [1986], trans. Seán Hand. Minneapolis: University of Minnesota Press, 1988.

———— "Immanence: A Life . . . ," trans. N. Millett. *Theory, Culture, and Society* 14 (1997): 3–9.

———— *The Logic of Sense* [1969], ed. Constantin V. Boundas, trans. Mark Lester with Charles Stivale. New York: Columbia University Press, 1990.

———— *Logique de la sensation.* Paris: Editions de la différence, 1981.

———— *Spinoza: Practical Philosophy* [1970], trans. Robert Hurley. San Francisco: City Lights Books, 1981.

Deleuze, Gilles, and Félix Guattari. *Anti-Oedipus: Capitalism and Schizophrenia* [1972], trans. Robert Hurley, Mark Seem, and Helen R. Lane. Minneapolis: University of Minnesota Press, 1983.

———— *A Thousand Plateaus: Capitalism and Schizophrenia* [1980], trans. Brian Massumi. Minneapolis: University of Minnesota Press, 1987.

———— *What Is Philosophy?* [1991], trans. Hugh Tomlinson and Graham Burchell. New York: Columbia University Press, 1994.

de Man, Paul. *Aesthetic Ideology,* ed. Andrzej Warminski. Minneapolis: University of Minnesota Press, 1996.

———— *Allegories of Reading: Figural Language in Rousseau, Nietzsche, Rilke, and Proust.* New Haven: Yale University Press, 1979.

———— *Blindness and Insight: Essays in the Rhetoric of Contemporary Criticism* [1971, 1983], 2nd ed. Minneapolis: University of Minnesota Press, 1983.

———— *The Rhetoric of Romanticism.* New York: Columbia University Press, 1984.

Dennett, Daniel C. "Back from the Drawing Board." In *Dennett and His Critics: Demystifying Mind,* ed. Bo Dahlbohm, 203–235. Oxford: Blackwell, 1993.

———— *Consciousness Explained.* Boston: Little, Brown, 1991.

———— *Darwin's Dangerous Idea: Evolution and the Meanings of Life.* New York: Simon & Schuster, 1995.

———— *The Intentional Stance.* Cambridge: MIT Press, 1987.

———— "Quining Qualia." In *Consciousness in Contemporary Science,* ed. A. J. Marcel and E. Bisiach, 42–77. Oxford: Clarendon Press, 1988.

———— "Why You Can't Make a Computer That Feels Pain" [1978]. In *Brainstorms: Philosophical Essays on Mind and Psychology,* 190–229. Cambridge: MIT Press, 1981.

Dennett, Daniel C., and Kathleen A. Akins. "Who May I Say Is Calling?" *Behavioral and Brain Sciences* 9 (1986): 517–518.

Derrida, Jacques. "Biodegradables: Seven Diary Fragments." *Critical Inquiry* 15 (1989): 812–873.

—— "But, beyond . . . (Open Letter to Anne McClintock and Rob Nixon)" [1986], trans. Peggy Kamuf. In *"Race," Writing, and Difference,* ed. Henry Louis Gates, Jr., 354–369. Chicago: University of Chicago Press, 1986.

—— "By Force of Mourning" [1993], trans. Pascale-Anne Brault and Michael Nass. *Critical Inquiry* 22 (1996): 171–192.

—— *Dissemination* [1972], trans. Barbara Johnson. Chicago: University of Chicago Press, 1981.

—— "'Eating Well': An Interview" with Jean-Luc Nancy, trans. Peter Connor and Avital Ronell. In *Who Comes After the Subject?,* ed. Eduardo Cadava, Peter Connor, and Jean-Luc Nancy, 96–119. New York: Routledge, 1991.

—— "Force and Signification" [1963], in *Writing and Difference,* trans. Alan Bass, 3–30. Chicago: University of Chicago Press, 1978.

—— "Like the Sound of the Sea Deep within a Shell: Paul de Man's War" [1988]. In *Responses: On Paul de Man's Wartime Journalism,* ed. Werner Hamacher, Neil Hertz, and Thomas Keenan, 127–164. Lincoln: University of Nebraska Press, 1989.

—— *Limited Inc* [1972, 1977, 1988], trans. Samuel Weber and Jeffrey Mehlman, ed. Gerald Graff. Evanston: Northwestern University Press, 1988.

—— "Living On: Border Lines," trans. James Hulbert. In *Deconstruction and Criticism,* ed. Harold Bloom, 75–176. New York: Seabury Press, 1979.

—— *Memoires for Paul de Man,* trans. Cecile Lindsay, Jonathan Culler, and Eduardo Cadava. New York: Columbia University Press, 1986.

—— *Of Grammatology* [1967], trans. Gayatri Chakravorty Spivak. Baltimore: Johns Hopkins University Press, 1976.

—— "On a Newly Arisen Apocalyptic Tone in Philosophy" [1981], trans. John Leavey, Jr. In *Raising the Tone of Philosophy: Late Essays by Immanuel Kant, Transformative Critique by Jacques Derrida,* ed. Peter Fenves, 117–171. Baltimore: Johns Hopkins University Press, 1993.

—— "Passions: An Oblique Offering," trans. David Wood. In *Derrida: A Critical Reader,* ed. David Wood, 5–35. Oxford: Blackwell, 1992.

—— *Points . . . Interviews, 1974–1994,* ed. Elisabeth Weber, trans. Peggy Kamuf et al. Stanford: Stanford University Press, 1995.

—— *The Post Card: From Socrates to Freud and Beyond* [1980], trans. Alan Bass. Chicago: University of Chicago Press, 1987.

—— "Psyche: Inventions of the Other" [1987], trans. Catherine Porter. In *Reading de Man Reading,* ed. Lindsay Waters and Wlad Godzich, 25–65. Minneapolis: University of Minnesota Press, 1989.

—— *Speech and Phenomena and Other Essays on Husserl's Theory of Signs* [1967], trans. David B. Allison. Evanston: Northwestern University Press, 1973.

—— *The Truth in Painting* [1978], trans. Geoff Bennington and Ian McLeod. Chicago: University of Chicago Press, 1987.

——— "Ulysses Gramophone: Hear Say Yes in Joyce" [1987], trans. Tina Kendall and Shari Benstock, 256–309. In *Acts of Literature*, ed. Derek Attridge. New York: Routledge, 1992.

——— "White Mythology: Metaphor in the Text of Philosophy," in *Margins of Philosophy* [1972], trans. Alan Bass, 207–272. Chicago: University of Chicago Press, 1982.

——— *Writing and Difference* [1967], trans. Alan Bass. Chicago: University of Chicago Press, 1978.

Derrida, Jacques, and Geoffrey Bennington. *Jacques Derrida*. Chicago: University of Chicago Press, 1993.

Descartes, René. *The Philosophical Writings of Descartes*, 3 vols., trans. John Cottingham, Robert Stoothoff, and Dugald Murdoch. Cambridge: Cambridge University Press, 1985.

Descombes, Vincent. "Apropos of the 'Critique of the Subject' and of the Critique of This Critique." In *Who Comes after the Subject?*, ed. Eduardo Cadava, Peter Connor, and Jean-Luc Nancy, 120–134. New York: Routledge, 1991.

de Sousa, Ronald. *The Rationality of Emotion*. Cambridge: MIT Press, 1987.

——— "Rational Homunculi." In *The Identities of Persons*, ed. Amélie Oksenberg Rorty, 217–238. Berkeley and Los Angeles: University of California Press, 1976.

Diderot, Denis. "Letter on the Blind for the Use of Those Who See" [1749]. In *Selected Writings*, trans. Derk Coltman, ed. Lester G. Crocker, 14–39. New York: Macmillan, 1966.

Dubos, Jean Baptiste (abbé). *Réflexions critiques sur la poésie et sur la peinture*, vol. 1. Paris, 1740.

Dufrenne, Mikel. *The Phenomenology of Aesthetic Experience* [1953], trans. Edward S. Casey, Albert A. Anderson, Willis Domingo, and Leon Jacobson. Evanston: Northwestern University Press, 1973.

Eagleton, Terry. *The Ideology of the Aesthetic*. Oxford: Blackwell, 1990.

Ellison, Julie. *Cato's Tears and the Making of Anglo-American Emotion*. Chicago: University of Chicago Press, 1999.

Fenves, Peter. "The Topicality of Tone." In *Raising the Tone of Philosophy: Late Essays by Immanuel Kant, Transformative Critique by Jacques Derrida*, ed. Peter Fenves, 1–48. Baltimore: Johns Hopkins University Press, 1993.

Ferry, Luc, and Alain Renaut. *French Philosophy of the Sixties: An Essay on Antihumanism* [1985], trans. Mary H. S. Cattani. Amherst: University of Massachusetts Press, 1990.

Flesch, William. "Ancestral Voices: De Man and His Defenders." In *Responses: On Paul de Man's Wartime Journalism*, ed. Werner Hamacher, Neil Hertz, and Thomas Keenan, 173–184. Lincoln: University of Nebraska Press, 1989.

Foucault, Michel. *The History of Sexuality*. Vol. 1: *An Introduction* [1976], trans. Robert Hurley. New York: Vintage, 1990.

—— *The History of Sexuality.* Vol. 2: *The Use of Pleasure* [1984], trans. Robert Hurley. New York: Vintage, 1986.

—— *The History of Sexuality.* Vol. 3: *The Care of the Self* [1984], trans. Robert Hurley. New York: Vintage, 1986.

—— "My Body, This Paper, This Fire" [1972], trans. Geoffrey Bennington. *Oxford Literary Review* 4 (1979): 9–28.

—— *The Order of Things: An Archaeology of the Human Sciences* [1966], trans. Alan Sheridan. New York: Vintage, 1994.

—— "Theatrum Philosophicum" [1970], trans. Donald F. Bouchard and Sherry Simon. In *Language, Counter-Memory, Practice: Selected Essays and Interviews,* ed. Donald F. Bouchard, 165–196. Ithaca, N.Y.: Cornell University Press, 1977.

Frank, Joseph. "Dialogical Introduction" to the symposium "A Turn away from 'Language'?" *Common Knowledge* 4 (1995): 24–27.

Frank, Manfred. *What Is Neostructuralism?* [1984], trans. Sabine Wilke and Richard Gray. Minneapolis: University of Minnesota Press, 1989.

Freud, Sigmund. *The Standard Edition of the Complete Psychological Works of Sigmund Freud,* 24 vols., ed. James Strachey et al. London: Hogarth Press, 1953–1974.

Frey, Hans-Jost. "Undecidability." *Yale French Studies* 69 (1985): 124–133.

Fried, Michael. *Absorption and Theatricality: Painting and Beholder in the Age of Diderot.* Berkeley and Los Angeles: University of California Press, 1980.

Gallagher, Catherine. *Nobody's Story: The Vanishing Acts of Women Writers in the Literary Marketplace.* Berkeley and Los Angeles: University of California Press, 1994.

Gasché, Rodolphe. *Inventions of Difference: On Jacques Derrida.* Cambridge: Harvard University Press, 1994.

—— "On Mere Sight: A Response to Paul de Man." In *The Textual Sublime: Deconstruction and Its Differences,* ed. Hugh J. Silverman and Gary E. Aylesworth, 109–115. Albany: SUNY Press, 1990.

—— *The Tain of the Mirror.* Cambridge: Harvard University Press, 1987.

—— *The Wild Card of Reading: On Paul de Man.* Cambridge: Harvard University Press, 1998.

Gearhart, Suzanne. "Philosophy *before* Literature: Deconstruction, Historicity, and the Work of Paul de Man." *Diacritics* 13 (1983): 63–77.

Gordon, Robert M. "The Passivity of Emotions." *Philosophical Review* 95 (1986): 371–392.

Greenspan, Patricia. *Emotions and Reasons: An Inquiry into Emotional Justification.* New York: Routledge, 1984.

Greimas, Algirdas Julien, and Jacques Fontanille. *The Semiotics of Passions: From States of Affairs to States of Feelings* [1991], trans. Paul Perron and Frank Collins. Minneapolis: University of Minnesota Press, 1993.

Griffiths, Paul. *What Emotions Really Are: The Problem of Psychological Categories.* Chicago: University of Chicago Press, 1997.

Grossberg, Lawrence. *We Gotta Get Out of This Place: Popular Conservatism and Postmodern Culture.* New York: Routledge, 1992.

Guillory, John. *Cultural Capital: The Problem of Literary Canon Formation.* Chicago: University of Chicago Press, 1993.

Hamacher, Werner. "'Lectio': de Man's Imperative." In *Premises: Essays on Philosophy and Literature from Kant to Celan,* trans. Peter Fenves, 181–221. Cambridge: Harvard University Press, 1996.

Hamacher, Werner, Neil Hertz, and Thomas Keenan, eds. *Responses: On Paul de Man's Wartime Journalism.* Lincoln: University of Nebraska Press, 1989.

Harding, Sandra, and Merrill B. Hintikka, eds. *Discovering Reality: Feminist Perspectives on Epistemology, Metaphysics, Methodology, and Philosophy of Science.* Dordrecht: D. Reidel, 1983.

Hardt, Michael. *Gilles Deleuze: An Apprenticeship in Philosophy.* Minneapolis: University of Minnesota Press, 1993.

Harth, Erica. *Cartesian Women: Versions and Subversions of Rational Discourse in the Old Regime.* Ithaca, N.Y.: Cornell University Press, 1992.

Harvey, Irene E. "Doubling the Space of Existence: Exemplarity in Derrida—the Case of Rousseau." In *Deconstruction and Philosophy: The Texts of Jacques Derrida,* ed. John Sallis, 60–70. Chicago: University of Chicago Press, 1987.

Haverkamp, Anselm, ed. *Deconstruction is/in America: A New Sense of the Political.* New York: New York University Press, 1995.

Hegel, G. W. F. *Introductory Lectures on Aesthetics* [1842], trans. Bernard Bosanquet, ed. Michael Inwood. Harmondsworth: Penguin, 1993.

Heidegger, Martin. *Being and Time* [1927–1957], trans. John Macquarrie and Edward Robinson. New York: Harper & Row, 1962.

Hertz, Neil. "Dr. Johnson's Forgetfulness, Descartes's Piece of Wax." *Eighteenth-Century Life* 16 (1992): 167–181.

—— *The End of the Line: Essays on Psychoanalysis and the Sublime.* New York: Columbia University Press, 1985.

—— "Lurid Figures." In *Reading de Man Reading,* ed. Lindsay Waters and Wlad Godzich, 82–105. Minneapolis: University of Minnesota Press, 1989.

—— "More Lurid Figures." *Diacritics* 20 (1990), 2–49.

Hiley, David S. *Philosophy in Question: Essays on a Pyrrhonian Theme.* Chicago: University of Chicago Press, 1988.

Holdheim, W. Wolfgang. "Jacques Derrida's Apologia." *Critical Inquiry* 15 (1989): 784–796.

Husserl, Edmund. *Ideas: General Introduction to Pure Phenomenology* [1922], 2 vols., trans. W. R. Boyce Gibson. London: Allen and Unwin, 1931.

—— *Logical Investigations,* 2nd ed. [1913–1921], 2 vols., trans. J. N. Findlay. New York: Humanities Press, 1970.

—— *The Phenomenology of Internal Time-Consciousness* [1905], ed. Martin Heidegger, trans. James S. Churchill. Bloomington: Indiana University Press, 1964.

Jackson, Frank. "Epiphenomenal Qualia." *Philosophical Quarterly* 32 (1982): 127–136.

Jacobs, Carol. *Telling Time: Lévi-Strauss, Ford, Lessing, Benjamin, de Man, Wordsworth, Rilke.* Baltimore: Johns Hopkins University Press, 1993.

Jaggar, Alison M. "Love and Knowledge: Emotion in Feminist Epistemology." In *Gender/Body/Knowledge: Feminist Reconstructions of Knowing and Being,* ed. Alison M. Jaggar and Susan Bordo. New Brunswick, N.J.: Rutgers University Press, 1989.

Jameson, Fredric. *Postmodernism, or, the Logic of Late Capitalism.* Durham: Duke University Press, 1991.

Kant, Immanuel. *Critique of Judgment* [1790], trans. Werner S. Pluhar. Indianapolis: Hackett, 1987.

Kaplan, Alice Yaeger. *French Lessons: A Memoir.* Chicago: University of Chicago Press, 1993.

Kay, Carol. "Hobbesian Fear: Richardson, de Man, Rousseau, and Burke." In *Critical Conditions: Regarding the Historical Moment,* ed. Michael Hays, 97–114. Minneapolis: University of Minnesota Press, 1992.

Keats, John. *Poetical Works,* ed. H. W. Garrod. Oxford: Oxford University Press, 1970.

Keenan, Thomas. *Fables of Responsibility: Aberrations and Predicaments in Ethics and Politics.* Stanford: Stanford University Press, 1997.

Kenny, Anthony. *Action, Emotion, and Will.* London: Routledge, 1963.

Kierkegaard, Søren. *The Concept of Irony, with Continual Reference to Socrates* [1841], ed. and trans. Howard V. Hong and Edna H. Hong. Princeton: Princeton University Press, 1989.

Kirk, Robert. *Raw Feeling: A Philosophical Account of the Essence of Consciousness.* Oxford: Oxford University Press, 1994.

Kivy, Peter. *The Corded Shell: Reflections on Musical Expression.* Princeton: Princeton University Press, 1980.

——— "The Quest for Musical Profundity." In *Philosophies of Arts: An Essay in Differences,* 140–213. Cambridge: Cambridge University Press, 1997.

Klein, Richard. "The Blindness of Hyperboles: The Ellipses of Insight." *Diacritics* 3 (1974): 33–44.

Kristeva, Julia. *Revolution in Poetic Language* [1974], trans. Margaret Waller. New York: Columbia University Press, 1984.

LaCapra, Dominick. *Soundings in Critical Theory.* Ithaca, N.Y.: Cornell University Press, 1989.

Lacoue-Labarthe, Philippe. *Typography: Mimesis, Philosophy, Politics,* trans. Eugenio Donato, ed. Christopher Fynsk. Cambridge: Harvard University Press, 1989.

Lacour, Claudia Brodsky. *Lines of Thought: Discourse, Architectonics, and the Origin of Modern Philosophy.* Durham, N.C.: Duke University Press, 1996.

Langer, Susanne K. *Feeling and Form: A Theory of Art Developed from Philosophy in a New Key.* New York: Charles Scribner's Sons, 1953.

Leclaire, Serge. *Psychoanalyzing: On the Order of the Unconscious and the Practice of the Letter* [1968], trans. Peggy Kamuf. Stanford: Stanford University Press, 1998.

Lem, Stanislaw. *Solaris* [1961], trans. Joanna Kilmartin and Steve Cox. New York: Berkley Publishing Corporation, 1970.

Levinas, Emmanuel. *Totality and Infinity* [1961], trans. Alphonso Lingis. Pittsburgh: Duquesne University Press, 1985.

Levinson, Jerrold. *Music, Art, and Metaphysics: Essays in Philosophical Aesthetics.* Ithaca, N.Y.: Cornell University Press, 1990.

——— "Musical Profundity Misplaced." *Journal of Aesthetics and Art Criticism* 50 (1992).

——— *The Pleasures of Aesthetics: Philosophical Essays.* Ithaca, N.Y.: Cornell University Press, 1996.

Lloyd, Genevieve. *The Man of Reason: "Male" and "Female" in Western Philosophy,* 2nd ed. Minneapolis: University of Minnesota Press, 1993.

Lucy, Niall. *Debating Derrida.* Victoria: Melbourne University Press, 1995.

Luhmann, Niklas. *Love as Passion: The Codification of Intimacy* [1982], trans. Jeremy Gaines and Doris L. Jones. Stanford: Stanford University Press, 1998.

Lynch, Deidre. *The Economy of Character: Novels, Market Culture, and the Business of Inner Meaning.* Chicago: University of Chicago Press, 1998.

MacCannell, Juliet Flower. "Portrait: de Man." *Genre* 17 (1984): 51–74.

Mallarmé, Stephane. *Oeuvres complètes,* ed. Henri Mondor and G. Jean-Aubry. Paris: Gallimard, 1945.

Marion, Jean-Luc. *Cartesian Questions.* Chicago: University of Chicago Press, 1999.

Marshall, David. *The Figure of Theater: Shaftesbury, Defoe, Adam Smith, and George Eliot.* New York: Columbia University Press, 1986.

——— *The Surprising Effects of Sympathy: Marivaux, Diderot, Rousseau, and Mary Shelley.* Chicago: University of Chicago Press, 1988.

Massumi, Brian. "The Autonomy of Affect." *Cultural Critique* 31 (1995): 83–109.

——— "Deleuze, Guattari, and the Philosophy of Expression." *Canadian Review of Comparative Literature/Revue Canadienne de Littérature Comparée* (1997): 745–782.

——— "Everywhere You Want to Be: Introduction to Fear." In *The Politics of Everyday Fear,* ed. Brian Massumi, 3–37. Minneapolis: University of Minnesota Press, 1993.

Matravers, Derek. *Art and Emotion.* Oxford: Oxford University Press, 1998.

McDowell, John. *Mind and World.* Cambridge: Harvard University Press, 1996.

McGann, Jerome J. *The Romantic Ideology: A Critical Investigation.* Chicago: University of Chicago Press, 1983.

Mehlman, Jeffrey. "Prosopopoeia Revisited." *Romanic Review* 81 (1990): 137–143.

Menninghaus, Winfried. *In Praise of Nonsense: Kant and Bluebeard* [1995], trans. Henry Pickford. Stanford: Stanford University Press, 1999.

Mizumura, Minae. "Renunciation." *Yale French Studies* 69 (1985): 81–97.

Moran, Richard. "The Expression of Feeling in Imagination." *Philosophical Review* 103 (1994): 75–106.

Morrison, James. "Deleuze and Film Semiotics." *Semiotica* 88 (1992): 269–290.

Murphy, Timothy S. "Quantum Ontology: A Virtual Mechanics of Becoming." In *Deleuze and Guattari: New Mappings in Politics, Philosophy, and Culture,* ed. Eleanor Kaufman and Kevin Jon Heller, 211–229. Minneapolis: University of Minnesota Press, 1998.

Nancy, Jean-Luc. "Dum Scribo," trans. Ian MacLeod. *Oxford Literary Review* 3 (1978): 6–21.

——— "Elliptical Sense," trans. Peter Connor. In *Derrida: A Critical Reader,* ed. David Wood, 36–51. Oxford: Blackwell, 1992.

——— "Introduction" to *Who Comes after the Subject?,* ed. Eduardo Cadava, Peter Connor, and Jean-Luc Nancy, 1–8. New York: Routledge, 1991.

Negri, Antonio. *The Savage Anomaly: The Power of Spinoza's Metaphysics and Politics* [1981], trans. Michael Hardt. Minneapolis: University of Minnesota Press, 1991.

Nietzsche, Friedrich. *The Birth of Tragedy* [1872], trans. Walter Kaufmann. New York: Vintage, 1967.

——— *The Gay Science* [1887], trans. Walter Kaufmann. New York: Vintage, 1974.

——— *The Twilight of the Idols* [1889], trans. R. J. Hollingdale, 2nd ed. Harmondsworth: Penguin Books, 1990.

Nissenbaum, Helen. *Emotion and Focus.* Stanford: Center for the Study of Language and Information, 1985.

Norris, Christopher. "Utopian Deconstruction: Ernst Bloch, Paul de Man, and the Politics of Music." *Paragraph* 11 (1988): 24–57.

Nussbaum, Martha C. *Love's Knowledge: Essays on Philosophy and Literature.* Oxford: Oxford University Press, 1990.

——— *The Therapy of Desire: Theory and Practice in Hellenistic Ethics.* Princeton: Princeton University Press, 1994.

Picard, Rosalind W. *Affective Computing.* Cambridge: MIT Press, 1997.

Pinch, Adela. *Strange Fits of Passion: Emotional Epistemologies from Hume to Austen.* Stanford: Stanford University Press, 1996.

Plato. *The Collected Dialogues of Plato,* ed. Edith Hamilton and Huntington Cairns, various trans. Princeton: Princeton University Press, 1961.

Polan, Dana. "Francis Bacon: The Logic of Sensation," in *Gilles Deleuze and the Theater of Philosophy,* ed. Constantin V. Boundas and Dorothea Olkowski, 229–254. New York: Routledge, 1994.

Prins, Yopie. *Victorian Sappho.* Princeton: Princeton University Press, 1999.

Proust, Marcel. *Remembrance of Things Past* [1913–1927], 3 vols., trans. C. K. Scott Moncrieff and A. Mayor, rev. Terence Kilmartin. New York: Vintage, 1981.

Redfield, Marc. "De Man, Schiller, and the Politics of Reception." *Diacritics* 23 (1990): 50–70.

Ricoeur, Paul. *Freedom and Nature: The Voluntary and the Involuntary* [1949], trans. Erazim V. Kohák. Evanston: Northwestern University Press, 1966.

Ridley, Aaron. *Music, Value, and the Passions*. Ithaca, N.Y.: Cornell University Press, 1995.

—— "Musical Sympathies: The Experience of Expressive Music." *Journal of Aesthetics and Art Criticism* 54 (1995): 49–57.

Robbins, Jill. *Altered Reading: Levinas and Literature*. Chicago: University of Chicago Press, 1999.

Rorty, Amélie Oksenberg. "Cartesian Passions and the Union of Mind and Body." In *Essays on Descartes' Meditations,* ed. Amélie Oksenberg Rorty, 513–534. Berkeley and Los Angeles: University of California Press, 1986.

—— "Explaining Emotions." In *Explaining Emotions,* ed. Amélie Oksenberg Rorty, 103–106. Berkeley and Los Angeles: University of California Press, 1980.

Rousseau, Jean-Jacques. *The Confessions* [1781], trans. J. M. Cohen. Harmondsworth: Penguin, 1953.

—— *Emile* [1762], trans. Barbara Foxley. London: Dent, 1911.

—— *Essay on the Origin of Languages* [1781], trans. John H. Moran and Alexander Gode. New York: Frederick Ungar Publishing Co., 1966.

—— *Letter to M. D'Alembert* [1758], trans. Allan Bloom as *Politics and the Arts,* ed. Allan Bloom. Ithaca, N.Y.: Cornell University Press, 1968.

—— *Oeuvres complètes,* 5 vols., ed. Bernard Gagnebin and Marcel Raymond. Paris: Gallimard, 1959.

—— *"The Social Contract" and Discourses,* trans. G. D. H. Cole. London: Dent, 1973.

Sadoff, Dianne F. Review of Cathy Caruth, *Unclaimed Experience: Trauma, Narrative, and History* and John O'Neill, ed., *Freud and the Passions. South Atlantic Review* 62 (1992).

Santner, Eric. *Stranded Objects: Mourning, Memory, and Film in Postwar Germany.* Ithaca, N.Y.: Cornell University Press, 1990.

Sartre, Jean-Paul. *The Emotions: Outline of a Theory* [1948], trans. Bernard Frechtman. New York: Philosophical Library, 1948.

Schacter, Stanley, and J. E. Singer. "Cognitive, Social, and Physiological Determinants of Emotional State." *Psychological Review* 69 (1962): 379–399.

Schiller, J. C. F. "On the Sublime (Toward the Further Development of Some Kantian Ideas)" [1801], trans. Daniel O. Dahlstrom. In *Essays,* ed. Walter Hinderer and Daniel O. Dahlstrom, 22–44. New York: Continuum, 1993.

Schopenhauer, Arthur. *The World as Will and Representation* [1859], 2 vols., trans. E. F. J. Payne. New York: Dover, 1969.

Schultz, William R., and Fried, Lewis L. B. *Jacques Derrida: An Annotated Primary and Secondary Bibliography.* New York: Garland Publishing, 1992.

Sedgwick, Eve Kosofsky, and Adam Frank. "Shame in the Cybernetic Fold: Reading Silvan Tomkins." In *Shame and Its Sisters: A Silvan Tomkins Reader,* ed. Eve Kosofsky Sedgwick and Adam Frank, 1–28. Durham: Duke University Press, 1995.

Shaviro, Steven. *The Cinematic Body.* Minneapolis: University of Minnesota Press, 1993.

Siebers, Tobin. "Mourning Becomes Paul de Man." In *Responses: On Paul de Man's Wartime Journalism,* ed. Werner Hamacher, Neil Hertz, and Thomas Keenan, 363–367. Lincoln: University of Nebraska Press, 1989.

Smith, Barbara Herrnstein. *Belief and Resistance: Dynamics of Contemporary Intellectual Controversy.* Cambridge: Harvard University Press, 1997.

―――― *Contingencies of Value: Alternative Perspectives for Critical Theory.* Cambridge: Harvard University Press, 1988.

Smith, Robert. *Derrida and Autobiography.* Cambridge: Cambridge University Press, 1995.

Sokolsky, Anita. "The Resistance to Sentimentality: Yeats, de Man, and the Aesthetic Education." *Yale Journal of Criticism* 1 (1987): 67–86.

Solomon, Robert C. "Emotions and Choice." In *Explaining Emotions,* ed. Amélie Oksenberg Rorty, 251–282. Berkeley and Los Angeles: University of California Press, 1980.

―――― *The Passions: Emotions and the Meaning of Life* [1976]. Indianapolis: Hackett, 1993.

Spinoza, Benedict [Baruch] de. *The Ethics* [1677]. In *A Spinoza Reader: The Ethics and Other Works,* ed. and trans. Edwin Curley, 85–265. Princeton: Princeton University Press, 1994.

―――― "From a Non-Geometric Draft of the *Ethics.*" In *A Spinoza Reader: The Ethics and Other Works,* ed. and trans. Edwin Curley, 55–66. Princeton: Princeton University Press, 1994.

Staten, Henry. "*The Birth of Tragedy* Reconstructed." *Studies in Romanticism* 29 (1990): 9–37.

―――― "Derrida and the Affect of Self." *Western Humanities Review* 50 (1997): 348–351.

Stern, Julia. *The Plight of Feeling: Sympathy and Dissent in the Early American Novel.* Chicago: University of Chicago Press, 1997.

Still, Judith. "The Disfigured Savage: Rousseau and de Man." *Nottingham French Studies* 24 (1985), 1–14.

Stocker, Michael, with Elizabeth Hegeman. *Valuing Emotions.* Cambridge: Cambridge University Press, 1996.

Strasser, Stephan. *The Phenomenology of Feeling.* Pittsburgh: Duquesne University Press, 1977.

Terada, Rei. "Passion and Mental Work." *PMLA* 114 (1999): 99.

Todd, Jane Marie. "Framing the *Second Discourse.*" *Comparative Literature* 38 (1986), 307–317.

Tomkins, Silvan. "The Primary Site of the Affects: The Face." In *Affect, Imagery, Consciousness.* Vol. 1, *The Positive Affects,* 204–242. New York: Springer Publishing Company, 1962.

Tompkins, Jane. "Criticism and Feeling." *College English* 39 (1977): 169–178.

Trembath, Paul. "Aesthetics without Art or Culture: Toward an Alternative Sense of Materialist Agency," *Strategies* 9/10 (1996): 122–151.

Turski, W. George. *Toward a Rationality of Emotions: An Essay in the Philosophy of Mind.* Athens: Ohio University Press, 1994.

Valéry, Paul. *Paul Valéry: An Anthology,* ed. James R. Lawler. Princeton: Princeton University Press, 1956.

Varela, Francisco. *Ethical Know-How: Action, Wisdom, and Cognition.* Stanford: Stanford University Press, 1999.

Walton, Kendall. *Mimesis as Make-Believe: On the Foundations of the Representational Arts.* Cambridge: Harvard University Press, 1990.

——— "Spelunking, Simulation, and Slime: On Being Moved by Fiction." In *Emotion and the Arts,* ed. Mette Hjort and Sue Laver, 37–49. Oxford: Oxford University Press, 1997.

Waters, Lindsay. "On Paul de Man's Effort to Re-Anchor a True Aesthetics in Our Feelings." *Boundary 2* 26 (1999): 133–156.

——— "Paul de Man: Life and Works." Introduction to Paul de Man, *Critical Writings, 1953–1978,* ed. Lindsay Waters, ix–lxxiv. Minneapolis: University of Minnesota Press, 1989.

——— "Professah de Man—he dead." *American Literary History* 7 (1995): 284–303.

Waters, Lindsay, and Wlad Godzich, eds. *Reading de Man Reading.* Minneapolis: University of Minnesota Press, 1989.

Wiener, Jon. "The Responsibilities of Friendship: Jacques Derrida on Paul de Man's Collaboration." *Critical Inquiry* 15 (1989): 797–803.

Wihl, Gary. *The Contingency of Theory: Pragmatism, Expressivism, and Deconstruction.* New Haven: Yale University Press, 1994.

Wimsatt, William K., and Monroe Beardsley. "The Affective Fallacy." In *The Verbal Icon: Studies in the Meaning of Poetry.* University of Kentucky Press, 1954.

Wittgenstein, Ludwig. *Philosophical Investigations,* 3rd ed., trans. G. E. M. Anscombe. New York: Macmillan, 1958.

——— *Tractatus Logico-Philosophicus* [1921], trans. D. F. Pears and B. F. McGuinness. London: Routledge & Kegan Paul, 1961.

Wolin, Richard. "Destruction at Auschwitz: Heidegger, de Man, and the New Revisionism." *South Central Review* 11 (1994): 2–22.

——— *The Terms of Cultural Criticism: The Frankfurt School, Existentialism, Poststructuralism.* New York: Columbia University Press, 1992.

Wollheim, Richard. *Art and Its Objects,* 2nd ed. Cambridge: Cambridge University Press, 1980.

Wordsworth, William. *The Poems,* 2 vols., ed. John O. Hayden. New Haven: Yale University Press, 1981.

Yeats, W. B. *Collected Poems,* ed. Richard J. Finneran. New York: Macmillan, 1989.

Youngquist, Paul. "De Quincey's Crazy Body." *PMLA* 114 (1999): 346–358.

Zajonc, R. B., and Hazel Markus. "Affect and Cognition: The Hard Interface." In *Emotions, Cognition, and Behavior,* ed. Carroll E. Izard, Jerome Kagan, and Robert B. Zajonc, 73–102. Cambridge: Cambridge University Press, 1984.

Žižek, Slavoj. "The Cartesian Subject versus the Cartesian Theater." In *Cogito and the Unconscious*, ed. Slavoj Žižek, 247–274. Durham: Duke University Press, 1998.

——— *The Ticklish Subject: The Absent Centre of Political Ontology.* London: Verso, 1999.

Index